Kilroy
Was Here

GW01425141

Kris Olsson is a Brisbane writer and journalist. She has worked for *The Australian* and *The Courier-Mail* and has been published extensively as a freelance. Her novel *In One Skin* was published in 2001.

Kilroy
Was Here

KRIS OLSSON

BANTAM
SYDNEY AUCKLAND TORONTO NEW YORK LONDON

KILROY WAS HERE
A BANTAM BOOK

First published in Australia and New Zealand in 2005
by Bantam

Copyright © Kris Olsson, 2005
Foreword © Angela Davis, 2005

All rights reserved. No part of this publication may be reproduced, stored in a retrieval
system, transmitted in any form or by any means, electronic, mechanical, photocopying,
recording or otherwise, without the prior written permission of the publisher.

National Library of Australia
Cataloguing-in-Publication Entry

Olsson, Kristina, 1956–.
Kilroy was here.

ISBN 1 86325 447 1.

1. Kilroy, Debbie. 2. Women prisoners – Australia –
Biography. 3. Women prisoners – Services for – Australia.
4. Social justice. I. Title.

365.43092

Transworld Publishers,
a division of Random House Australia Pty Ltd
20 Alfred Street, Milsons Point, NSW 2061
http://www.randomhouse.com.au

Random House New Zealand Limited
18 Poland Road, Glenfield, Auckland

Transworld Publishers,
a division of The Random House Group Ltd
61-63 Uxbridge Road, Ealing, London W5 5SA

Random House Inc
1745 Broadway, New York, New York 10036

Typeset by Midland Typesetters, Maryborough, Victoria
Printed and bound by Griffin Press, Netley, South Australia

10 9 8 7 6 5 4 3 2 1

Contents

For Dad – I will forever carry you in my heart; for Mum – your love never faltered, I love you; for Joe – love binds us together through thick and thin; for Jody and Josh – my children, my strength; and for all the strong women in my life, for the journeys we've travelled together, both inside prison and in the free world.

Foreword

This remarkable book introduces us to a woman who, over the years, has made and remade a life that, in turn, has touched and transformed so many lives around her. At the same time, Debbie Kilroy's humility is such that she would never represent herself as having accomplished any more than what life has demanded of her. This combination of uncommon ingenuity and tenacity on the one hand, and a deep understanding of the collaborative character of her efforts and achievements on the other, reveals why her story is so exceptional and why it must be shared with those who have not yet come to know her.

Debbie Kilroy describes her life as having been fashioned within the context of her relations with others – and especially her sisters whose destinies have been moulded by their experiences in prison. In this way, her life makes sense as an itinerary – circuitous at times, single-mindedly driven at others – leading to the creation of that extraordinary organisation Sisters Inside.

During early 2001, I received a number of email messages about a statewide conference on women in prison scheduled to take place in Queensland, Australia during the latter part of November. Although I inadvertently overlooked the first two messages, Debbie Kilroy was persistent (a trait I later learnt to appreciate, especially after attending that first conference), and eventually she prodded me to answer her request. In identifying herself as the director of a community organisation that worked with women in prison, she also indicated that she herself had been incarcerated for a number of years and that some nine years previously she and other women serving long-term prison sentences had founded Sisters Inside. She described Sisters Inside as an organisation specifically focused on the needs of women prisoners, which addressed a range of issues that were obscured by the existing campaigns to defend prisoners' rights.

After reading the string of messages, what most impressed me was the direct involvement of imprisoned women in the work of Sisters Inside. That is to say, the names of women prisoners were not obligatorily added to a leadership roster that relied on prisoners for legitimacy, but did not necessarily consider what it would mean for them to participate in management on an equal basis. As I learnt, the core leadership of Sisters Inside consisted of prisoners, former prisoners, and their allies. For me, this recognition generated enormous excitement because it addressed so many of the thorny problems we were confronting in the anti-prison movement in the United States: the marginalisation of women, for example, and the conflicts between those who prioritised campaigns around 'political' prisoners and those who argued that the plight of individuals convicted for their political beliefs was intrinsically linked to that of nearly two million men and women being held captive by a system of punishment primarily reserved for the poor and racially subjugated. I was anxious to find out how the work of Sisters Inside was proceeding in a part of the world, and in a part of Australia, with which I was unfamiliar.

So the stage was set for my visit to Queensland, Australia in November 2001, and my first meeting with Debbie Kilroy at Brisbane Airport. I had no trouble identifying her, although no one had described her to me as blonde, physically fit and forthright in every way. Her unassuming manner immediately drew me to her, as well as her capacity to make one feel as if she was a long-lost friend – no protocol intervened between our initial introductions and the issues at hand. During the ride in Debbie's black souped-up pick-up truck to the hotel where the conference was being held, my partner and I were treated to a quick, abbreviated history of Sisters Inside. We learnt about Anne Warner, the former MP and Minister from the Labor Party, who was one of the organisation's major leaders, and by the end of the conversation we could identify the names of women in leadership who were locked up in the nearby prison, the Brisbane Women's Correctional Centre. Debbie also informed us about some of the immediate difficulties the organisation was confronting, the foremost of which was the prison's refusal to authorise short furloughs for the imprisoned members of the Sisters Inside Management Committee so that they could participate in the conference as previously planned. By the time we reached the hotel, we had been sufficiently briefed and were ready for a weekend of hard work.

The conference itself provided dramatic evidence of Debbie's ability to create alliances among people who came from such diverse communities that one would not ordinarily expect them to work together. Former prisoners – both white and indigenous – were not afraid to openly challenge government officials, who, in turn, did not seem to be irritated by the critiques they encountered. Elders from Aboriginal and Torres Strait Island communities concerned about the rising percentage of indigenous prisoners engaged in conversation with white activists. Scholars and artists reflected on how they might use their talents and skills to further the cause of women prisoners. When Debbie later became the first former prisoner to receive the Medal of Australia, it was clear that this was an honour long overdue.

At this conference, Debbie and her colleagues formally introduced their campaign against the strip-search in women's prisons, which they provocatively called 'state sexual assault'. This campaign, which is now making its way around the world, links the violence that women suffer in intimate settings to the routine violence inherent in prison regimes. She and her colleagues emphasised the importance of breaking through the ideological barriers that prevent those of us who inhabit the free world from recognising abuses that are at the very core of prison practices. If we are opposed to domestic violence and sexual assault, they argued, then we ought to be equally willing to speak out against the practice of strip-searching.

Because the imprisoned members of the Sisters Inside Management Committee were prevented from attending the conference in person, their speeches were compassionately presented by their sisters outside. But as moving as these presentations proved to be, Debbie and her colleagues did not accept them as an adequate level of participation in the conference by those in the name of whom the gathering had been convened. If they could not come to the conference, Debbie announced, the conference must be brought to them. As a result, a rather large group of conference presenters were shuttled to the Brisbane Women's Correctional Centre, where we summarised our papers and engaged in an extended discussion with other members and supporters of the organisation.

My memories of this initial encounter with Debbie Kilroy have been brought to the fore in writing the Foreword to Kris Olsson's biography. The subject of this biography has little time for the preliminary niceties that prevent one from engaging straight-forwardly with injustice. She demands an immersion without fanfare in the work of contesting the conditions that damage individuals, whose lives – for many complicated reasons, including, but not limited to their own actions – are sacrificially offered up to punishment systems all over the world.

The value of this biography is that it allows us to follow the trajectory of a person who had firsthand experience with this system as a child and who was thus placed on a track that led her to spend important years of her adulthood within an institution that claimed the life of one of her closest friends, and very nearly claimed her own. What she did to circumvent her own spiritual – and possibly physical – death is at the hub of the story you are about to read. It is what makes Debbie Kilroy's life meaningful for us all.

Angela Davis
December 2004

Prologue

The attackers came from behind. Later, this is what Debbie Kilroy will find hardest to forgive. Gutless, she'll say in a terrible pun, but at the time it meant the women with the sharpened barbecue forks could quickly achieve their aim: murder.

Sunday lunch on a soupy summer's day inside Brisbane Women's Correctional Centre at Boggo Road. Boggo Road is not only the jail's location – five minutes south of the city centre and another five to the salubrious riverside suburbs. To most people, that's also its name. Prisoners pronounce it 'Bogga', and the sound carries all their own suspicions about their lives: bogged, sucked down, swallowed up by the quicksand of defeat.

This feeling is endemic in jails, but in January 1990, among the women of Boggo Road, it was just one ingredient in a deadly brew of emotions stirred up by overcrowding, growing factionalism among the women, and the grief and anger that always accompanies the festive season for anyone separated from their children. Over all this, a humid tension hung like a prickly blanket, one that can't be kicked off.

This Sunday, 7 January, was much like any other. In their free time in the morning, the sixty women in B block played cards in desultory groups on the covered concrete verandah that ran beside the kitchen and dining room, or watched *Rage* on television in the recreation room.

At eleven-thirty they drifted to the dining room where they sat, four or five to a table, for a barely edible lunch. No one dallied over the processed meat, tomato and lettuce. Lethargic, they all went back to what they had been doing, to wait for the prison officers to escort them back to their cells for the 12 to 1 pm lockdown. A lot of waiting gets done in prison. It's factored in to the daily routine.

Debbie Kilroy and her friends Debbie Dick and Janelle Scognomiglio slumped down around a plastic table on the verandah. They made small talk. Kilroy was wishing the time away: it was a visits day, and she knew Joshua, her three-year-old son, would be waiting in the visits area at two o'clock. At that moment she couldn't know that the next few hours would indeed evaporate, collapsing together to form one horrific memory that would never, ever leave her.

It began with the alarm bells. They rang out shrilly from the top section of the jail, signalling some kind of serious trouble in the other blocks. The prison officers heading towards the verandah froze momentarily, then in one movement turned and bolted towards the bells, locking the bottom section behind them.

The women waiting for escorts to their cells watched them go, muttering impatiently. More waiting. At their table, Debbie Dick lowered her head onto her folded arms. She was bored and listless. 'I feel like I could sleep forever,' she sighed.

Prophetic last words. As Dick closed her eyes, two shadows moved as one from behind the kitchen wall. Storm Brooke and Amali Badenoch had seen their chance. They pulled out their sharpened forks, and advanced at a run.

The blades found their first target easily. Debbie Dick was slightly built and caught completely off-guard. From the moment the deadly prongs struck her, she didn't stand a chance.

But Debbie Kilroy, strong and alert from a life of aerobics and street fighting, wasn't such easy prey. At the first sting of steel, she shrugged out of her attacker's hold and was up, swinging her plastic chair above her head. Surprised by Kilroy's animal swiftness and strength, Badenoch fled as Scogs had done. But any rationality left in Storm Brooke had deserted her. She stood over Debbie Dick, plunging a fork into Dick's chest in a blind frenzy. Again and again and again.

Kilroy still clutched the chair above her and now she brought it crashing down on Brooke's head with a force that had little to do with fitness and everything to do with adrenalin and fury and shock. The blow snapped Brooke out of her blind rage. She stopped stabbing and stared at Kilroy, gripping the bloody fork. Then she ran, in through the kitchen, and was gone.

Debbie Dick's limp body was slumped on the concrete floor. She was unconscious, bleeding profusely. Kilroy was bleeding too, but hadn't noticed the wounds. Out of the thundering silence she suddenly heard her own voice, yelling, screaming: 'Get a doctor! Someone get a fuckin' doctor!' The concrete prison echoed the sounds back to her, a brutal riposte.

She crouched beside her friend, holding her. This is the moment, visual and terrifying, when reality and memory will kick in, all through the days, months and years to come. It is the moment she realised, watching Debbie Dick's face turn a fearsome grey, that she was witnessing a life ebbing away, that she was watching her friend die.

But not without a fight. Fighting was Kilroy's instinctive reaction to any threat, and now she gathered all her anger and fear and fight into a terrible howl to ward off death. She screamed out a stream of expletives and demands and questions: 'What the fuck are you all doing, my mate's been stabbed/get the doctor now you dogs/I want the ambulance fuck you/where the FUCK is the ambulance/My mate's been stabbed. My mate, my mate . . . ' Fighting and grieving with each painful breath.

When the ambulance officers finally arrived, they went straight to work on Debbie Dick, and bundled her away. Kilroy was genuinely surprised to find herself on a gurney, her white T-shirt blotched with blood she didn't recognise. Was it hers? She had no idea. But as they loaded her into the second ambulance and switched on the siren, she felt oddly detached from the blood and from the attentions of the paramedics, and impatient with it all. She wanted to know only one thing: *what's happened to my mate?*

Her fears would be confirmed hours later, the words spilling carelessly from the mouth of a young policeman as she lay surrounded by other patients in an open public hospital ward. *Dead.* The word slipped sharp and final between her ribs, hitting a place her assailant's clumsy blades could not.

Though the pain in her heart was real enough, there would be no tears. There would be no outward sign of anguish, not then. But in the appalling silence that took its place, one word would resonate, over and over, soothing her, numbing her grief with its promise:

payback. It was her obligation and her privilege now and, back in her cell at Bogga, the only thing she could see. She dreamed of her own beautifully sharpened knife.

1

An Ordinary Childhood

There are footsteps on the back stairs. Heavy, deliberate. In the kitchen, where weak winter sunlight falls in yellow planks on the linoleum, the child in the grey school tunic hears them, and freezes.

Two young Queensland police officers in their blue serge uniforms climb the stairs of the wooden house in suburban Brisbane. It is 1974, and they are looking for a child. The child is a tearaway, a troublemaker, a truant, and home is the last place they expect to find her. But here they are at the top of the stairs and the back door is open, and they've got her. There's the piece of paper in one of their pockets and the open door. She's theirs.

They know this house. It is a modest, post-war timber home in Kedron, in Brisbane's north, with an above-ground swimming pool in the backyard and azaleas out the front. The tidy garden, the clothes swinging on the Hills hoist – it is all unexceptional, and on this quiet July morning, it offers no clue to the trouble that has been brewing here for months, the anger and desperation that has brought them here several times already, looking for Deborah Harding.

Usually, it's because she's taken off from school on a Friday and not bothered to go home all weekend. No phone calls, no messages. Her frantic parents – Kevin, a bricklaying contractor, and Pat, a clerk – spend whole days scouring the surrounding suburbs for the thirteen-year-old, but she is as clever as Houdini. They never find her. When she's ready, she'll stroll back into the house, chin raised for the inevitable screaming match. Then disappear again a fortnight later.

1

In between, she wags school and hangs out with rough types at the local Dandy Burger or the Valley pool hall, where it's all larrikin-ism and bluff. They play 'instant squash' – throwing cans of soft drink beneath the wheels of moving trucks – and stuff paper into the recesses of public telephones, returning in the afternoons to remove the paper and a stash of trapped coins.

To a young police officer, Deborah Harding is a wild little bitch. She's a troublemaker mixing with the wrong crowd, a delinquent in the making. But she's no criminal. Not yet. She just does what she likes and mouths off at anyone who tries to get in her way. Mainly, that's her mother. The police know this because, in the past six months, Pat Harding has become a regular in the corridors of the Juvenile Aid Bureau in the city, where she agonises over what to do next.

Debbie's erratic behaviour – the constant truancy, the daily slanging matches about school and bad company, her weekend disappearances – have all begun to make Pat feel like she's bouncing off walls. That's how she describes life with Debbie: like living inside a pinball machine. She tells the police this when she's summonsed yet again to discuss the latest misdemeanour. She's desperate now to find answers to her daughter's rages, her unpredictable behaviour. She'll try anything. That's what she says.

Her two children have always been the most important things in Pat's life. She'd wanted to be the perfect wife and mother. Since her marriage to Kevin at twenty-two, all her energies have been directed at that, at creating a home where nothing would be lacking, where everything was provided. Hot meals on the table, clean clothes on the line and happy children playing rounders in the backyard. This would be her achievement. In the uniformly working class world they inhabited, this would be the measure of her success.

But Debbie had set her up for failure. Her growing delinquency challenged the truism that had guided Pat's generation: if you were a good mother, you would have good children. And, of course, the reverse. Plainly, she'd begun to believe, she had failed. It didn't seem fair.

At thirteen, Debbie Harding is not afraid of anything. That's what she likes to believe. But she doesn't trust anyone either, apart from her mates, so as the footsteps on the stairs grow heavier, so does the odd sense of foreboding she feels standing there, alone in the quiet house.

There is no one else at home. That's why she's here, of course. If she'd come back before her mother had gone to work there would have been hell to pay and today, she isn't in the mood. Going to school wasn't exactly what she'd intended either, but there had been a strange feeling in the house from the time she'd walked in. She'd wanted to get out again, straight away.

She'd made a sandwich and gone down to grab her school uniform from the line. Upstairs again she felt briefly gladdened, as she pulled the tunic over her head, by the flash of surprise she would surely see on her mother's face that afternoon when she realised she had actually gone to school. On a Monday. Without a brawl.

The feeling evaporated with the sounds from the back stairs. She listened: there were two sets of footsteps. No voices. She stood immobilised in the kitchen, staring at the open doorway, her hand on the low sideboard. She'd dropped two clothes pegs there as she walked past with her uniform just a minute ago. Now her fingers closed around them, the only part of her body that moved.

As the two police officers stepped into the bright rectangle of the doorway, she looked them in the eyes, and her hands moved to her pockets in a gesture of half-hearted defiance. Later that day, when the nightmare was in full swing and everything she had owned was being taken from her, she would reach into her pockets to empty them, as directed, and pull out two plastic clothes pegs.

They stand in the doorway and remove their hats. From here they're looking straight into the kitchen, past a round veneered table with four chairs, the tidy benchtops. The child is standing on the other side of the room, looking straight at them. Unbelievably, she is wearing her school uniform: yellow blouse beneath a grey tunic. Of course, that's where it stops. She wouldn't be seen dead in school shoes. Despite the coolness of the morning, she's wearing thongs. Uncombed blonde hair splays over her shoulders. She shoves her hands in her pockets and cocks her head.

'G'day, Debbie.' The girl is stone. She doesn't blink. 'Off to school?'

She still doesn't blink, but her lips move. 'Maybe.'

'Not like you.'

'What's it to you?'

'Didn't think you liked school.' The two officers, a male and a female who has long, crimson fingernails, are taking it in turns. Trying not to spook her. She doesn't reply.

'Or home either, from the sounds of it. Where'd they pick you up last week? Cunnamulla?'

'Just went for a drive.'

'In a stolen car.'

She shrugs.

'With a couple of blokes.'

'Mates.'

She's addressing her answers to the kitchen sink. She hasn't moved her hands.

'How d'you think your parents felt? Eh? Don't suppose you did think.'

A barely perceptible shrug.

'Well, your luck's in, Deb. We're giving you a break from school. And from your mum and dad.' It's the female with the long, pointy fingernails. She's waving a piece of paper in front of her like a prize. 'Here's your ticket. We're going to take you with us.'

'I'm going to school.'

'Not today.'

'I *want* to go.'

The two officers exchange grins. 'Yeah,' says the man. 'Come on.'

Her face is suddenly animated. 'You fuckin' idiots.' She's not shouting but she's loud. 'All the time you're tellin' me to go to school. Should be at school.' She waggles her head. 'Now I'm goin' to school and you say I'm not. What are ya, stupid?'

The two police officers look at her. There's an irritating undertone of truth to what she's saying. And there's this other thing: she's not afraid. Not of them, not of wherever it is they are taking her.

Then suddenly the girl seems to deflate a bit. She looks at them. 'Does my mother know you're here? Does Dad?' The answer seems to come from the fridge, which begins to rumble in the silence. 'Does Nana?'

'Your father signed.' It's Fingernails holding up the bit of paper again. But they're already walking her towards the door, and out into the strangeness of the morning. Her thongs slap against her feet and her skin prickles. It's probably the cold. The policewoman guides her into the back seat of the car and there are the long, crimson nails again, this time on her shoulder. She shrugs them off. Before the door shuts she says 'Fuckers!', just loud enough. Then they drive away.

Looking back on this day, the adult Debbie is struck most by the memory of the pegs, and by her own innocence. The stark image of the pegs isn't surprising: they were the only things she took with her from the old life to the new. They became ciphers for what would happen to her: hung out to dry. But the innocence is all in hindsight. With its benefit she can see that, at thirteen, she'd done nothing that could possibly account for this: this abrupt but legal abduction, and the years of sanctioned abuse and humiliation she would endure in its wake inside the locked walls of the coyly named Wilson Youth Hospital.

At the time, she was ready to believe she was a 'bad' girl. Since she'd started high school the year before, she'd been fashioning herself as an outlaw, as someone who stood apart. As someone who, unlike her parents and most thirteen-year-olds she knew, had no trust or faith in the institutions that govern our lives – school, church, family – or in any authority that promised rewards for obeying the rules. Curiously, she also had grave suspicions even then about anyone who claimed they loved her.

This put her parents, Kevin and Pat, in the front line. Debbie's belligerence towards them through her childhood is something Pat still frets about – it's become a one-sided interrogation that's never really stopped. What went wrong? How had they failed? What cocktail of genes and experiences led her daughter away from the decent, predictable life they had strived for and into one mined with trouble, violence and tragedy? Pat doesn't know, but after years of soul searching, she's discovered that the earliest clues can be those most easily overlooked, and sometimes the most telling.

Pat and Kevin Harding were delighted when their first child was born on a hot summer night in January 1961. She was a breech birth and a long time coming but she was fair-haired and pretty. Perfect. The way they saw their lives. When her brother Michael arrived two years later, they thought they had it all. It was the family from central casting.

Like all baby photos from that time, the Hardings' reflect back an ideal, in pictures that are rose-tinted and oddly adult in their compositions. Debbie, in a home-stitched dress of spotted blue and white voile, smiles gravely back at a photographer who is no doubt waving a small toy to keep her happy. Michael, in a little blue suit, holds the obligatory ball. But the ideal hides the everyday drama that was already plotting against Pat's 'perfect family'. Just before Michael's birth, one-year-old Debbie was diagnosed with 'wry neck', or torticollis. At that age, it meant only that she couldn't turn her head properly, but the condition, left untreated, can cause permanent paralysis of the neck and facial muscles, and almost certain disfigurement. Debbie underwent corrective surgery before her second birthday, followed by months of painful manipulation. Initially, this was carried out by doctors, but they soon handed responsibility for the procedure over to her parents.

Each day Kevin would hold a wriggling, crying Debbie on the dining room table while Pat reluctantly kneaded the muscles on her daughter's neck. It was traumatic for all of them, but no one could have foreseen the repercussions. Unknowingly, Pat and Kevin had begun to destroy their daughter's trust in the word 'love'.

Debbie, like Pat, is surprised at the vivid memories she has of that time. She was just a toddler, after all, but the images are clearer than many from her later childhood: 'I remember lying on a table. Dad was holding me, and Mum was squeezing my neck. Squeeze, squeeze. The pain was awful. I was screaming. And at the end of it Mum's saying, "It's all right, darling," and "We love you, darling". The two things stuck in my mind. People could love you but still hurt you. Love meant pain. Even then,' she says grimly, 'something was telling me not to trust anyone.'

Pat isn't sure if it was that early experience that led to the wild tantrums Debbie began to have soon after. The tantrums were cyclical, she says, and between them Debbie was manageable. But once or twice a month her daughter would seem possessed by some furious anger at the world, and nothing would dilute it. She would cry and scream inconsolably, and throw herself to the ground at the tiniest setback, or at the prospect of doing something she didn't care to do. Her mother was at a loss. No attempt at calming her would work.

As Debbie got older and the explosive rages continued, Pat would lock her in her bedroom, which Debbie would systematically destroy. Toys were hurled at the walls, the bed pulled apart. Pat would walk out of the house and into the garden to dig or water, not just to escape the screaming, but 'to prove to the neighbours that I wasn't in there, belting her'. 'The noise was incredible,' she remembers. 'When it stopped I'd open the door to her room and she'd be cowering in a corner, sobbing, worn out. But she was a very strong-willed little girl from the beginning. We had a constant battle of wills. I clearly remember taking her to get her hair cut when she was about three. Well, trying to. It took six adults to get her in there and in the end, we lost.'

By the time she entered primary school, however, Debbie's rages were being fuelled from another quarter. Pat's mother, Beryl Grey, moved in and lived with the family in Kedron for extended periods after Debbie and Michael were born. Beryl herself had been a Depression baby born to a large farming family in Kyogle. From an early age she'd learned to stick up for herself, and has never been afraid to call a spade a spade. If strong wills are genetic, it isn't hard to trace the origin of Debbie's.

Debbie says Nana had – and has – an 'incredibly strong personality': 'She's always been anti-authority. She's a tearaway, tough.' By contrast, Pat had always been quiet and compliant, a 'real goody-two-shoes'. Squeezed between the larger-than-life personalities of her mother and her daughter, Pat fought bravely to run an ordinary, peaceful household. That's all she wanted. But her voice was drowned out by louder ones.

'Nana was always the matriarch,' Debbie says. 'From the earliest time she used the divide-and-rule technique with Mum and me. It was an open competition. If Mum wouldn't give me something, Nana would. She absolutely spoiled me. She'd give me anything.'

At eighty-five, and still a straight-talker, Beryl doesn't disagree. She adored Debbie, possibly seeing in her fiery, take-no-prisoners granddaughter a kindred spirit, someone who would not be cowed. 'She wasn't a bad girl. But they were way too strict on her,' she sniffs.

By the time she enrolled in infant school at St Anthony's, a small Catholic primary school in Kedron, Debbie's disdain for authority was well established. It was obvious even at church where, after her parents placed their money in the collection bowl at each service, the five-year-old would carefully remove it. But in the robed nuns of St Anthony's she was about to collide with the kind of assertion and discipline she'd never known at home, or anywhere else.

It started with tree-climbing. The schoolyard boasted several massive trees, probably Moreton Bay figs which, with their branching limbs and snaking surface roots, are open invitations to children to climb. Of course, Debbie climbed them. Always the tomboy, always hanging out with the boys, she didn't think twice. That's what trees were for. Until the day – she was only little, perhaps in grade two – one of the nuns hauled her down. Such behaviour was totally inappropriate for a girl, she was told. Little Debbie was given six of the best. Six crisp straps across the hand. Only boys climbed trees, was the mantra. She reeled, not from the strap, but from the insult.

What did they mean, 'only boys'? It was another stupid, meaningless rule. So Debbie kept climbing, and the beltings continued, each blow striking hard against her sense of justice. The unfairness of it, the arbitrary nature of the rules, hurt more than the strap's hard edge. 'I was shocked by it even then, I think,' she says. 'I'd never experienced anything like that at home. I wasn't belted. There wasn't any violence in my life. I didn't even see my parents argue.' In the end she devised a way to take the sting out of the strap: she would bide her time until the end of the punishment, then reach up and pull the veil from the nun's head.

Many things would eventually influence Debbie's later behaviour, but she believes her early treatment at the hands of the nuns effectively diminished her sense of right and wrong. 'The people who preached right and wrong, good and bad, were these nuns, and what did they know?' she asks now. 'They bashed little kids. No wonder I hated authority.'

At home, things seemed to follow the cycle Pat had identified when Debbie was little. There would be periods of peace – Pat remembers 'lots of good times, Christmases and holidays we all had together' – punctuated by regular bouts of bruising verbal stoushes. Debbie's brother Michael, now forty-one, remembers his sister picking fights with him and 'niggling' but, from a distance, doesn't see their childhood relationship as any worse than other siblings. He was too preoccupied with football to take much notice, he says. 'Dad would take me training and to games on weekends. That was my whole life,' he says.

Every now and then, Pat and Kevin would dispatch Debbie to Kevin's sister Melba and her husband Rex for the weekend, to give everyone a break. 'She played up on her mother, but she never did with me,' says Melba, now in her early eighties. 'They'd send her over to me and she'd sleep between us, lying there reading a *Reader's Digest* out loud. It was great fun. I didn't have a daughter of my own, and I loved it.'

But at home the rages continued, complicated by Debbie's growing reliance on Nana as her ally, and the sure knowledge that, whenever she was in trouble with her mother, Nana would take her side. One day, ten-year-old Debbie came home from school demanding to have her ears pierced. Her parents declined. She continued the verbal assault until Kevin looked at her firmly and said, 'If God intended you to wear earrings, you would've been born with holes in your ears.' Debbie was devastated, and flew into the room she shared with Nana to see what could be done.

Within two minutes Nana's not insubstantial voice came booming through the walls at Kevin and Pat. She fumed about the stupidity of Kevin's ruling and then made her own decision. 'I'm taking her to have them done in the morning,' she called. Inside their bedroom she hugged Debbie to her side. 'Don't worry, darling,' she said. A shiny pair of gold sleepers was duly fitted the next day.

It is easy to forget, in these days of robust political debate and sophisticated lifestyles, that the country in which Debbie Harding grew up was a place still quite isolated from global upheaval, a place still in thrall to a new young Queen, a white picket fence place where cynicism had not yet entered the wider vocabulary. Australia was still a country where buying a house meant buying a home and not an investment; where the vast majority of women were at the gates of those homes to greet their children after school; where it was entirely normal not to have a telephone at home.

Debbie was in her early years of primary school when the Beatles played to feverish and hysterical crowds around the country, when dollars replaced pounds in our purses, when Armstrong walked on the moon. In 1970, when she was nine, you could buy a dozen eggs for forty-eight cents, a copy of the local paper for seven cents, and build a new house in Sydney with 'septic and double carport' for $15 000.

A year later – in 1971 – US president Richard Nixon was named *Time* magazine's 'Man of the Year' and haemorrhoid creams were advertised on the front pages of newspapers. Fashions at the

Melbourne Cup included 'well-cut slack suits', 'dresses in silk, spotted with navy or red, with a pleated skirt or floral sheers with ruffles'. We are told that 'Mrs Andrew Peacock wore a bright splash of tangerine in a finely pintucked Swiss voile dress' for Lady's Day in 1972.

If she'd been ten years older, Debbie might have been lured into the public scrums that were the anti-Vietnam moratorium marches and anti-apartheid demonstrations of the early seventies. The teenagers of that era were perhaps our most politicised, and loudly shook off the apathy they perceived and so abhorred in their parents and in those in authority. As a member of that generation, she might have found easy outlets for her anger.

In that sense, the entire Harding family's timing was bad. Pat and Kevin missed the protest generation too, born ten years too soon. They were wartime babies; the generation captured by austerity, by the work ethic and by respect for the established hierarchies: you deferred to your boss, to your local member of parliament, to teachers, doctors and the law. You even believed – mostly – what you read in the daily papers, and what you heard on the six o'clock news.

Pat and Kevin belonged to a generation that admired compliance and conformity, for whom dissent and rebellion were grave concerns. They were appalled by the idea of standing out in a crowd. That would mean drawing attention to yourself, putting yourself outside the norm. You groomed your children to fit in, to be accepted, to toe the line, as you did. So if, despite all your best efforts, your child became wayward, or showed any signs of deviating from the norm you'd worked hard to achieve, you did two things. First, you blamed yourself, and assumed everyone else in the street did, too. Second, you sought help from the institutions you believed in: church, the medical establishment, government, the law. These were the experts, people with university educations and qualifications, people you could trust. That's how it was in the suburbs of Australia in the 1970s.

The family staggered through Debbie's primary school days. Academically, she was regarded as bright but underachieving. Her report cards, all carefully preserved by Pat, show a preponderance of Bs and Cs, and similar remarks repeated right through to grade seven: 'Could do much better if she applied herself'; 'Satisfactory, but capable of much better work'; 'needs supervision' and 'lacks concentration'. They were the kind of report cards most parents find slightly exasperating: the child is passing, after all, not failing, but there is obvious potential for more. Debbie's tempestuousness, however, had already taken Pat and Kevin to the brink. They weren't going to get angry about her results, which revealed, at least, that she was intellectually 'normal', perhaps even clever. 'She went to school, she did her homework. That was enough,' Pat says.

Their relief at this was palpable. Her academic results – Bs and Cs with very little effort made – meant she had a good brain, but even better, it meant they could dismiss for a while a secret anxiety they had harboured since Debbie's first wild, unmanageable tantrum. Was there madness in the family?

Colourful stories had circulated for many years about Kevin's father, Cecil James, who had fought in World War II and returned, so the rumours went, an utterly changed man. Some said he retreated completely into himself, some said he chased his wife around the house with an axe. The general consensus in the family was that he was crazed with shell-shock: Beryl remembers accusations of 'moon madness', and Melba believes it was the last stages of syphilis. At any rate, he was admitted to what was then called the Goodna Mental Asylum, west of Brisbane, where he spent fifteen years. The following generation began to look closely at any aberrant behaviour that might mean the madness had been passed down.

The thought that some inherited madness or fearful psychiatric condition might have produced Debbie's alarming behaviour plagued Pat and Kevin throughout Debbie's childhood. Getting her through primary school without any major incidents was a huge relief, but it was short-lived. At the end of year seven, there was a decision to be made between the nearby Catholic girls' college, Mt Alvernia, and the local state high school. A gargantuan battle between parents and child ensued.

Pat and Kevin were adamant that Mt Alvernia, with its discipline and pastoral care, was the better option. Debbie, sick of the discipline of nuns and keen to follow her mates, campaigned hard for Kedron State High. It was a relatively new school with no track record. It was further away and Debbie would have a good walk to the bus stop and back. They were reluctant to let her go. But Debbie was determined: she would hate it at Mt Alvernia, she would hate the nuns and have no friends, and life, Kevin and Pat could see, would be hell. For them all. They gave in. It was, Pat believes, one of the most significant decisions of their lives.

First year at high school brings a culture shock for most teenagers, after the relative shelter of classrooms with just one or two teachers, and playgrounds where everyone knows your name. Suddenly there is a different teacher for each subject, the buzz of different faces and ideas, new responsibilities like catching public transport. There is the crisp new uniform, new subjects and, best of all, the absence of the close and restrictive scrutiny of nuns. Debbie could smell liberation.

But Debbie came to Kedron High with a major disadvantage: she was a year younger than most of her fellow year eight students. Born in January, she'd entered primary school at barely five years old. Most of her contemporaries had turned five the year before. While it didn't impact on her then, it had enormous repercussions later: by year eight, her lower level of emotional maturity was obvious. At twelve, she didn't see high school as the beginning of an adventure in education – only that she was now free of the shackles of the nuns, free to do what she liked.

Things began to go wrong halfway through that first year. To Kevin and Pat's mounting horror, Debbie began to hang around with older kids who appeared to live their own lives unfettered by parental guidance. Sometimes they'd go to school, sometimes they wouldn't; unlike Debbie, they were allowed to go out at night, and to go to the Valley, an inner city shopping district full of pinball arcades, pool halls and a growing number of prostitutes and drug dealers.

Kevin was particularly perturbed that many of these older friends of Debbie's were Aboriginal. But these were the very friends Debbie identified with most. She was drawn to them as outsiders, as people just like her: different, uncomfortable in mainstream structures, square pegs refusing to be pushed and shoved into round holes. She felt an immediate affinity with their openness and honesty. Most critically for her, they were very loyal mates.

She knew, though, that her father was incensed by her friendship with 'blacks', and she would taunt him not just by bringing them home but by alleging she was not his daughter but the adopted child of an Aboriginal family. It came to a head one night when the usually soft-spoken Kevin lost his temper with her and, picking up a black ashtray, yelled, 'I don't want my daughter running around with a bloke as black as this!' and hurled it against the wall.

The fights between mother and daughter began to escalate too, as Debbie, flexing her newly adolescent muscles, demanded to know why she shouldn't go out at night to parties with her friends. Pat began to receive calls from the principal at Kedron High reporting Debbie absent from school. A new and pernicious pattern settled on the Hardings' daily lives: Pat would fight with Debbie in the morning, go to work, come home, and fight with Debbie again.

Kevin, working long hours as a bricklaying contractor, missed most of them. He left home at six every morning and returned at six every night. 'He often went for a drink after work with his mates,' Pat says. 'Why wouldn't he? There was only brawling at home.'

But Debbie was enjoying herself. She'd found a whole new life with her new friends, all of whom shared her hostility towards school and teachers and the rigid rules they imposed. Debbie despised her teachers. When she did turn up for school, she would disrupt classes with arguments and insults until she was sent to the principal's office for punishment. This became such a regular event that a desk was set up for her there. She didn't mind at all. At least she was out of class. She'd give it ten minutes, wait until his back was turned and then head for the gates.

More and more, however, Debbie was wagging, and spending whole days and whatever money she had – mainly collected from the phone boxes they blocked – at the Valley pool hall. She and her mates would play music and pool and, in the evenings, 'run around the streets'. 'I'd been so protected as a kid – Catholic upbringing, Catholic school – that when I got to high school I discovered all this other good stuff you could do – run around, go to parties. Get on a bus and visit some of the older kids we'd met in the Valley,' she says. Of course, her parents assumed the worst. She was just a young girl, barely a teenager, running around with older girls and boys. But it was all good, clean fun, according to Debbie. She didn't get drunk. She wasn't even much of a smoker. She certainly didn't see herself as being in any kind of 'moral danger'.

She survived year eight, but in year nine she upped the ante. Every few weeks she'd nick off from school some time on Friday and seemingly disappear into the ether. Whole weekends would go by without any sign of her. Pat and Kevin, and frequently Melba and Rex, would scour the surrounding suburbs, spending all day Saturday and all day Sunday looking, knocking on doors, ringing the police. Debbie would stroll in casually on Sunday night or return on Monday, when no one was home.

The first couple of times, they were desperately worried. They wouldn't sleep. Then anger set in. They were already on first name terms with officers from the newly formed Juvenile Aid Bureau (JAB) – Pat still remembers the look of the long corridor in the JAB's building in Herschel Street in the city – but now they seemed to be in constant touch. No one seemed to have any answers. 'The police were always around then,' Pat recalls. 'I was bouncing off walls, and I hated it, I really did. I thought it was all my parenting. I'd tried to be a good mother. I didn't know where I'd gone wrong, but I felt like I'd failed, and I hate failing.'

The Hardings were appalled when, after one weekend of frantic searching, they finally found Debbie asleep on the floor of an untidy flat in the outer suburb of Northgate. Two teenage boys were asleep on the floor nearby. Kevin was livid, but terrified too, imagining any number of scenarios. Debbie just seemed confused. They were her mates, she was in no danger, she told him in defensive tones. Still, she could see that Kevin had almost reached the limit of his patience. She assured him she wouldn't run away again.

She was right about her father. The last straw came one weekend shortly afterwards when, predictably, Debbie hadn't come home. This time, though, the police eventually found her. She and two friends – both boys – had decided to go for a drive. Debbie didn't know the car was stolen, or how far they intended to go. It just seemed like a lot of fun at the time. Then drove west, out of Brisbane, and when they hit the open highway they decided to keep going. Inglewood, Goondiwindi, St George. Now they were really in the bush. They were finally stopped in Thargomindah, about 800 kilometres away.

They were taken to the police station in Charleville, which is where a tired and exasperated Kevin Harding, along with Melba and Rex, finally arrived to pick up his daughter. Debbie had already appeared in the local court, charged with unlawful use of a motor vehicle, and had been admonished and discharged, along with the others. She was nonplussed by the entire event. When Kevin, Melba and Rex walked in, flustered from the long, dusty drive, she was sitting on a desk in the police station, swinging her legs.

By July 1975, Pat and Kevin had reached the limits of their tolerance. Daily life had become a nightmare but, more than this, they'd begun to believe their daughter needed help of some kind – some professional intervention and assistance, something they had not been able to give her themselves. The officers at the JAB readily agreed. A psychiatric assessment, they suggested. It might isolate some undiagnosed problem that could be treated. A four-week assessment could be done at the Wilson Youth Hospital. Debbie could be admitted as an in-patient.

Pat and Kevin received the suggestion with the open minds and hopeful optimism of parents offered a cure for a very sick child. Maybe this would work. Maybe this would reveal something concrete. 'When they said this would help I believed them,' Pat says. 'But at the time I would have painted the house hot pink if the social workers had told me it would fix her. We'd have done anything.'

The 'four-week assessment' required a parent's authorisation. Debbie would need to be signed over to the state's care for the assessment, which was actually a prelude to an order for care and control. Kevin was required to give a written statement to Juvenile Aid, and to attend a specially convened court hearing so that a magistrate could make the order.

It's fairly obvious that Kevin's statement, dated 7 July 1975, was not actually written by him. It is a trite, official summary of the events that led an ordinary suburban family to the brink, written in the stiff, formal language of the police. Words like 'located' and 'youths' are not in the everyday vocabulary of a working class bricklayer, and the statement feels oddly contrived, as if Kevin is making a speech in front a group of people he sees as his superiors:

I am the father of Deborah May Harding who is 14 years of age. We have been having trouble with Deborah for the past year and in the last two months her behaviour has become worse. The main trouble has been that she will not accept any authority from myself and my wife.

One month ago my wife and I took Deborah to the Juvenile Aid Bureau because of her bad behaviour. Earlier that morning she had been located by Police at a flat at Northgate. When found she was sleeping on the lounge floor of the flat and there were also two youths sleeping on the lounge floor. After she was spoken to she assured my wife and I that she would behave herself and we decided to give her another chance. Realising that her behaviour was not normal an appointment was made for Deborah as an out-patient at Wilson Youth Hospital. This appointment was made for Friday, 11th July, 1975.

On the 17th June, 1975 Deborah went to school and she did not come home. She was reported as a Missing Person. On the 19th June, 1975 Deborah was located with two other youths in a stolen vehicle. That day she appeared at court in Charleville charged with Unlawfully Using the Vehicle. Later we collected Deborah and brought her home. On the last weekend in June I told her that she was not allowed to go out and she defied my instructions and went. She did the same this weekend and even though she gave explanations of her actions I have checked these stories out and found them to be untrue.

It has now got to the stage where she is completely uncontrollable and I think that for the sake of my wife's health and for her own good, Deborah should be put somewhere to be helped. She has been telling us for months that she wants to go into a home, but it sounds like a dare to us. K.L. Harding.

On the morning of 8 July 1975, Kevin drove to the Inala Magistrates Court alone where the order was made. The official application was brought by the female arresting officer, on the grounds that Deborah May Harding 'appeared to be uncontrollable'. Pat didn't go. 'I just couldn't,' she says. Kevin signed the statement, effectively relinquishing control of his daughter to the state. It took no longer than ten minutes. Too easy, Pat thinks now, but at the time she was able to convince herself it was the right thing for her child. And for the survival of her family.

The official documents sign into being a different Deborah Harding. The child who detested every institution she encountered was now controlled by the most powerful of them: the state. It would be years before she could shrug off its insidious hold, and in that time she would lose her faith, her trust and her innocence. And gain a whole new understanding of the word 'power'.

2

A Prison Term for Wagging School

Wilson Youth Hospital 8.07.75 Day Shift Admissions: Deborah Harding

New admission 11.30 am. Brought in by J.A.B. for being uncontrollable. Has appeared in court today and to appear again on the 4th August.
Age: 14 years Religion: R/C
Next of kin: Parents
Address: Patomar Street, Kedron
On Admission: Tidy in school uniform
Cooperative. Has settled in well. First hair treatment commenced.

There is an eerie quiet in adjourned courtrooms. Police and solicitors bat words and gestures back and forward, observers murmur, but there is a heightened sense of deference in the air, a kind of hush that emanates from the bench temporarily vacated by His or Her Honour. Even adults hardened by a thousand television court dramas feel chastened when they first enter a courtroom. Before a charge is read, before a witness is called.

Imagine a child led into such a room in the company of two police officers. Led past the portrait of the Queen, the rows of seats, to the bar table, where she is told to sit. She slumps in a wooden chair, head down, but not low enough to prevent her eyeing the empty bench in front of her, its timber panels emblazoned with the coat of arms. To the right of the bench is a small desk with recording instruments and notebooks carefully arranged, in front of that a raised carrel she recognises from television as the witness box. There is no one in it, of course; in fact the whole place is empty except for her, and the two police officers now conferring in low tones at the other end of the long table.

Presently a man in shorts, long socks and a brown tie enters and faces the room. 'Ready?' he says to the police. They nod. He throws his head back. 'All stand! This court is now in session!' he booms, as a man wearing a Dracula-like robe floats up behind the bench and sits. Even now that she's standing, all the child can see is his disembodied head bent over something in front of him, thick-framed glasses obscuring much of his face.

He sits, and the police follow suit, motioning her to do the same. The magistrate shuffles some papers in front of him and begins to speak; among the jumble of foreign-sounding words she hears her name. Fear begins to stew in her belly, a fear compounded by the odd suspicion that she isn't really here, that it's a dream. The others reinforce this by behaving as if she isn't in the room. They talk about her but not to her, as if this Deborah May Harding is some kind of absent acquaintance they are concerned for, worried about. But no one even looks at her; she might be invisible. It is a feeling with which, over the ensuing few years, she will become horribly familiar.

It is all over very quickly. Dracula is on his feet again and the man in the shorts is up, commanding, 'All rise! This court is now adjourned.' The policewoman looks at her for the first time, waving her to her feet. She has no idea what has just occurred. But as she is led away towards a side door she glances down at the sheaf of papers the policewoman is shuffling into order on the long table. On the top sheet, in carbon-copied blue type, is her father's name, Kevin Leo Harding. Above it is his signature, sudden proof that whatever has happened to her here has been done with his approval. That whatever is about to happen will happen with her parents' authority. For once in her life she stays quiet, doesn't say a thing as she is taken, but a small aperture of tenderness in her closes silently over.

Debbie: I was probably in a state of shock, I think. But I know I went quietly that time. After that I decided they were going to do it hard too, with a few smacks in the face. But then, the first time, I didn't know what had hit me. I do remember the nit cap and the pegs. You had to empty your pockets and then take your clothes off, in front of them. They'd just brought me straight from home, so I didn't have anything, but I turned my pockets out and there were these two clothes pegs. That's all I had. I handed them over.

Then I had to have a shower with this antiseptic stuff, like hospital pre-op stuff, and put this detergent in my hair, it probably had DDT in it, for nits. I put on the prison clothes, grey shorts and a T-shirt, and the nit cap. You had to wear that for three days, so everyone always knew who the new kids were. It was like a shining spotlight on your head. You knew what they thought: you're here, so you must be dirty. You're scum so we're going to de-nit you. They'd say it was about germs and diseases, but it was just another part of the shaming process.

Every girl had to have a gynaecological examination too. That was so we could swim in the pool. Where else in the world do you have to have a gynaecological check to swim in the local swimming pool? To me it felt disgusting: you got dressed in this white medical gown, you had to be naked underneath, and they used this horrible duck's bill thing, metallic. Most of us were virgins in there, but they assumed we were all little sluts. And these were the people who were supposed to be 'taking care' of us. Even now, I avoid going to gynaecologists.

Apart from those clear spikes of memory – the pegs, the nit cap, the medical exam – Debbie will block out much of her first traumatic entry to Wilson. The selective amnesia she develops will serve her well in the years to come, erasing the most painful experiences from the shallows of her memory. What she is left with will be impressions, like faded images in a fast-moving slide show, so that months and sometimes years of her life become indistinguishable from others.

These days, this first experience of Wilson has melded partly into the subsequent ones. Each time she was locked up the experience overrode the preceding one. With each fresh admission, she knew what was coming: she anticipated the foul smells that accompanied the shower, the shame that accompanied the hair treatments, the humiliation and sense of assault she felt when enduring the gynaecological examination. As a child, her only retaliatory weapons were her fists and her mouth, and they provoked further punishment. The months and years became, she says, 'one massive blur of never-ending horror'.

The institution Debbie Harding entered as an 'uncontrollable' fourteen-year-old in 1975 was already under the scrutiny of professionals concerned about the basic functions of Wilson Youth Hospital and the daily treatment of children incarcerated there. Wilson had opened in 1961 with accommodation for thirty-five boys, and was touted by Queensland's health department as 'the first child guidance hospital for the treatment of delinquency in the world'. Its approach was to be psychiatric rather than reformatory, and its staff were psychiatrists, doctors and nurses as well as warders and security officers. As such it became the dual responsibility of the departments of health and children's services.

The girls' section opened in May 1971, after its notorious predecessor, Karala House, was closed in response to allegations of 'inhumane, unjust and unlawful treatment' of inmates, and public outrage at reports of girls enduring three months of solitary confinement and other 'medieval punishments'. The transfer of girls to the new centre in the suburb of Wilson, however, was 'progressive'. In a letter dated 4 August 1971 to the undersecretary of the department of health, the then director of the children's services department, Mr C. Clark, explained that although 'staff had undergone a training course, they have not had actual experience of handling delinquent girls'.

But inexperienced staff weren't the only problem identified by a growing number of people including social workers, psychiatrists, chaplains, students and people directly involved with children in care, at Wilson and elsewhere. By 1975, many of them were worried enough to take their concerns about Wilson to the Inquiry into Youth in Queensland conducted by Judge Demack. At around the same time the Wilson Protest Group, comprising students and a number of church-based workers who frequently visited Wilson, was formed to raise awareness of what they saw as the 'brutalising' treatment handed out behind its walls.

Wally Dethlus, who was the Roman Catholic chaplain at Wilson between 1973 and 1976, spearheaded the formation of the group. He is still in no doubt about the institution and the way it was run. Wilson was 'isolated, controlled by drugs and violence and with little access to parents or loved ones': 'That was my first impression,' he says. 'I couldn't believe it. Kids who had no criminal convictions were being locked up and treated psychiatrically. The only other place in the world they did that was in the Russian gulags.'

In August 1973 Dethlus and another priest, Pat Tynan, began going into Wilson after a request from one of the girls to see a Catholic priest. There hadn't been a priest there in six months; Dethlus was told the previous incumbent had been discharged after being caught with a whip for 'enforcing discipline'. Dethlus isn't sure about the truth of the claim, but the things he saw in his first few visits soon overshadowed it.

They included the detention of children as young as eight years old; the forcible administration of antidepressant, sedative and tranquillising drugs, often by injection; violence between staff and children, and the use of harsh restraints; the almost total absence of education or training; the isolation of children from their families, and the confusion of children admitted for 'psychiatric assessment' to an institution that looked and functioned like a prison. Then there was the use of solitary confinement. 'For me it was one shock after another,' he says.

Dethlus and Tynan saw girls and boys individually. The children would come in 'just to chat'; the younger ones would sit and draw in the priest's notebook and those who couldn't read would ask for letters from home to be read aloud, and for help with writing replies. 'We'd often just talk about what they did during the day, their friends. Once they trusted you they would talk about more substantive issues, like sexual assaults at home. Some young women were having nightmares and they'd talk to me, and I'd try to help them get a measure of peace,' Dethlus says. 'Each one had a psychiatrist but I wasn't allowed to talk to them, and the kids didn't trust them. But I did get permission to approach them about a couple of kids, and I'd go to the manager, again and again, to advocate for them. Management hated my guts for doing that, for questioning them. But I saw that as my role: the one-on-one sessions with the kids, and advocating for them.'

At the core of the problems at Wilson, according to Dethlus and the rest of the protest group, were the disparate functions assigned to the institution, which served at once as an assessment centre, a remand centre, a treatment centre and a jail, all of this complicated by the location of the Children's Court in the same building. In a paper prepared in response to Judge Demack's report and recommendations (released in 1976 after a two-year inquiry into juvenile justice) the protest group pointed out that children on remand had only to walk through a door to appear in court, and that while this was convenient, this must 'cast doubt and fear in the parent's and child's minds about the quality of justice likely to be received in the Court'.

The group's concerns about the assessment process, however, would have rung loud alarm bells with Debbie Harding's parents if they had been in a position to read them at the time. How could proper assessments be made, the group asked, when many children didn't require a secure or closed environment, which itself might actually provoke antisocial behaviour in them? They quoted Judge Demack: 'It is important that he [sic] is assessed in relation to the conduct that brought him into Court, rather than his response to being held in a closed institution.'

For many children, that response was twofold, according to Wally Dethlus:

> It became entrenched in their psyche that they were both mad and bad; mad because they'd been sent to a psychiatric institution, and bad because they'd been locked up with kids who had committed criminal offences. Most of the girls went in without criminal convictions, they were in there for running away from home, things like that.
>
> Family Services would just 'pop' them in there for a four-week assessment because it solved their problems – they were incredibly underfunded and dealing with impossible case loads. We really fought those assessments. Because later, the same girls would be back, and for other, more serious things, robbery with violence, breaking and entering.

The official accounts of Debbie's initial month at Wilson reveal little more than she remembers herself. Comments range from 'reasonable behaviour, disobedient at times' to 'cheeky and defiant', 'weepy' and 'well behaved and pleasant'; and indeed, the hospital report prepared for her Children's Court appearance at the end of the four weeks concludes that, although 'no real change has occurred in the attitude of the parents or child, [her] remaining in Wilson will not improve this'. The recommendation was for Debbie to return home 'with the hope that communication between mother and daughter will improve'. She was still labelled as 'uncontrollable' and was ordered to live at home under the supervision of the director of Children's Services until she was eighteen.

The arrangement lasted less than three months. By the end of October, the optimism the Hardings had begun with on Debbie's release had deteriorated, and the situation seemed irretrievable. There were huge fights about her attitude and about her Aboriginal friends, even with Nana. Inevitably, Debbie took off. When she turned up again, she agreed she couldn't stay at home. Instead a place was found for her at a Children's Services hostel at Kelvin Grove, from which she absconded in early November. By the middle of that month, she was back inside Wilson.

What of the much touted 'psychiatric assessment'? The promised treatment that would 'fix' Debbie's behaviour? Neither was ever mentioned, to Debbie or her parents, although they did see a psychiatrist at Wilson who suggested Pat should make 'a really strong effort to try to be consistent in handling Deborah', and that Deborah and Nana should not be sharing a bed in the family home. These comments are made in reports by a Wilson psychiatrist, and by Janne McGaw, the child care officer assigned to Debbie, who visited the family a month after her initial release from Wilson. McGaw observed at that time that 'communication between members of the family seems to have improved only minimally', and that Debbie's father 'seems unable to convey any warmth or affection when relating to his daughter'.

Kevin Harding is referred to in various documents as a 'hard' and 'distant' man who appeared to have 'opted out' of his role in Debbie's upbringing. In one report, Debbie was said to be tearful after her father claimed she couldn't possibly be his child, that there must have been a mix-up at the hospital where she was born. But Debbie's memories of her father at this time don't gel with the official line: she remembers a 'softie' who she could twist around her little finger, who would take her side if she was fighting with her little brother, Michael.

Nonetheless, although most of the fights at home were between Debbie and Pat, Debbie could feel the huge gulf that had opened up between Kevin and herself. More than anything else, it was the fractured and cool relationship with her father that she would anguish over and regret in the months to come. It would become the focus of the next few terrifying years. She didn't know it then, but when she walked through the gates of Wilson again in November 1975, Debbie's life would spiral into a grief-fuelled vortex which, nearly thirty years later, still shadows her waking life and her dreams.

It's an ordinary afternoon in late November. Inside the high brick walls lashed with wire, girls mill around the stuffy 'therapy' room, twirling strips of nylon or knitting lengths of wool into shapes that might become slippers or might not. A couple of them are reading, someone is sketching in a school exercise book. With these novel forms of therapy, young female inmates of Wilson are meant to help improve themselves. To cure whatever is ailing them. To become better, nicer girls.

Debbie Harding doesn't even pretend to do any of these things. She isn't interested in knitting or reading. She's slouched against the back wall, surly, the clack of knitting needles grating in her ears. She hates them all for being so good, for doing what they're told. She's got half a mind to provoke a couple of them until they're angry enough for a fight. Something to liven things up. She's terminally bored, bored with the stupefying routine and with everyone's mute compliance with it. And she's itching to shatter it, just for some entertainment. Something to pass the time.

Before she has a chance to, a white-uniformed nurse appears at the door. 'Debbie, the psychiatrist wants to see you,' she says, swivelling on her flatties, waiting. 'Now.' She stands eyeing the skinny, blonde-haired child, and her look is part impatience, part contempt. 'Come on.'

The child returns the stare and for a moment doesn't move. Two things go rapidly through her head: at least the stupid bitch is taking me out of this boring room, and fuck, what if they're going to tell me they're keeping me here for years? What the hell, she rationalises, it will kill the boredom for a few minutes. She pushes herself out of her slouch and moves away from the wall. As she reaches the door two long whistles issue from the group of knitters, and she turns momentarily, thrusts two fingers savagely in the air. Then she saunters up the stairs, towards the psychiatrist's office.

Inside, it's immediately obvious something serious is going down. It's the psychiatrist's face. It's usually shut up tight, as if it's a mask that holds everything snugly behind it, something he can put on in the mornings and take off when he gets home at night. Right now it looks as if someone has loosened it around the edges; his lips, usually a straight, hard line, are kind of sloppy, and his eyes are wandering all over the room.

Finally he lets them rest on a spot somewhere near the wall clock ticking into the silence. The child stands there with her arms folded. She wants to say, get it over. Usually the psychiatrist will tell her to unfold her arms but when he opens his mouth this time, he says something odd, something that doesn't make immediate sense. He says: 'There's no easy way to say this, Deborah. It's your father. He died suddenly last night.'

The nurse who has brought her watches the girl, something like pity replacing the contempt. The girl's body twitches slightly, as if she has been sharply smacked. But she doesn't make any sound. There is just silence and the ticking; and then all hell breaks loose as the girl erupts into the air, lunging towards the psychiatrist and screaming he's a liar, he's a lying cunt, he's a filthy dog, as her arms flail about and the psychiatrist raises his own in defence, shouting for help.

The nurse is on her in one loud heartbeat, yelling over her shoulder for back-up as the child throws wild punches, still screaming. When two male nurses arrive and hold the wild-eyed girl on the floor, the psychiatrist regains his composure, pats down his mask. When it is safely back in place, he looks at the girl, and raises his voice above the obscenities streaming from her. 'Take her down,' he says.

Deborah Harding is half carried, half dragged to the detention unit where tantrums are controlled and punishments meted out. She is locked in a padded cell. The cell is empty apart from a bare mattress on the floor. There is one high window, barred and shuttered. She barely acknowledges where she is.

Hours pass as she throws her body around the room, using her arms and legs and voice as weapons, peppering the walls and the ceiling with expletives. Wishing they were bullets so that her grief would be visual, that this room would be marked by it, scarred by it. As if the pain was a solid thing, and could be evicted from inside her. Out, out of her. If she can't get it out she wants to die, just disappear, becomes there and then and forever unafraid of anything, unafraid of death. Afraid only that she will not die. That she will live forever, solitary, with this spear of guilt at her chest.

Does she dream it, hallucinate it, or is that the matron's face at the window? Now she's coming in the door, coolly observing. She says: 'No wonder the poor man had a heart attack. Look at you. You've driven him to an early grave.' The matron ignores the stream of expletives this produces, just raises her voice a little as she says it again, telling her that she's killed her father, that *it's your fault, Deborah, now will you start to behave?*

The matron leaves but returns with the same message, as if the words will somehow still her. They don't, of course. She continues to scream for hours. Faces appear at the door to tell her just how bad she is, and after a while she doesn't know if it is matron's face or a nurse's or, perhaps, her own. She has lost all sense of anything but hate and pain, they are all that exist. Darkness does not diminish them. For hours into the night she kicks the cell door, then curls up in a foetal position, sobbing.

Some time before dawn, the nurse she calls Peachy enters the cell, crouches beside her, opens her hands. She expects more medication, pills; but her palms are full of sweets. She pulls more out of her pockets. She sits with her for a long time in the dark, talking quietly, her voice a salve on her own rawness. The words are kind, patient. Her body feels as if it has been skinned, but slowly her breath stops searing her throat. Her wary eyes flick a look at Peachy. A human being. In this house of horror. She feels her eyes close and she lets them, and briefly sleeps.

Debbie: After Dad died it was just a blur of violence. I wanted to kill the matron. I told them, never let her near me, because I'll just kill her, and when she did come near I would leap over tables and hurl chairs, I just wanted to get my hands on her. Just the sight of her. She just kept telling me I'd done it. *You killed your father.* Over and over. And that's what I swallowed. That's what I played out in my life for years, until I was thirty: I killed my father so I must be bad. I must need punishment. And the way you get punishment is to be really bad, to become violent. So that's what I did.

She wasn't even going to let me out for the funeral. I was locked up in the padded cell, and I was being treated like an animal so I acted like one: I'd smash things, and lie on the floor and kick the door for hours and hours. I'd get a rhythm up after a while.

In the next day or so the matron's decision was reversed and they discharged me to Mum's care on permanent release. I went to the funeral. I stood looking down at the hole in the ground, and there was this urge to jump in there with him. Nothing else, no other feeling. After that, it's a blur of horror again. I was back in Wilson not long afterwards.

The official records of that year make no reference to the death of Kevin Harding. It is mentioned in Debbie's files only in retrospect, a footnote in a drama that was rapidly becoming larger-than-life. 'Name: Deborah May Harding. Charge: Break, enter and steal/ robbery with violence/steal/receive. Next of kin: mother, Patricia Harding, Patomar Street, Kedron. Father: Kevin Harding, deceased.' That is all. But the day of Kevin's premature death from a massive heart attack, at age thirty-nine, drew an indelible line beneath Debbie's childhood. Until then, she was a confused and bad-tempered little girl, a rebel with various small causes whose grand-mother still persisted in buying her dolls. But in accepting the blame for her father's death she accepted a terrifying power. That kind of power and capacity for 'badness' most surely belonged to the world of adults. After November 1975, still in the tender skin of a fourteen-year-old, she stepped firmly away from childish truanting and shoplifting and into the serious role of a violent offender, a young woman looking for trouble. Wilson gave her all the right contacts.

Debbie doesn't remember exactly when she met Bimbo, but by the time of Kevin's death the two were firm friends, and thereafter liter-ally partners in crime. Bimbo was a wild and larrikin Aboriginal girl whose brash and open character Debbie was immediately drawn to. She was also a Wilson veteran, a seasoned operator on the streets and a familiar face in the Children's Court. Debbie felt easy in her company, and never in danger of being bored.

In the early days of their acquaintance, they hung out together when their stays at Wilson overlapped, occasionally meeting up outside at the fun parlour, falling in and out of touch. Debbie knew instinctively, though, that Bimbo would always be a 'mate', someone to be relied on, someone – maybe the only one – she could see herself reflected in. Someone real.

On the weekend after Kevin's death, when Debbie was released to her mother's care in preparation for the funeral, the girls met up. A day or two later, with the funeral over and the atmosphere at home as cold as a grave, Debbie disappeared. The new and unassailable feeling of guilt had followed her from Wilson; it was in the eyes of everyone she knew. Except her mates. With them the guilt was transformed into something else, something hard and unfettered, unafraid. That's how she felt when she was with them. Immune to all the emotions required of her elsewhere, and to all the rules.

Living on the streets, camping in the homes of friends, her life became a day-to-day matter of survival outside the law: breaking in to houses, picking fights and 'hanging out' during the day, then off to the fun parlour and pool hall to spend their booty at night. In the five weeks she was outside the institution after Kevin's death, Debbie managed to accumulate six charges that police brought against her in January 1976: three of break and enter, one of stealing, one of unlawful damage and, remarkably, one of possessing a firearm. A policeman's gun.

Debbie: We'd broken into a copper's house, and we got this gun as well as some money, and we knew they were after us so we thought we'd hide. Where do you hide with a gun? We were at this house in Gladstone Road at Highgate Hill, so we got up on the roof. It was real kids' stuff, you know? Oh, we'll just get up on the roof and hide. They won't find us here! So we're up there and there's a hundred cops around, or it felt like it to us anyway, and we've got this cop's gun, and they're all freaking out because they think we're going to shoot someone. We weren't going to shoot anyone! We were just kids, mucking around.

That's how Bimbo and I spent our days, running amok around the place. We'd break into houses and steal money – we only wanted cash – and then go play pool and pinball all night. We'd get busted but you didn't bring all the others down with you, you'd just take responsibility for the lot. It was better to have one locked up than two or three of you. It drove Mum and Nana barmy, that I'd take the rap for lots of things I hadn't necessarily done, but it was about being staunch with your mates, true to the code. People don't understand that, the code; adults think they know everything, but they know shit. That's why I was always so much closer to my mates than anyone else. Mates stand by you, and by the code.

We knew that breaking into houses wasn't right; but I believed they'd pushed me so far that I had no other choice but to live out there, because I wasn't accepted in here. Because in here it was so wrong, so biased and unjust and on their rules, which weren't fair. So fuck it; we'd go live in the culture of criminals – at least you knew it was straight down the line, no bullshit there. There were rules, it was a code. There was no code in formal authorities, we thought it was just bullshit, lies. I remember thinking that when the old nun flogged me; they said one thing and did another.

We didn't spare our victims any thought. To me, they gave us no other choice, that's the only way for me to survive. We weren't hurting the victim, anyway, just taking their money. We never demolished or wrecked their houses; we didn't steal TVs, only cash, or took their bank books and stole their money that way.

We couldn't stand it when other kids wrecked places, left shit on things, threw things around. That's disgusting. I'd say to those kids, why are you doing that? If you want the money to eat and live, take the money and get out of their house, there's no need to demolish it. The only time we did some demolishing was the cop's house, but he was a cop. At the time I had no idea where the path was leading. I just lived day to day, not counting the days, and so it's all just blurred into one thing. Survival.

The day she is picked up and charged after a month-long spree of petty crime is vivid in her memory. For some reason, she has returned home from Bimbo's to see her mother. It is January 1976. Nana is there, of course, and so is a male relative, Arthur, a man she will later come to despise. She is told the police are looking for her. Of course, she has no intention of reporting in. But everyone encourages her, they all assure her it will be nothing, that they will just want to talk to her and she might as well get it out of the way. Finally, they persuade her. Debbie and Pat climb into Arthur's car; he drives them to the Woolloongabba police station in Brisbane's south.

The building is two-storey, old red brick with arched windows and timber trim, backing onto the Gabba Cricket Ground. They pull up outside and Arthur suggests Pat stays in the car; he will go in with Debbie. They won't be long. Debbie is already suspicious, is kicking herself for giving in to this. Why does she want to talk to these dogs anyway? But some part of her wants to make her mother happy, to mollify her.

She and Arthur walk towards the double glass doors that front the footpath. Through the doors and straight up a steep set of steps lined with brown linoleum. She remembers the murky colour of them, the papery smell of polish and officialdom. The sound of her feet and his, an irregular echo in her head.

At the top of the stairs there is a desk, and to the side a whole room of desks; fans tick over the humid January air and the windows to Ipswich Road are open. Cars swish by beneath them. As soon as they reach the first desk and the grinning copper behind it, Arthur leans down to her. 'Got you, you little bitch,' he whispers. 'Now you're going back to Wilson.'

She is stunned, but she hadn't realised how ready she was for betrayal, that she'd expected it, that her whole body was on high alert. She yells and swings a punch at him. 'Fuckin' arsehole! Ya fuckin' filthy dog! You're all dogs!' Then she's striding among the desks with their piles of paper and files which she's brushing to the floor, scattering by the handful, but there is still this blind fury, so one by one she seizes the heavy manual typewriters and hurls them towards the open windows. At least one sails out, tumbling, and meets the hot cement of the footpath with a satisfying smash.

Her arms are gripped then by two policemen, one on each side, they've got her in a firm hold and even though she's struggling and still screaming obscenities at them, at Arthur, who is nowhere to be seen, they manage to march her back down those hateful brown stairs. She is livid with anger and resentment and furious at herself, twisting her body to make it as hard as she can for them. They get her to the bottom. She looks wildly about – surely her mother will help her – but knows instinctively she won't, that no one will.

For one long moment she sees her own flailing body reflected in the glass of the doors, her face contorted with shock and fury. Helpless. But not, she knows suddenly, powerless. While the officers hesitate over how to open the doors without releasing her, she gathers all her fierce energy into her legs and kicks out. There is a loud crack as the glass in both doors shatters, spraying shards out

onto the footpath where they glint triumphantly in the hard sun.
Her heart leaps. They might have got her, but they've got her on her
terms. With the help of two more officers, they manhandle her out
and into a police car.

It is January 10. She is driven back to Wilson via the detested
courtroom where, this time, as the grey-haired magistrate signs the
order for her admission, her fury erupts again and she up-ends the
table at which she is made to stand. Two days later she is back.
The magistrate commits her to stand trial in the Supreme Court
on a charge of robbery with violence. She is taken back to Wilson.
It is her fifteenth birthday.

Wilson Youth Hospital, Treatment Section: Saturday 10.1.76.
Debbie Harding admitted 12.45 pm. For Children's Court on
Monday. Unkempt appearance and upset about admission.
First hair treatment done. Evening: telling stories about how
she and mates bashed up all the old Wilson girls. Trying out
strangle holds on other girls, watch she may be dangerous.

Sunday: Bragging constantly of her 'tough' activities, and
successfully getting attentive audience. Demonstrating throat
grips etc and frequently raised arm as if to punch, to test peer
reaction. 2nd hair treatment done. Given aspirin for sore arm
and ribs – claims police hurt her.

Monday 12.1.76: To court 9.40 am. Brought back from court
screaming and upset, to Closed Tantrum at 10.45 am. To Open
Tantrum 11 am to 11.15 pm. 3rd hair treatment.

Tuesday: Became abusive; ordered to her room. Knocked
chairs over in process and using foul language. Banging and
kicking on door. Evening: trouble from 3 pm onwards.
Constantly stirring and urging others to join her. Rude and
un-cooperative, asking to go to detention. Refused to do
therapy. Dr Foley notified and IMI Largactil 25 mgm ordered
as a p. measure for extreme bad behaviour. Debbie continued
to misbehave and had the whole place in uproar. At 7 pm
viciously slapped another girl across the face. Lashed out
violently at staff and called Sister a 'moll' and a 'slut'.

Absolutely unable to reason with her. To Room 13 and IMI Largactil given 7.10 pm with no effect. Continued to bang and scream abuse for an hour. Night: slipped and fell on floor in sitting position. Using obscene language fluently.

Wednesday 14.1.76: very lethargic and pale this morning. Slept till lunchtime. Complained of sore leg, no bruising or swelling evident.

The ongoing, living nightmare of Wilson begins here. For the next two years, Debbie Harding's life will be a revolving door of crime, violence, incarceration and punishment, inside Wilson and on the streets, as she lives out her image of the kind of badness that might have killed a man. Her father.

Those first six charges will be followed with predictable regularity by similar ones: robbery with violence, break and enter with intent, break and enter, steal. There were long months in Wilson, broken occasionally by 'trials' of living at home with Pat, Michael and Nana. But Kevin's death had done little to improve the relationship between mother and daughter. Several months after Debbie's readmission to Wilson, well-meaning relatives took Pat overseas, hoping to help her recover not just from the sudden loss of a young husband, but from the slow loss of her daughter. Gradually, she and Debbie had become more and more estranged.

Pat was in no state to make predictions then, but even so she could not have forecast the destructive effect her short holiday would have on both her children. Left abruptly by their father, Debbie and thirteen-year-old Michael now felt abandoned by their mother. Michael's trauma would sit like a molten rock inside him for years before it exploded. For Debbie, though, it was simply part of life's ongoing insistence that she needed to be punished. Inside Wilson, that was easily dealt with. Punishment echoed back at her from the walls she kicked, the girls she punched, the plates she hurled. And from the eyes of the staff that were always on her, watching. Despising.

Back inside, her behaviour deteriorated as she became convinced that the way to deal with the violence of forced imprisonment was more violence, more provocation. The fire alarms studding the low ceilings were an easy target; she would be rewarded for punching them by the arrival of two screaming fire trucks and the inevitable detention in isolation. Everything was worth the punishment, though: blocking up the shower so that the bathroom flooded or, if she was angry, smashing the television.

She would be held variously in sections with names like 'treatment', 'the glass room', 'open tantrum' and 'closed tantrum'. In the glass room, staff would stand and watch as she hurled whatever she could find around the room; but when they locked her in 'open tantrum' it would be 'on for young and old': 'They'd have to get the orderlies. They'd come in all the time and give me injections – but it would take six or seven of them to hold me down,' she remembers. 'If I'd been out, they'd always lock me up in there because I'd flip out as soon as I got in. I'd be straight in with an injection. Once, I slept for a whole day because I wasn't focused, but then a week later, they gave me another one and I thought, I'm not going to sleep on this shit. And I didn't. I stayed awake kicking the door all night, then had a bit of a nap the next day, then started up again. And that would start everyone else up. Everyone would be kicking walls and doors.'

For Debbie, survival became increasingly tied up with how tough she could be, and how cunning. Or in her parlance, 'acting insane to stay sane'. Instinctively she knew she had to have strategies, but despite her growing street-smarts and desensitisation to pain, she was essentially still a little girl reacting tit-for-tat to the heavy hand of authority – and usually losing.

She can't remember how long she spent in detention inside Wilson. She does recall there was a long block of time when she was banned by matron from walking on any carpet. Effectively, this meant she could never leave open or closed tantrum. Occasionally she would get around this by jumping between doorways or by crawling – rather than walking – along the carpeted hall.

Debbie: It was all bullshit. You did things to get a reaction, to shock. It was just yahooing, and if they'd ignored me, I probably would have stopped. But they'd lock me up for things like running up the hallway, so then I'd turn it up. I was on centre stage. Bring it on. Then they'd use the drugs. Mogadon, Largactil, and that's a heavy-duty psych drug. Girls would walk around like zombies on it. We called it the Largactil Shuffle.

Indeed, in a confidential document 'for the use of Wilson Youth Hospital Staff Only', Dr Phillips, the senior medical director of youth welfare and guidance, states candidly that 'the types of cases detained in Wilson Youth Hospital for treatment are the psychiatrically disturbed ones in the juvenile delinquent population . . . admitted because of the usual offences, ie, stealing, running away from home, offences against the person and property and so on'. About two-thirds of these, he estimates, will need 'child psychiatry treatment'; the drugs 'usually used are the anti-convulsants, the sedatives and the tranquillisers'.

Despite the drugs, which she believes destroyed swathes of her memories of this time, Debbie does have a clear image of the day she up-ended the bench in front of the Children's Court magistrate:

> The stupid old prick, he was pissing me off. You knew the old dog was going to lock you up so you'd just boot the table, create a bit of excitement, instead of just standing there like a mullet going, oh, thank you for sending me back to that hole.
>
> They'd expect you to sit there subdued, and accept their authority, authority that was so fucked and made no sense. They could abuse you all they liked in there, and then they'd expect you to sit in court and cop it on the chin. Well, no way, cop *this* on the chin – there goes the table, boot! and the chairs, boot! Eventually they didn't even take me into court, because I'd either escape down the stairs or wreck their room.
>
> You had to do something, or you'd be a blithering mess, you'd be broken. But my arcing up got worse and worse and more violent, because of their violence back at me. It became tit-for-tat. If they'd just backed off and left me alone . . . but they just had to keep upping it, because they've got to make out they're smarter. So you'd have to outsmart them all.
>
> Like when the coppers brought us in and went upstairs to big-note themselves, leaving us for five minutes, Bimbo and I would leap straight out onto the verandah and jump down into the street, gone. Or out through the matron's office – she always left the door open – out the window, onto the roof, into the yard next door.

By her sixteenth birthday, no one was pretending that Debbie would ever live permanently at home again. Pat had bought another house, in Vale Street, Wilston, and Nana moved permanently into the old family home at Kedron. This was the house Debbie would be released to for the all-too-brief patches of freedom she wrested from the authorities. Despite the steady escalation in her criminal activities, Nana was always prepared to take her on. She never believed Debbie's behaviour was as bad as it was portrayed. She would back her, support her financially and emotionally. And lie for her, if necessary.

There was really only one thing that Nana found disagreeable or distasteful in Debbie's actions: her insistence on bringing home her Aboriginal friends. It was easy at that stage to blame Bimbo for the constant trouble Debbie had been in since Kevin's death, Bimbo and the extended mob of family and friends that had become her granddaughter's familiars.

But even Beryl Grey, expecting the worst from such associations, didn't see bigger trouble looming, in the shape of a young Aboriginal man Debbie had teamed up with late in 1976. Or maybe she did see it, and Debbie, perennially dismissive of warnings – especially where she sniffed any skerrick of racism or criticism of her friends – ignored it. Whichever way it was, Debbie walked blithely into the quicksand of her first truly violent personal relationship. The self-imposed regime of punishment intensified dangerously.

3

Once Violence Becomes a Possibility

Wilson Youth Hospital: Deborah May Harding. DOB: 12 January 1961

July 8 1975: admitted to WYH on remand

Aug 4: placed under supervision until 18 yrs by Children's Court Brisbane as uncontrollable – Patomar St Kedron

Oct 21: transferred to Kelvin Grove Hostel

Nov 7: appeared before Children's Court Brisbane, admonished and discharged

Nov 10: absconded

Nov 16: remanded at WYH

Dec 3: placed in mother's custody, Patomar St Kedron

Dec 6: absconded

Jan 10 1976: admitted to WYH

Jan 12: appeared before Children's Court Brisbane, committed to trial to Supreme Court in March

Jan 12: re-admitted to WYH

Feb 16: appeared before Children's Court Brisbane, admonished and discharged. Re-admitted to WYH

Apr 13: appeared before Children's Court Brisbane, admonished and discharged. Re-admitted to WYH

Jun 3: placed on trial with mother at Patomar St Kedron

Sep 24: admitted to WYH

Sep 27: committed to Care and Control for 2 years by Children's Court Brisbane. Re-admitted to WYH

Nov 17: trial with mother, Patomar St Kedron

Dec 20: new address: Vale St Wilston

Feb 21 1977: admitted to WYH on remand until 3.3.77 by

Children's Court Coolangatta

Mar 3: appeared before Children's Court Coolangatta, remanded until 7.4.77

Mar 14: appeared before Children's Court Brisbane, admonished and discharged. Re-admitted to WYH

April 1: appeared before Children's Court Brisbane, admonished and discharged. Re-admitted to WYH

Apr 7: committed to Care and Control for 2 years by Children's Court Coolangatta. Re-admitted to WYH

May 9: trial with grandmother, Mrs Grey, Patomar St Kedron

Feb 22 1978: placed under Supervision for 1 year by Children's Court Petrie, Patomar St Kedron

Mar 15: exact address unknown, boyfriend's flat in Rockhampton

May 5: trial with grandmother, Mrs Grey, Patomar St Kedron

April 7 1979: discharged from Care and Control

If there is any such thing as a 'normal adolescent', you wouldn't have found one in the vicinity of Debbie Harding in the mid to late 1970s. What constitutes 'normal' anyway? Despite their protestations, 'normal' is something most fourteen- and fifteen-year-olds of any era will crave: the assurance that they fit in, are just like others, that they have a 'normal' mother and father, a 'normal' body, a life not too different to their friends'. But Debbie Harding was the exception that made the rule. As a teenager, she really didn't have a concept of what 'normal' was. Apart from a rejection of the 'straight' kids or the 'vegies' – kids who toed the line, obeyed their parents, went to school and ballet and Girl Guides – 'normal' life wasn't something she gave any thought to. Even before the catastrophic changes that came with her father's death, her view of the world was split not so much between normal and abnormal, as between us and them. Friend or foe. Strong or weak.

Even now, the adult Debbie has to look to her son, Joshua, to track the habits and patterns of normal teenagers, to find out what their interests are, how they occupy their time. Joshua belongs to a tribe she knows little about, to a country from which she was exiled before she became a resident. One in which young people move happily (mostly) between the worlds of school and home and friendships, making plans for a future they are confident of enjoying, even of owning. Debbie watches Joshua carefully. Admiring his progress, mostly, but also maintaining vigilant guard. There are patches of quicksand in that country for any teenager, and Debbie has seen more of them than most.

Debbie: I have no concept of what a normal adolescent is, or what they do. I never have. I suppose they come home, watch telly, listen to music, do homework. If that's normal, I didn't do any of that. My teenage life was on the streets, with my mates . . . In and out of Wilson, running amok, going to bed late, sleeping late, getting up at lunchtime, breaking into people's houses all afternoon or night, then going and spending the money, yahooing.

Up until I was fourteen or so, Nana would buy me a doll every birthday and Christmas, and they just sat at her place. I'd say to her, stop buying me dolls, I don't play with the stupid things. I don't remember playing at all.

With the money we stole we'd go to the pinball parlour, play pool, listen to the jukebox, buy clothes, but I gave lots of money away. There was no big thing I wanted money for; it was more about 'fuck you'. We were being treated like these bad-arsed criminals, and the way I interpreted that as a teenager was to break into people's houses and steal their purses. That was my interpretation of a big, bad-arsed criminal.

But because of the way we were treated, with absolute violence, we'd get smashed around, locked up in the watch-house, locked up again, you got in this cycle, same ol', same ol'. Playing the role. You'd be interlocked with these coppers on this merry-go-round and you couldn't get off. So I acted the part. All that stuff I was told – 'you're bad, you're bad', so okay, what will I do that's bad? Steal, belt other kids if they looked sideways at me, that sort of thing. I didn't have any fear. I was never scared, not of the dark, or of being alone. All those things get removed from you.

So she certainly didn't admit to any trepidation when, aged fifteen and hanging around at Keperra with the 'Keperra boys' – a loose group of white and Aboriginal youths who ran the streets of the outer northern suburbs – she encountered the wild and unpredictable Matthew Parson (not his real name).

Parson was a young Aboriginal boy who had been adopted at birth by a white couple already well into their sixties. Even at fifteen he was known for his violence and quick temper, but Debbie was drawn, as usual, to his wildness, his antisocial personality, his contempt for institutions of all kinds. By the end of 1976, despite Debbie's ricocheting in and out of Wilson, they were boyfriend and girlfriend, a young and unlikely Bonnie and Clyde. For this Bonnie, however, there would never be that kind of glamour in the relationship. Instead, its trademarks would be black eyes, split lips and broken bones, and the abject humiliation that accompanies terrible and regular beatings.

They began soon after the relationship did. Debbie: 'We were coming home on the train one day. He was so jealous and irrational that I'd only have to look sideways to set him off. Mostly I'd have no idea what happened. This day he just flipped out, I've no idea why, and started bashing me on the train. Between the city and Keperra he gave me two black eyes and two split lips.'

That day was the beginning of Debbie's descent into a hell of unpredictable, brutal bashings that would continue for several years. Shortly afterwards, as the two were 'mucking around' in Nana's backyard one afternoon, it happened again. Something caused a boilover in Parson's brain and, without warning, he'd grabbed a long piece of wood and brought it down with all his strength over Debbie's head. Instinctively, she held up her arm to block the blow, and in that second she felt the bone in her forearm snap in one clean break.

In severe pain, she asked him to take her to a hospital. Nope, he said calmly, get in the car, we're going to Ipswich. Debbie's pleas fell on deaf ears. You'll tell, he scoffed. I won't, she promised. She bore the pain all day until finally, that night, she escaped from him and literally ran to Ipswich Hospital. When doctors asked her what had happened, she told them she'd fallen down the stairs.

Back then, she didn't think of it as domestic violence, and has trouble labelling it even now. 'I wasn't brought up with violence, so that thought wasn't in my head,' she says. 'That's not why I lied to the doctors; it was more about not telling on anyone. Not just because it's your boyfriend; you just don't tell. Besides, in my head I thought it was what I deserved. This was just after Dad died, I thought I had it coming.'

Domestic violence, say the texts, usually involves a 'cycle of violence' in which the perpetrator's anger and frustrations grow and peak in physical abuse, followed by apology, remorse, and a 'honeymoon' period in which amends are made or attempted with gifts, kindness, good behaviour. Parson, though, showed no sign of remorse or shame over his brutality to Debbie; there was no kindness and certainly no gifts. She was his possession, he believed; he was her master, but in an ironic reversal of the slave relationship, it was Parson who wore the stamp of ownership: a huge tattoo of her name inscribed in blue across his back. It was visual and permanent proof not of his devotion but of his rights. Perhaps in the beginning Debbie was meant to be impressed. Instead she simply lived in a heightened state of anxiety from day to day while Matthew was around; she knew others did too, although no one would concede it.

Somehow, between the beatings, between sojourns in Wilson, Debbie found herself pregnant. She was sixteen. This revelation rattled even the imperturbable Nana, possibly because of her own history: she had borne Pat out of wedlock, at the same age Debbie now was. Together, Nana and Pat arranged a hasty abortion at a clinic in Sydney.

For Debbie, the memory is like something out of a bad movie: 'I was put on a plane alone, then in a cab at the other end, taken to a place that was like a corner shop. Then getting put on a trolley and knocked out. Then next thing, being wheeled out again and given a cup of tea. Put back in a cab, back on a plane, and there you are home again, where no one mentions it, no one talks about it at all.' Like her father's death, the loss – albeit unacknowledged – became merely a footnote in her conscious mind. In her subconscious, though, it added to a growing weight that, at some unpredictable time, would become impossible to bear.

But out of the sad, confusing days around the abortion, Debbie brought one thing: a determination not to allow anyone to make decisions for her again. Even then, at sixteen, she'd surprised herself with her ready cooperation with the abortion plans, her willingness to concede that her elders knew best. She vowed never to make a slip like that again.

Just months later, she was pregnant once more. This time, she was determined no one would interfere. 'It wasn't really about having a baby at all, but about them not telling me what to do,' she recalls. That summed up her attitude: there was no real excitement about the prospect of a baby, but no nervousness either. 'I wasn't worried about it, or freaked out about it,' she says now. 'I didn't worry about anything much in the world then. I was still living in and out of home, still doing break and enters. No one actually knew that I was pregnant. I wore my ordinary clothes the whole time. I was pretty well straight up and down.'

Perhaps because Debbie's baby was 'transverse' – lying across rather than upside down – and because her girlish shape barely changed, it was easy for both her and Matthew to continue living as they had been since they met, mainly on the streets. Neither of them made any concessions for the tiny life they were responsible for. Debbie didn't bother attending antenatal appointments at the hospital, didn't prepare a nursery. And Matthew didn't let the notion of a developing baby dilute his volatility, or his rages against the mother of his child.

Sometimes, Debbie would feel a tremor of fear when Matthew came near her, unable to predict his mood or the next blow. On the rare occasions she was able to acknowledge her fright, she would resolve to leave him, to get away. It never worked. Once, when they were driving and she bravely announced the relationship was over, he accelerated through the dark suburb and drove 'like a madman' to the top of the local quarry. Speeding towards the cliff edge, he screamed that he would kill them all, all three of them. 'All right! I'll come back!' she'd assured him, clutching the dashboard, the seat belt undone over the slight swell of her belly. Only then had he allowed the car to slow.

One day he sauntered into Nana's house and said he needed help to clutch-start the car. Outside the December sun beat mercilessly in a washed-out sky. She slid her swollen belly beneath the steering wheel, conscious of the growing baby, and began to work the pedals, easing them in and out. She was sweating, but nothing like him. He was carrying too much weight and suffering as he tried to push and bully the car into submission. The third attempt failed. It was enough. When she looked up his bulk suddenly filled the driver's window and she didn't even see the fist coming. Her body slumped sideways across the gearstick.

She knew nothing until she woke up, hours later, in a hospital bed. Her face was bruised and broken, her right eye a slit against angry skin, black and blue. She was told later that she staggered around for a while after the king-hit as if nothing had happened, until one of his friends arrived and noticed something was wrong. Insisted on taking her to casualty. Where, when she was properly awake, she promptly eased her body, now eight months pregnant, off the trolley and walked out, hailing a cab home to Nana's house.

All the way back she cursed herself. Not for failing with the clutch, but for failing to see the fist coming. She should have known by now. She should have been able to pick it. But couldn't. Just a month earlier he thought she was looking at another boy and smashed a chair across her stomach. Later she will be able to distinguish between violence against her children's bodies and violence against her own, but then, at sixteen, the child growing under her ribs was just a part of her. She couldn't separate it out.

But she learnt to pick it, because she couldn't fight back. She tried. Some time before the chair incident, Matthew had been thrown through the windscreen in a car accident, leaving his face punctured with dozens of minute shards of glass. He was more subdued as he lay on his bed at his parents' house, but hurling insults all the same, using his mouth rather than his fists. Blinking against the verbal assault, Debbie had seen her moment, looked around and grabbed an old softball bat, bringing it down hard across his back. *The bastard.* Elation in her veins as the heavy bat fell through the air.

But it was short-lived. She'd miscalculated badly. In seconds he was on his feet and almost on her as she fled, out the door, down the front steps, sprinting down the footpath. Knowing what was coming, feeling sick. Pregnancy slowed her down, but she'd torn through several backyards and over three fences before he finally got her, tackling her to the ground. He held her down effortlessly with his bulk while his eyes searched out a weapon, anything. Despite his own injuries he managed to keep her there, lean across and rip a paling from a nearby fence. Then he gave her the flogging of her life.

Nothing changed right up to the day the baby was born. The beatings continued – he would blacken one or both eyes every couple of weeks – and so did their ventures into crime. Just weeks before the birth, they were caught red-handed inside a house at Dayboro, where Matthew gave the excuse that his girlfriend was pregnant and hungry. It didn't wash with the police, who charged them anyway.

Another day – on one of her escapades from Wilson – Debbie managed to find her way to Matthew's home at Keperra, and when the police inevitably knocked on their door, their quarry was crouching in a cupboard, willing herself to be invisible. Like a small, frightened child. It took them just minutes to find her: a simple game of hide-and-seek.

Then one day in February 1978, Debbie was taking the car to a mechanic for repairs. It broke down before she reached the garage, so she got out and pushed it the last couple of miles. No one stopped to help, but she was used to that. No one helped when she was beaten in public, either.

Debbie: I finally got the car there and then realised I was having these pains in the stomach. There was a public phone so I rang a girlfriend. She asked how often they were coming and I said, about every five minutes. Christ, she said, get in a cab and go to the hospital, that baby will be born at the servo. How was I going to know I was in labour? It didn't seem like any big deal to me.

So I go off to the hospital, it's about three in the afternoon. And it's horrible, disgusting. It's so clinical, and no one's friendly, they just leave me on this bed with this pain and my legs up in these stirrups. No one was gentle with me because I was a child; in fact they treated me really badly because I was a child. It was like, you're only seventeen, how dare you?

Then there's the matron standing there saying, they're causing a riot out there in the waiting room, do something about it. Matthew and his mates had come up and were waiting out there, getting bored, so they're mucking around and throwing coffee at each other from the coffee machine, like kids. Nana's there too, trying to get in to be with me. And she's arguing with Matthew, who's saying he's the one going in.

In the end they didn't let anyone in. I was there alone. With the matron going off at me, yelling at me to do something about it. What can I do about it? I ask her, I'm here trying to have this baby. Eventually they get security guards to remove Matthew and his mates. And I'm in there, on my own. Not knowing what the fuck is happening to me.

Eventually they must have given me an epidural, because it killed my body from the waist down and I couldn't move. It was the worst experience of my life, and I'd been through some serious shit by then. I swore I'd never have another child as long as I lived. I will never forget the humiliation and the pain. The stirrups and the matron, and her words, screaming at me. The public shaming.

Debbie would not see her baby, a little girl she called Jody, for twenty-four hours. When a nurse brought her in next morning, a tiny bundle screaming hungrily, she deposited her unceremoniously in her mother's lap and left. Debbie looked at her baby, and at the nurse's retreating back, appalled. What was she supposed to do? No one had bothered to explain how to feed a baby. Women in the other beds around her, 'all good respectable married women', looked on.

She concentrated all her energies on getting out of hospital. Despite developing mastitis, she discharged herself and took her baby home to Nana's, only to be rushed back to outpatients the same night with a high temperature and unbearable pain in her breasts. Debbie recalls: 'Nana had to get a cab up to the Albion day and night chemist to buy a bottle and teat because of course we didn't have any of that. While she's away my little brother Michael is left alone to look after Jody, who's just crying and crying. He would only have been fifteen. He told Nana he'd pick her up and she'd stop crying, he'd put her down and she'd start again. Pick her up, put her down, pick her up, put her down. I can laugh at that now.'

There are photographs of the first few months of Jody's life, and they tell a vastly different story to the one Debbie was living out. Here is a picture of Debbie, so young it stops your heart, cradling a dark-haired baby, looking at the camera the way she looked at life: without flinching, but without expecting much. Here are several of Matthew Parson holding his daughter. There is nothing in the arrangement of his arms, nothing in his unpolished good looks, that hints at the cruelty he is capable of. The demons aren't apparent in these ordinary images. But they were lurking in the moments and hours before and after the camera recorded its lies. That's where Debbie's memory snapshots were made – in terrifying reality, not through the artificial means of lens and film.

'He never acted the role of father to Jody. The photos mean nothing; he was never there,' she says. 'When he was it was horrible; it was all fear and bruises and not being able to see out of my eyes. I just kept my head down all the time. I was still living at Nana's and she saw the bruises, but there wasn't much she could do. He'd just make threats, to kill me, to kill us all.'

There was even less anyone could do when Debbie decided to move to Rockhampton with Matthew, taking their month-old baby with her. Away from family and friends, the violence only escalated. Debbie wonders now how she survived. On one occasion, she leapt from a third storey unit to escape him. The jarring left her temporarily paralysed, but at the time she thought she'd broken both legs and wondered briefly if she'd ever walk again. After a terrifying month, she returned to Brisbane with Jody. Inevitably, Parson followed.

She tried hard to evade him but somehow he always found her, and the regular round of black eyes and split lips resumed. She endured bottles smashed across her back and a broken bone in her chest from his kicks. The vicious attacks would often happen in front of people: he would haul her out of the pub by the hair and, despite her calls for help, the bouncers would ignore them. Others in the bar or on the street would turn their backs. Debbie found their callousness hard to believe, and learned never to rely on others for rescue. But she would not be silent herself. Despite the injuries he inflicted, she would not shut up, would give it right back to him, hanging on to some sense of fight.

Of course, her taunts would only escalate the violence. Once, behind the wheel of a car and feeling pretty safe because Matthew was more than thirty metres away, she paused and yelled at him, giving him cheek. 'He's gone ballistic as I've started to drive off, he's picked up this rock and pegged it as hard as he could,' she says. 'It's smashed through the car and hit me in the head – I've still got the lump. And his old father was standing there near him, yelling at him to leave me alone, because he's going absolutely mad.'

Tellingly, it wasn't until Parson turned on their child that Debbie was able to stand up to him properly. Towards the end of 1978, when Jody was sitting up and crawling, Debbie moved into her own flat at Kedron, close to Nana. Once more, she thought she might have escaped, but of course Parson found her. He broke into the flat while she was shopping with Jody and was there waiting for her when she returned home.

> **Debbie**: He started demolishing everything, smashing me up. Jody was only little and she started to cry. He had hold of this broomstick – I'd bought a new broom and it wasn't attached to the handle – and he shoved her in the chest with it, sent her flying across the kitchen. She was crying hard; I thought he'd really hurt her. That was it for me. I just flipped, and somehow gathered the strength, and got him out of there. That was a pattern for me, but I didn't know it at the time: you can belt the hell out of me because I killed Dad, but touch my kid and you're out. It's amazing; and that's how it was with the violence in my life. I couldn't walk out when someone belted me; but if they raise their hand to my kids, they're gone. And he was, finally. The low-life scum.

Another factor that ensured Parson did not reappear was the friend-ship Debbie had formed with an older man, John Parker, a mechanic who was also the national president of the Rebels motorbike club. She'd met him at the Breakfast Creek Hotel, and although it occurred to her automatically that he would be a 'good catch', the two initially struck up a warm platonic friendship.

Parker, from all accounts a gentle, mild-mannered man who eschewed drugs and violence, had heard about Parson's rages, and would follow Debbie home at night in his big F100 ute to scare Parson off. It worked. 'I wasn't even going out with John then,' Debbie says, 'but when Matthew thought there was another bloke on the scene, a bloke with a bit of power, he disappeared off the face of the earth. Typical. He was really just a gutless wimp.'

The departure of Parson heralded a short period of calm in the lives of Debbie and her baby daughter. They moved back in with Nana, and Debbie, who had been an ardent aerobics fan for years, started work teaching aerobics at a local gym. She also began helping John Parker with the bookkeeping for his workshop. They were clearly very attracted to each other, and spent a lot of time together drinking at the Breakfast Creek, or at the drag track, or the Rebels clubhouse. They soon became lovers and it wasn't long before he moved in at Nana's place.

Debbie: John was the calmest and most peaceful man you'd ever meet in your life. He was a hard-working man who owned his own business. He wasn't into drugs, he wasn't into anything – only drinking, and that was limited to Friday and Saturday. He wasn't a drunk – there wasn't any alcohol in the fridge at home. He didn't even smoke. So I stopped doing everything too. Settled into a routine. I'd do the gym in the morning, the washing and cleaning in the afternoon. Go drinking at the clubhouse or the Brekky Creek with my mates.

If someone gave me the shits I'd punch them, but that's all. John had a lot of power but he was very mild-mannered. He wasn't scary at all; he was a sook. That's the great myth about bikies, that's the bullshit. Men in bike clubs are like men anywhere. It's like a football club – you'll get the dickheads, the highly intelligent ones, the unemployed ones, people with small businesses, some who do drugs and some who don't.

I've always felt safe with bikies. I know lots of women who don't, and lots who have been badly treated, but I never felt that. I always played my own power though, and that was probably about John being the president, but I could give someone a smack in the head and they wouldn't retaliate. I was learning about power, who's got it, who hasn't, where to align yourself, what you can and can't get away with. Which is all institutional stuff too, it's about learning how to survive.

During this time, Debbie and Pat tentatively began to patch up the differences that had prised them apart and kept them estranged for nearly five years. It was obvious to Pat that Debbie's lifestyle had stabilised and that, even though her wildness hadn't completely dissipated, she was taking good care of the little granddaughter she'd never had a chance to know. Pat's own personal circumstances had brightened significantly too; a couple of years earlier, she had met Len Jones (not his real name), a quiet and unassuming man fourteen years her senior, and they had settled at Tarragindi on Brisbane's south side. Both mother and daughter had safe places from which to approach each other, and to become reacquainted with each other's lives.

Officially, Debbie was still under the care and control of the department of children's services, an order that would be in force until after her eighteenth birthday. But with a baby to look after, the relative order of her life, and the presence of a man who didn't need to prove his love by hitting her, she fell out of the habit of crime. When her birthday rolled around, she hadn't been inside Wilson for nearly two years. Three months later, the state relinquished their control. She was free.

But not totally. The police had decided to hold over some old charges, which meant she would be eligible for 'the big house', or adult jail, because she was now over eighteen. The charges related to a robbery committed in company with two others, both of whom had fled the state. So Debbie fronted court alone, and was remanded in custody pending the apprehension of her co-accused.

'Boggo Road held no fear for me then. I was a cocky eighteen-year-old, ten feet tall and bulletproof,' she says. Luckily, she needed that bravado for less than forty-eight hours. In that time Nana, who was also looking after Jody, plucked her jars of fifty-cent pieces from their hiding places and took the swag of coins to the police. There was enough of the carefully saved coins to pay the $300 bail. Debbie walked out of Boggo Road, back to her life with John.

For Pat, though, life seemed fated to deliver heartache. While her daughter was showing vague signs of slowing down, her son, Michael, was still mixing with the wrong crowd and continuing the spiral that had begun with his father's death. Just before his eighteenth birthday, he was horsing around with friends jumping off the Bribie Island bridge, when he tragically misjudged the depth of water. When Michael failed to surface after a dive, one of the other boys leapt in to retrieve him. He was alive, but his neck was broken, his spinal cord hanging by a thread.

When Debbie saw her brother in hospital, metal attachments holding his head, she prayed that he would die. He looked like a trapped animal, unable to move. Doctors told Pat her son would not walk again. But Michael had other ideas. Slowly, some of the paralysis left him. He remained in traction for two years, but afterwards he would learn to move his limbs and to walk with help, although his body would never completely recover. He would be left with a debilitating limp and other complications, including arthritis, for the rest of his life.

By then Jody was old enough to sense that John Parker was a 'nice' man, but also to realise that her mother wasn't doing an enormous amount of mothering. 'I didn't see Mum much,' she says now. 'Nana looked after me mainly. She did everything for me, and let me get away with murder. I loved being with her.' She was also old enough to remember the very last time that her biological father came to the house. 'He came with these flowers. But they had someone else's funeral notice on them – he'd stolen them from the cemetery. He wanted to take the cat, which was called Mrs Grey. That was Nana's name too. I vividly remember her getting out my great-grandfather's shotgun, and chasing my father down the street. It was a sawn-off shottie, and she was seventy years old or more,' she says.

Slowly, though, the happiness in the house began to erode. Violence stepped in to remind Debbie that for her, life wasn't meant to be this good, this untroubled. It is easy in retrospect to see alcohol as the fuel that ignited the violent brawls that marred the relative peace Debbie and John had established. But Debbie knows now there was another, more insidious trigger for their behaviour. And while she is at pains not to make excuses for John's physical aggression towards her – or anyone else's, for that matter – she has the insight and the psychological tools these days to identify her own part in it.

These were the days when Debbie was at the peak of her fitness. She was busy running several aerobics classes a day at the local gym and was also lifting weights. Later she would add touch football, rugby union and soccer to her repertoire, and these team sports would suit her garrulous nature. Her strength, agility and fearlessness made her a valuable player. Off the field, she'd be known for the same qualities, which she took with her to post-match drinking sessions or to nights on the town with team-mates. In her later days with John, however, she didn't need a game to celebrate the night away. Any occasion would do.

'We had crazy times, really,' says her friend Gill Campbell, who Debbie met in the months leading up to her twenty-first birthday. 'We were constantly nightclubbing and running amok. We partied *hard*. We were either thrown out of places, chased by guys or bashed by our boyfriends. It never stopped. We lived on the borderline which was a great adrenalin rush and a lot of fun.'

Campbell first spoke to Debbie at a dinner organised by members of the Rebels bike club and their girlfriends at the Newmarket Hotel in Brisbane's inner north. She has always remembered what Debbie wore that evening: a very short skirt and top, with a plaited headband à la Olivia Newton-John in the film clip of her hit "Let's Get Physical". 'She just stood out in the crowd,' Campbell remembers. 'I thought she was stunning.'

Soon afterwards Campbell, Debbie and her friend Anita Hamilton began to get together to go partying around the city. It wasn't long before Campbell, who describes herself at the time as 'fairly quiet and well-mannered', got to witness Debbie's street-fighting abilities:

> Campbell: One night we were out at our usual all-nighter, Swizzles in Elizabeth Street, when two girls came up to Deb at our table, trying to be friendly. Deb knew one of them had slept with John, and she told her to go away before she lost it. But this stupid girl hung around, so Deb just smashed a glass into the nape of her neck. Anita and I were a bit stunned, but to give Deb her due, she always warned someone before she physically attacked them and if they decided to stay, they had to accept the consequences.
>
> Another night at Swizzles these three big girls gave Deb a hard time in the toilets. Deb told us she was going back in, so I picked up a wine bottle and kept it in my hands and stood by the toilet doors. I wasn't a fighter – Anita and I were scaredy cats, really – but I wanted to make sure three didn't get into one. I shouldn't have worried. These three girls started verballing and pushing Deb and the next thing Deb had slammed one of their heads into the mirror, another one she slammed into a cubicle with all her might and the third, she slammed her head into the wall, got her on the ground and banged her head into the ground. That sorted them out.
>
> But the following Friday night when we got to Swizzles, there were these three girls again, so Deb, half pissed, went up to them and said, 'Good evening, ladies, how are we tonight?' Later, these three and some guys tried to get Deb as she was getting into a cab. They clipped her but didn't do any damage. She could hold her own in a street fight, and when she lost control, God help male or female.

According to Campbell, Debbie had 'a tongue and a wit about her that could demean anyone in seconds'. Men would flock towards her, but the moment they displayed any arrogance or foolishness she would cut them down with her own brand of ridicule. Debbie could, she says, talk men into removing their pants and showing off their penises, only to throw herself onto the floor laughing and pointing. 'It was great to see a girl with so many comebacks,' Campbell says, 'but in the end guys would really get the shits and want to just kill her.'

Swizzles was their preferred drinking spot. It was one of the few establishments open past midnight in Brisbane then; Debbie and her friends would inevitably end up there after drinking hard at other venues. Inevitably, too, it would be the scene of over-heated brawls and casual punch-ups. As Debbie's relationship with John deteriorated, this is where he would often find her after a long, futile wait at home. On at least two occasions, he strode into the nightclub – resembling an enraged Nordic god with his long hair and flowing beard – and literally dragged her out by the hair.

They began to argue about how often Debbie was out. According to Debbie, what Parker really wanted was a docile housewife who'd be waiting for him whenever he came home. He'd told her as much. That didn't wash with Debbie, who was in love with the life she had, mainly spent 'out yahooing with my mates'. 'I told him I wasn't his mother and I wasn't going to do that. I was only twenty years old,' she says. 'I was still a kid, running around.'

In retrospect, Debbie believes she didn't take the relationship seriously. She was having far too good a time outside it. And besides, the nine-year age gap was beginning to impact on them both. It was driven home to Debbie when she told Parker, who loved cars and raced them at the drag track, that she wanted to get a convertible. 'No, you don't,' he said. 'I've had one, you get wet when it rains.' Debbie didn't care. She'd never had one.

Debbie: But he'd been there, done that. And although he was this calm and gentle man, I just knew how to hit the buttons. It's no excuse for what he did, but I knew – I'd kick his Harley over, or throw a table onto the bonnet of his Corvette. He had a workshop with hundreds of thousands of dollars worth of cars in it. I knew what would get him going.

For me it was about pushing people to their limits, to see if they'd be violent, what they would do, could I trust them? It's all connected to the neck manipulation when I was a baby: I love you and I'm hurting you. If they say they love you, well righto, let's see, because I know you're going to punish me somehow. You're going to hurt me so I'm going to push you to the limit, so do it.

The major cause of discontent in the relationship, however, was John's ongoing infidelity. Debbie is at pains to explain that he 'wasn't a sleazebag – he was a Casanova. Just wanted to sleep with other sheilas all the time'. In one memorable example of this, well into the relationship, Debbie and John came to serious blows over another woman. They had arranged to meet at the pub, but when John didn't show up, Debbie believed she knew what he was up to.

Debbie: I knew he'd be back at the workshop with some sheila. And I've got the keys because I did his books for him, and I'm not having any of this shit. So I've gone round there and yeah, he's there with her, and I've smacked the hell out of her and chased her around, picking up axles and tools and hurling them across the workshop at her. He's trying to stop me but I've finally caught her, and I've bitten her on the face. He's yelling, let go! And I'm yelling, I'm going to bite her fuckin' cheek off! I finally let her go and ran out, smashing every window of every one of his cars on the way.

Gill takes up the story: 'Deb's got back into the driver's seat, and next thing John's come running up, thrown himself through the front passenger window past me to get to Deb. She flies out of the car, John says, "Oh, sorry," to me and then he's off after Deb again. It was like a Laurel and Hardy movie.'

Deb enraged many of the members of the Rebels, going out of her way to call them 'The Pebbles' and escaping their wrath only because she was the president's girlfriend. They rarely interceded in fights between Debbie and John, although Debbie remembers one exception:

We were at the Rebels clubhouse, and we're up at this big stainless steel bar, and he's giving me shit. I'm pissed, so I just grab his beard and smash his head into the bar. The whole place goes quiet, because I've just smashed the president's head into the bar. And he just stands up, and quietly walks around to me, and hits me. So then I go calmly and pick up a pool ball, I'm going to crack him with it but someone came up to me, took it off me. We were probably arguing about some sheila he was running around with. One of them worked next door, he ended up living with her later and he did it to her, too. I mean, you'd never take it personally.

It went on and on. One Friday night at the Breakfast Creek Hotel, Debbie caught a woman staring at her, smirking. She guessed this was the woman John had been with several nights before, when he hadn't come home. Then suddenly the woman approached her, and began to goad: 'I was with your boyfriend the other night.' But Debbie was ready. 'Big deal, you pig,' she replied, 'he came home to me, didn't he?' Within seconds, the two women were trading punches around the tables. John just watched.

But years of his unfaithfulness were finally taking their toll. One morning, after being out all night, John came home and slipped into the shower. Debbie was calm. She wasn't after a fight, not now. She walked into the bathroom, looked him in the eye and said, 'That's it. Get out. Don't come back.'

Some months previously, around the time of her twenty-first birthday, she and John had attended a wild Rebels party in a bush clearing near the little town of Aratula, an hour south-west of Brisbane in the shadow of the Great Dividing Range. By now the relationship was strung out and tense as taut wire. The site, on top of a hill, was overflowing with bikies and their friends. Naturally, as alcohol took over from reason, she and John needled each other to the point of fury. After an energetic round of verbal abuse they began to grapple with each other, punching and kicking, and within minutes were hurtling down the hill in a flurry of thrashing limbs and screamed obscenities. The others at the party barely registered the event.

But Gill did. It stayed with her all her life because, despite the frenzied partying she'd enjoyed with Deb, this was the first time she had ever seen a woman punched by a man. 'Deb was pretty drunk and they were having a big fight, and next thing I saw was John just punching Deb in the head. She went down,' Gill says. 'I was in shock, but what was even more astounding was that Deb got up and went for John again. I couldn't believe that this girl was having another go when this guy obviously had no qualms about hitting a girl. I was warned by other club members not to get involved, but I was really upset. Luckily Deb disappeared and crashed out.'

One of the people who didn't witness the B-grade movie scene between the Rebels president and his girlfriend was a young man who had known Debbie slightly and watched her for years, but declined an invitation to the party at Aratula. Joe Kilroy was a bikie too, a Black Uhlan, who had been in one of the vague and inter-locking circles of mutual teenage acquaintances the two shared between Keperra, the Stafford and Red Hill skating rinks, and the Valley.

In those days Joe was serious about two things: his football and his bike, but he kept distant tabs on Debbie. He'd just played in a representative Queensland rugby league side in a tour of England; back in Brisbane, as two clubs vied for the fast and talented fullback, he would drop into the pubs he knew Debbie frequented. They'd run into each other occasionally, have a drink and a chat. That was all.

It didn't take long on the bikie grapevine for news of Debbie's and John's bust-up to get around. Joe heard about it along with everyone else, and shortly afterwards, he saw Debbie with some friends at the Breakfast Creek Hotel. Joe was no smooth operator, but he wasn't going to waste this opportunity. He'd been waiting a long time for it. He got up and joined her rowdy group for a drink. As soon as he got a chance, he asked her out to Brothers Leagues Club in the suburb of the Grange the following Sunday night.

4

Joe Kilroy

Joe: When I first saw Debbie, she was running with the Keperra mob. Parson, and some of my cousins. They'd be everywhere, at every party you went to. It was the same sort of circle. I'd see her in the Valley, at the fun parlour, or up at the Dandy Burger, hangin' around. She was a bit of a maniac. Amongst the parents she was described as 'bad news'.

But I just liked her, so I kept a bit of an eye on her. Something drew me to her, she had this . . . something, whatever it was. It wasn't her loudness. I saw her quiet more than I saw her loud. I saw the other side. I saw that she had a heart. That she was scared, just like everyone else. I knew, because I grew up in an orphanage, lonely. So I kept an eye on her. She never knew. I'm an observer, I've always been like that. And I'm patient with people, because I've seen all sorts.

Joe Kilroy was born in June 1960, the third child of a white Australian farm labourer, Tich Kilroy, and Joan Darby, a Batchula woman from the Hervey Bay area. Joan's father had been brought to Australia from Vanuatu by the infamous 'blackbirders' to slave in the cane fields of southern Queensland. He married Joan's mother, from the Batchula tribe, and stayed.

Joe was just two years old when his mother was hit by a drunk driver as she walked near their home outside Hervey Bay. She was killed instantly. Joe was too young to know how catastrophic that split second would prove to his entire life. The loss of a young mother is an immeasurable tragedy, but Joan's death would strike a double blow to the Kilroy children.

Within two days – even before their mother was buried – they had been packed up and dispatched to St Vincent's Orphanage at Nudgee, run by the Brisbane congregation of the Sisters of Mercy. Their father, who was working in central Australia, had declared himself unable to care for the motherless children, and attempts by Joan's family to take them were blocked by the state.

It was the early 1960s; throughout Australia, Aboriginal children were being removed from their families under the policy of assimilation. In some parts of Queensland, whole communities of Aboriginal people were still being forced from their lands and moved on. It wasn't until 1967 that they were recognised as Australian citizens and given the right to vote. The prevailing attitude was strongly patriarchal. In that spirit, Joan's family was seen as unfit to take responsibility for the three Kilroy children, Robert, then five, Kym, then four, and Joe.

Joe was barely out of nappies. Within the dour red brick walls of Nudgee orphanage, he was separated from his siblings and placed in the nursery with other very young children. Nudgee would become his home, and the nuns his mothers, until he was a teenager.

Unlike many of those who gave evidence to the 1999 Forde Inquiry into the abuse of children in Queensland institutions, Joe Kilroy says he did not suffer mistreatment or abuse during his childhood years at Nudgee. His memories of the nuns who brought him up are warm and affectionate; they seemed to be genuinely fond of him, and he of them.

One of them, Sister Leonie Wyatt, gave him his first feel of a football, kicking it around with the little boy in the playground and teaching him about the game. When he was named man of the match in the 1980 Brisbane A-grade rugby league final, he returned to Nudgee to personally thank Leonie. Even now, he occasionally visits the surviving nuns who still live in the convent on the hilltop site in Brisbane's north.

But Joe Kilroy would not escape a lonely childhood and institutional life unscathed. The early family deprivation and a sharp sense of abandonment would affect everything he did and felt as a child and as an adult, and the anger and isolation he experienced would only be compounded by the racism – overt and covert – he encountered everywhere around him. This sad legacy of his childhood would play a role in the turbulent marriage he would eventually enter with Debbie Harding, and be used, years later, to defend him before a sentencing judge in the Supreme Court of Australia.

A rare treat for children in such institutions was a weekend outing with a volunteer family. Ironically, it was Leneen Forde, who would go on to become Queensland's first female governor and the author of the controversial report on abuse of children in institutions, who occasionally whisked young Joe away from Nudgee to join her own five children for picnics and games at their St Lucia home. The Forde children liked Joe: Leneen still jokes about discovering them applying fake tan to their limbs after one of his visits, to make themselves look like him.

Joe enjoyed the visits too, but for him they were double-edged. He laughs now when he recalls one Easter weekend at the Fordes' when all the children – Leneen's five plus two from Nudgee – were let loose in the yard to hunt for Easter eggs. At the time he couldn't figure out why Leneen's kids were successfully plucking eggs out of nowhere. He couldn't find any, and neither could Susie, the other visitor from the orphanage. They were given some, eventually, but only as an adult did it occur to Joe that, of course, Leneen's kids did this every year. They knew where the eggs would be hidden.

Several years earlier, Joe and his siblings had been given a tantalising taste of real belonging when their father, Tich, teamed up with an Aboriginal woman named Rita Huggins. One of Rita's daughters, Jackie Huggins, now a well-known and highly respected academic and writer, was a teenager at the time and remembers Tich taking his three children out of the orphanage each weekend to join the family at their Inala home: 'Joe was only about four at the time, a cute, curly-headed boy who sucked his thumb. They'd come and we'd play with them, go down to the creek, do all the things you did in those days,' she says. 'We tried to show them what it was like to be in a family and to be loved and nurtured. It seemed very unfair that they had to go back every weekend; there'd be tears because they wanted to stay with us. And I always considered the three of them as my stepbrothers and sister.'

When the relationship between Rita and Tich broke down after three years, the visits ended. But Huggins and her family stayed in touch with the Kilroy kids, always knowing vaguely where each of them was and what they were doing. For the most part, though,

Robert, Kym and Joe were left to their own devices and their feeling of aloneness in the world. The fleeting sense of family and security offered by the weekends away from the orphanage seemed to underline their own isolation, rather than diminish it. For Joe, they made the abandonment all the more cruel.

At twelve, Joe was transferred from Nudgee to Boystown, an institution for wayward boys run by the de la Salle Brothers at Beaudesert, southwest of Brisbane. Bob also went to Boystown, and was there when Joe arrived. Kym stayed on at the orphanage, like most girls, until she was about fifteen. On the cusp of adolescence, Joe was deemed too old for the orphanage, and even though he'd shown no signs of waywardness, there was nowhere else for him to go but Boystown. It was a very different institution from the one he'd left. Joe remembers the brutality of floggings handed out not just by the Brothers but by other boys who were appointed to deputise in order to maintain control.

Straps – often with a steel science ruler folded into them – jockeys' whips, fists and open hands were used in most beatings, but the Friday night boxing matches were also seen as a form of punishment. Nearly thirty years later, the Forde Inquiry would hear that 'boys with no boxing skills were forced into the ring with bigger boys who were obliged to keep punching until the Director chose to stop the fight'. In his first year there, he was 'little, six and a half stone', but that didn't save him from the ring.

Often boys were also forced into mindless physical labour – such as digging deep holes in the grounds and then filling them in again – as discipline. 'They had a piggery, poultry pens and a dairy, and horses. You could spend all day carrying endless buckets of shit, chook shit, cow shit, horse shit, from one section to the other, round and round,' he recalls. 'What was that supposed to teach me? I'll tell you, it taught me resentment.'

Joe despised Boystown and at fifteen, as soon as he was legally able, he left. He wanted to try his hand as a welder, but his prospective employers all asked the same question: what were you in Boystown for? Even in the employment rich seventies, there was no job for him. He couldn't understand why. 'I just couldn't join the dots up,' he says, shaking his head. So finally, he went back to school, to erase the Boystown stamp and replace it with something more credible.

At Kelvin Grove High, in Brisbane's inner north, he repeated year ten and then, enjoying this new experience, went on to year eleven. He was living at a nearby hostel, St Martin's Centre, run by Father Leo Wright, who had known him at Boystown, and was working nights to pay his way, inserting brochures into weekend newspapers or doing industrial cleaning. But it wasn't enough, and when his 'double orphan's' pension was mistakenly cut off mid-way through year twelve and no one seemed able to sort out the bureaucratic mess, Joe quit school.

Football had always been a big part of his life, from the day Sister Wyatt began to throw the ball around with him. He was playing for Norths-St Joseph's while he still lived at the orphanage, and continued on up the ranks for Norths as a teenager, until he hit A-grade. One of his career highlights remains the 1980 rugby league grand final which pitted Norths against the Brisbane favourites, Souths. A rampaging Kilroy try gave Norths an unexpected victory, and the twenty-year-old the Man of the Match award.

Joe bloomed with Norths, and he loved the club he had grown up with. But after being named as the world's best fullback by an international football magazine in 1983, it became clearer that, if the right offer or enticement came along, he would have to move. In 1984, that enticement came from Brothers – an A-grade league club in Brisbane's north – in the shape of a brand new black Harley-Davidson motorbike. The offer was unprecedented in the club's history. Bikes had always been a passion for Joe, and his mates in the Black Uhlans were the closest he'd ever come to a family. The combination of football and a dream bike was irresistible. He grabbed the offer and ran.

At this point Joe was living in Norman Park, sharing a house with Robert and Kym. By the time he bumped into Debbie again after her break from John Parker in 1983, Debbie and Jody had moved into an old Queenslander at Kalinga, an inner northern suburb of Brisbane. Dismayed at the failure of the long-running relationship, Pat had been urging Debbie to consider buying a house. It would break the nexus of dependency with Nana and provide a stable base for Jody, who had started school the year before.

Debbie agreed and, with Pat's help, bought the classic, highset wooden house with a full-length front verandah in Emma Street.

Things looked hopeful: Debbie had a house, a job teaching aerobics, and a beautiful little girl. Moreover, she'd managed to stay out of serious trouble since her last stint in Wilson as a sixteen-year-old more than five years previously. She was even getting on better with her mother. An outsider observing Debbie the night Joe Kilroy invited her out might have ventured the opinion that she was 'settling down', or words to that effect. But that notion would have been quite misplaced.

Joe Kilroy probably knew that better than most. Perhaps that is why he was nonplussed when Debbie failed to show up for their first date at Brothers, standing him up in favour of John Parker, who had called unexpectedly and asked to see her, coincidentally on the same night. Nothing came of the meeting with Parker. But Joe decided on a more informal approach anyway, and began dropping in casually at Debbie's place on his way to work or on his way home. He'd do odd jobs to help her out, muck around with Jody, drink tea. She regarded him as a mate.

'There was just something lonely about her. You could see that through all that was going on,' Joe says. 'You know the way you look at someone and you're attracted to them and you just like them, always. It was almost like we were on parallel courses. I could see a lot of similarities between us. We shared the same sort of trauma, but she was reacting one way, me another.'

Debbie thought Joe was 'nice enough, quite charming', but her trust in people – virtually nonexistent to start with – had almost been erased by John Parker's rampant infidelities, and by the ongoing violence in her life. She noted Joe's attentions with interest, but she wasn't about to trade her hard-won independence and hard-drinking lifestyle for any bloke, even a handsome and charismatic footballer: 'It wasn't the usual Hollywood love story,' she recalls. 'I was too suspicious about relationships. Every one I'd had was fucked. They were violent and untrustworthy. Jody was very suspicious of Joe too, at the beginning. I'd been with John for nearly five years and she'd started calling him Daddy.'

But it didn't take long for Jody and Joe to team up. Within a couple of months the big footballer and the little girl had established a firm and easygoing friendship. Joe loved kids; it wasn't hard for him to fall in love with Debbie's bright, dark-haired little daughter. It was the beginning of a strong and trusting relationship between the two that would survive the confronting and tough times ahead. Debbie says that, after Jody's initial wariness, they never looked back: 'He's always been there for her, the only one who has. She sees him as her father, and he's always accepted her as his own and never faltered, ever. Ever. I probably falter more as her natural mother than Joe does.'

Joe's visits to the Emma Street house became more regular and lasted longer until after about six months, he 'just moved in'. Their lives barely registered the event: Jody went to school; Joe was playing for Brothers, working at various jobs including the Commonwealth Employment Service or Aboriginal Legal Service, and spending his spare time with the Uhlans; Debbie was working at the gym, running aerobics classes for Joe's A-grade team-mates and going out on the weekends, raising hell.

Gill Campbell remembers how the wild female threesome gradually became a foursome, which the girls didn't mind, realising 'we had a guy to back us up when we got into deep water – it was either the three of us or none of us so I suppose Joe really didn't have much option. Poor Joe would shake his head most of the time, as if to say, what can I do with this girl? Deb was definitely the life of the party wherever she went – if you didn't see her you could certainly hear her,' she says.

The three joined Joe in Sydney when he took part in a club bike run around this time, following him down together in Gill's 1968 Standard Chevrolet. (They all drove Chevs: Debbie a Chevrolet Nova, Anita a Pillarless '68.) They'd taken 'a heap of speed', Gill says, and she drove nearly all the way, with Deb taking over for the last two or three hours. 'I wouldn't let Deb drive my car much. She was a maniac driver – brilliant but a maniac,' she says.

They had a narrow escape from a nightclub one evening after Joe had left, when a group of men 'who were being smart-arses' surrounded them. They ran, hiding beneath bushes in a park while they watched the men searching for them in their car, then 'ran for all our might, stopped a cabbie, dived in and managed to get home unhurt'. After a speed-fuelled long weekend and four hours sleep, they drove home.

Alcohol was still Debbie's drug of choice but it wasn't unusual for her to buy a hundred 'trips' (LSD) during the week, then go out with the girls and sell them around the bars on Friday night for

$10 each. With $1000 in their pockets, they'd head for Pip's or Hollywood's or Swizzles. More often than not, the night would end in a violent brawl, often among the women.

Debbie: 'People knew me around the traps. As soon as anyone raised a hand to me I'd drop them – if you get held down by six to eight orderlies as a kid, you learn how to fight people off really quickly. These Rebel-ettes would be hanging around, they'd reckon they'd come in to punch me up and the blokes would say, don't go near her, she'll kill you, but they'd try it on so you'd have to drop 'em, every time. They'd start at about three in the morning. I'd never start it. They'd push up – once, one of them was pushing up about having slept with John, so I threw a drink over her and said, next time you'll wear the jug around your head.

She stayed there, so I dropped her with the jug, just picked it up and crack! Now, fuck off! They were fairly violent days. There were always punch-ups – by closing time Pip's was like a bar in a Western movie. At three am it would be on, brawls, people being thrown across tables, kicking and screaming. The place would be full of bikies and army jerks, and that's a bad mix, I can tell you.

In the middle of one of these brawls, one in which Debbie and a group of women were trading blows, Debbie glanced down to see a flick-knife lying on the floor. She swooped on it, and in a split second had it against the face of one of her opponents. Everyone was very, very drunk, but one of the bikies observing the women's antics managed to see clearly for a moment. 'Don't say a word,' he breathed to the besieged woman, 'or she'll slit your throat.'

At that moment a biker named Dumbo, a member of the Black Uhlans, suddenly grabbed Debbie, hoisting her up and over his shoulder and carrying her out onto the street. Debbie was livid, and surprised to find herself muscled roughly into the back of a cab. 'Get in there and get home,' Dumbo hissed.

As the cab drove off, the group of women from inside emerged to run alongside the car, beating on the window. 'Come on!' Debbie yelled, and began kicking the door of the cab, trying to get out. When it finally swung open she threw a wild punch at the woman that landed where it was aimed, and the cab accelerated away, leaving the woman prostrate on the footpath. 'It was wild,' Debbie concedes.

'I was never injured, though. I had a lot of energy, a lot of don't-fuck-with-me energy and a lot of personal power from going out with the Rebels and the Uhlans. There's a lot of status in those worlds.'

Joe: She was unreal. The hardest woman in the world to love in those days. A real pain in the arse with a gut full of vodka. I'd be home in bed asleep, and she'd come home pissed as a parrot and start accusing me of stuff, screaming, and playing the stereo right up loud. She'd start abusing me and wouldn't stop. I wasn't experienced in life like I am now. We were in our twenties, we were kids. Even though you have all this street-wise experience you've got no relationship experience, and no one around to help.

I look back and shake my head and wonder how we survived the early years. We just stuck with it. Because of my values and my background, there was no way in the world I was going to let my family fail. I didn't ever think I'd made a big mistake, but I wondered why. Why is this happening to me? What have I done? She'd come home and accuse me of sleeping with some sheila, shit like that.

Initially, the violence between Debbie and Joe was verbal, with the occasional physical stoush thrown in. True to her patterns, Debbie would push and test, push and test, usually after a night out at Pip's: 'It was bizarre behaviour, alien to me,' Joe says. 'Even though I'd been in institutions, to me her behaviour was out of left field, she was like someone who wasn't getting their medication. Only she wasn't on medication. She had a lot of anger in her, this one, a lot of stuff from her own childhood. I did too, from when I was a kid. What a great pair we were: we both got betrayed, we didn't trust anyone and we found each other – what a collision.'

Several bouts of physical violence between them occurred while they were out of the country, away from the friends and clubs and the growing interest of the media in Joe's football career. At the end of the 1985 football season, officials from the English club Halifax invited Joe to play a guest season with them, beginning in October. Joe had met them during the representative tour of England in 1983 and was keen to take up the opportunity. Debbie was happy to go, too: it would be her first overseas trip, and fun for all of them.

Joe went on ahead, with Debbie and Jody to follow. The night before Debbie's flight, she said farewell to Anita and Gill with a prolonged drinking session that hadn't finished when the sun came up. 'We were all still drunk when we poured Deb onto the plane,' Gill remembers. 'I think she threw up most of the way to England.'

But even those few physical confrontations in Halifax – booze-fuelled, button-pushing, angry – didn't overwhelm the positive aspects of the trip. Generally, their time in the Midlands was calm, and valuable for them as a family unit. For Debbie it was like a six-month-long holiday: Joe played a bit of football and they spent a lot of time socialising and partying with other Australians and the local players from Halifax. Often, they'd fill in their mornings at home, then go drinking all afternoon. At Christmas, the three of them enjoyed their first snowfall, and played around with snowmen and snowballs with Jody, then nearly seven.

Joe still believes the trip was good for them: 'We got away from all the external influences, good and bad. We only had each other. In my world, that's all we ever had anyway. But we'd never had the space to be us. For the first time in our lives in England I felt completely comfortable, whole. It just reaffirmed what I'd always felt. It sounds corny, I know, but I looked at Deb and saw there was a normal person beneath this schizoid exterior. It just melted away over there.'

Jody remembers the time fondly, too. 'We had a great time in England. I remember the hot lunches at school, and mucking around in the snow, and Mum wanting Vegemite and Nana sending it over. I don't remember any violence then. It just felt like a nice, normal family to me. And that's what I wanted,' she says.

Something must have convinced them the future might be bright, because shortly after arriving in England they began to talk again about having another child. Joe had argued long and hard for this; he was keen to have several children. For Debbie, though, memories of the shocking pregnancy with Jody and the disastrous events surrounding her birth meant the whole notion of producing another child was fraught with fear and intimidation. Not for her the merciful amnesia that often follows a traumatic childbirth experience: all she could see was a humiliated little girl with her legs locked in stirrups, gripped by pain, the condescension on the faces of grim nurses. She'd sworn over and over never to endure it again. In Halifax, though, positive outcomes seemed possible. She agreed to try.

It didn't happen straight away. Several months went by with no results. They were concerned, at first, and Joe submitted to fertility tests before finally, just prior to their departure for Australia in March 1986, one of the endless pregnancy tests came back positive. It was early days: Debbie was barely six weeks pregnant. But Joe was over the moon, and couldn't be contained. Not for the first time, he asked Debbie to marry him. The answer was still no. Marriage was an institution as far as she was concerned, and damned if she was going to get locked into another one.

Back at home in Brisbane, with life picking up the same routine it had before – football, bikies' parties, looking after Jody – Debbie announced the pregnancy to her mother. They were having dinner with Pat and Len. Pat was delighted, but horrified that Debbie would have another child without the protection of marriage. Distressed, she told her daughter she really couldn't have another baby 'out of wedlock'.

The atmosphere around the table was suddenly thick with appre-hension, as everyone waited for Debbie to react. For a whole minute she was silent, her lips tight as if she was blocking an explosion from within. Then: 'Jesus,' Debbie breathed. She turned to Joe. 'You want to get married, then?' she asked between clenched teeth. Joe was grinning. 'Yep,' he said.

Debbie stood up from the table. 'Okay then. But you two can organise it.' She turned and left the room. The other three could hear her muttering 'Fuck it' before she slid into a lounge chair and flicked on the TV.

So the big, traditional white wedding was set down for 31 May, at the Little Flower Church at Kedron, complete with bridesmaids, groomsmen, and Jody as flower-girl. Debbie would be four months pregnant. In the spirit of trying to preserve the fragile peace with her mother, Debbie had even submitted to a fitting for a frothy white bridal gown at a salon in the city.

The sales assistant was effusive, telling Debbie how beautiful the figure-hugging dress looked and assuring Pat it would be even more so at the wedding 'because she'll lose a few pounds – all brides do'. 'Not this one,' Pat muttered as she nodded and smiled at her daughter, whose face above the sweetheart neckline was crimson with rage.

> **Debbie**: I felt like I was getting dragged kicking and screaming into marriage, railroaded, because I certainly wasn't conscious of wanting to do it at the time. They wanted me to do all this traditional stuff – the service was at the church Dad was buried from and it was the church we'd always been to. So on the day we pull up in the car – the bride is supposed to be late but I was early, I wanted it all over and done with – and Joe's not there.
>
> So we drive around the block, and he's still not there. Joe had stayed over at a mate's, and I'm thinking, they'll all be off their tits. So I said to Len, who's driving, that's it, we're off. I'm not hanging around for him. And Len says, we'll go round one more time. And he goes around this big long block and when we get back Joe's there. But I'm pissed off by now and the dress is killing me. I'd had to pull the zip up with a wire coathanger. It was as tight as.

The wedding of the handsome bachelor footballer to the pretty blonde gym teacher was duly noted and photographed by Brisbane's *Sunday Mail*. To readers of the newspaper, and the world at large, it was another glossy celebrity wedding with all the requisite ingredients: a good-looking couple, high-profile guests – footballers and coaches – and the frisson of romance. In the published picture, bride and groom even manage to look happy and delighted with each other. But Joe's wide grin might have been related to the fact that, walking back up the aisle of the church after the ceremony, his hand on Debbie's back, he felt the dress give slightly. The zip had popped.

Debbie, busy planning to reward herself for her endurance, wasn't aware of this. She smiled her way through it all, and as soon as they hit the reception centre, at the Lawnton greyhounds club on Brisbane's northern outskirts, she headed for the bar. Accordingly, she can't remember a great deal about the party that ensued. She knows that Pat was happy to have pulled the whole thing off – although worried about how Joe's family would behave along with the footballers and bikies who'd been invited along with one hundred and fifty others. Unbelievably, given the mix of guests, there were no drunken brawls and no police raids, but the bikies and other friends at table 10 had a loud and riotous time with the assistance of some suspect chemicals.

> **Debbie**: We did all the speeches. In those days brides didn't give speeches but I did. I can't remember what I said – I was too pissed. Pregnant and pissed. I just wanted to get it over and get this dress off. When it came time for me to get changed the bridesmaids are trying to get the zip down but it's broken, they can't get it to move. I couldn't bear it so I just grabbed the dress by both shoulders and ripped the whole back and zip out. Dropped it. And then off we go to the Sheraton.

There is no argument about what happened on their wedding night: Debbie was drunk, Joe had to stay sober in order to drive them back to town and there was some general disharmony about raucous behaviour. Once in the bridal suite, where chilled champagne waited, Joe discarded his own formal wedding attire to have a shower. Now, at last, he could relax, have a drink and romance his bride. Or so he thought. 'When I came out, five minutes later, she's ripped off her dress and flaked out on the bed, out cold,' he says. 'So there I am with my bottle of champagne, sitting down at the pool on my own on my wedding night, drinking it by myself. Wonderful. I've never let her forget it.'

> **Debbie**: It was only one night – he had to get up and play for Brothers in the morning. Anyway I've just hit the pillow and gone out like a light. Next morning he's saying, we didn't consummate the marriage, we're not married; and I'm saying, what? I'm pregnant, it's not as if we haven't done it before! And he's saying, well, sorry, it's nothing like that, because we've never been married before. Then we packed our bags and went home.

For Debbie's friends, though, there was a collective sigh of relief at the sound of wedding bells and particularly at the news of the pregnancy. 'She actually stopped drinking and yahooing and it gave the rest of us time to recuperate,' says Gill. 'Up until then I thought Deb was never going to slow down and I'd drop dead from over-partying.'

The months leading up to Joshua's birth were unexceptional, but for one thing. Joe was ill with severe nausea, every morning from six, when they got up, until mid-morning at work. It had started in England, after the pregnancy was confirmed, but when it continued to plague him for months after they returned he consulted a doctor for tests. Everything came back normal.

Finally, after exhausting all lines of inquiry, the doctor asked Joe about his wife. Was she, by any chance, pregnant? Joe looked at him and nodded, wondering at the connection. Well, there it is, replied the doctor, ushering him out. You've got morning sickness, lad. Joe was disbelieving, but still, the nausea persisted, right up until 30 October 1986, when their baby boy was born. Then it disappeared.

> **Debbie**: We knew we must be having a boy because of the way I was carrying him. Jody had been lying across, and this one was right out front, huge. But the pregnancy was a breeze compared to the last one. I didn't know about dates, I never counted days, but one morning I had a show and I said, hey, I'm going to have this baby today. Joe was having conniptions, because he wanted me to go to the hospital right away, but I wasn't about to go up and wait nine hours like I did the last time.
>
> So I had a shower and fooled around, and got up there around eleven thirty. The nurses were much nicer this time – I was older, and I was married to Joe Kilroy, after all. The first nurse checked me and said, well, you're not going to have this baby on my shift, probably not until four. So I said, I'm off then, I hate hospitals and I'm not waiting. But before I had a chance they changed their minds. Not long after they checked me again and the same nurse said, actually, you're going to have this baby now. He was born at one fifteen.

Compared with Jody's arrival at the same hospital – the Royal Brisbane Women's – this birth was calm and joyous. Joe didn't leave Debbie's side. He watched as his son's head first appeared, announcing that the baby had black hair. The midwife carefully guided the tiny body into the world, then scooped him up and into his father's waiting arms: 'His eyes opened in three stages as I wiped them, these long eyelashes unfolding, chink, chink, chink,' Joe recalls. 'He had a little mark on his chest where he was folded over in the foetal position. We had a few names picked out but we both just said, he's a Joshua, and that was it. And Kevin, after her dad. He looked a little bit like her dad, a little bit like mine.'

This time the hospital stay was actually pleasant for Debbie, who felt she was treated much more gently as a respectable married woman and Joe Kilroy's wife. The nurses took time to explain the processes of breastfeeding to her, but despite her efforts with her hungry little son, her earlier experiences with Jody cast a long, negative shadow. Six weeks later, she had another bout of mastitis, with its accompanying pain and high fever. That was the end of it.

Within days, Joshua was thriving on Nana's prescription for a healthy baby: diluted cow's milk and sugar. You don't buy that formula shit, she'd told Debbie years before, after mastitis killed off her attempts to breastfeed Jody. You do it the old way: as they get older you put less and less water in the milk, and then you slowly add a melted arrowroot biscuit and cut the teat bigger. It had worked for her kids, she said, and it would work for Debbie's.

There followed a brief period of peace in the Kilroy household after Joshua's birth, broken only by a frightening few days during which Debbie and the baby were hospitalised with a severe virus. Joshua was about six months old, and separated from his mother in the children's wing, where he underwent a lumbar puncture. Debbie, delirious from the effects of pneumonia and a soaring temperature, lay in an adult ward in the damp stupor of fever, hallucinatory images edging her dreams.

Whose life do they belong to? she wonders. Not to hers: the images are frightening, and she has never been frightened in her life. Monstrous hands, arms, flap around her, she is struggling for air. She tries to turn her head, to shake them off, to breathe, but movement hurts her throat, her neck. There is only one person who can help her, she knows that now, and with the breath she has left she calls her: Mum! Mum! Help me! Please! Mum! Her grandmother, who has been mother and grandmother, is at her side, murmuring, I'm here. She is shocked: she knows this grown woman in the hospital bed has never called out for her mother in her life, but that it is plainly her mother she wants now. When she whimpers Mum, the grandmother repeats again, I'm here. But the grown woman, who looks suddenly like the child she recently was, is adamant. No, she says, no. I want my mother.

But by the time Pat Harding arrived at her bedside, Debbie's fever had finally broken. She had discharged herself and rushed to Joshua, still very ill, listlessly propped in a wire mesh cot in the children's wing. Neither Joe nor Debbie has ever forgotten those worrying few days. When Joe saw his son he was 'sitting there in a cot by the window, just looking at us, that little face just looking at us'. It was, he says, 'the most useless I've ever felt in my life'.

The trauma they'd shared as children made both Debbie and Joe fiercely protective parents. They might tear each other – and anyone on the periphery – to shreds during highly volatile times, but no one would lay a hand on their children. They would be spared the brutality Debbie and Joe had known so young. But protecting them didn't mean wrapping them in cotton wool. In Jody's mind, her life in the two years that followed Joshua's birth was split in two: days and nights spent tagging along with Debbie or Joe at football or bikie venues, or endless days when she and her brother were left with Nana, wishing their mother would come back.

> Jody: I used to get dragged along everywhere, to Lang Park, to the clubhouse, heaps of places. I loved it at Nana's but hated being left there for days. Sometimes I'd tag along with Joe to the Uhlans, and go to sleep there. Bikies would be passed out on the lounge and Joe would kick them, say, get up, my daughter wants to have a sleep. And they'd leave all their change on the couch – I used to pocket heaps.
>
> If I wanted to go home I'd ring Nana and cry poor and say, can I get a cab over? Yellow cabs were just in front of the clubhouse, so I'd go up the back stairs around midnight. I was seven or eight years old, and the cabbies would look at me, I could tell they were thinking, where did this child come from? I'd tell them I was with the Uhlans, over the back. 'Oh, with the bikies,' they'd say. 'Great.' But they were great.

Parental love and vigilance take many forms, and Debbie's and Joe's would be steadily undermined in the next few years, not by any lack of care or good intentions, but by their own failure to deal with the past. The old, unresolved issues lay just beneath the skin of the fragile marriage, and would inevitably come to the surface like infected splinters. Ironically, Debbie and Joe soon began to lay the groundwork for history to repeat itself, and for their own early heartbreak and tragedy to be visited upon their children.

5

Bad Company

Violence – or the inference of it – is the silent third party to more relationships than most of us will dare to admit. Between spouses, between siblings, even between parent and child: no one with a difficult or overactive child is a stranger to the unspoken impulse to use superior parental strength and authority to control them. We all own a capacity to express anger physically, to lessen our pain by inflicting it on others.

Debbie Kilroy had learned about violence early, its uses, its effects, its macabre satisfactions. The shock of it. But her experiences inside Wilson meant she would inevitably make violence and trust into deadly twins. One became dependent on the other, a terrible symbiosis in her dealings with those who tried to get close to her. With hindsight, it is obvious her marriage to Joe would be mined with potential problems from the start.

Throughout 1987, a pattern began to emerge in the Kilroys' lives. During the week, life was fairly ordered. It centred around the demands of work, football training, the children. But weekends were becoming a battleground of drinking and argument, raging over various territories: the Uhlans' clubhouse, pre- and post-football sessions at the pub, and Emma Street.

Marriage and two children hadn't blunted Debbie's predilection for going out and raising hell. She still frequented the same places – the Uhlans' clubhouse, the city nightclubs, various pubs – with the same girlfriends. And the year after Joshua was born she began to play touch football again for a south-side club, which brought another set of drinking friends into her life. Tanya Sale, who first met Debbie on the football field and has remained a staunch friend, remembers her as 'a ratbag' at the time, vocal and passionate and with an opinion about everything. Marriage and children, she recalls, didn't slow Debbie down at all.

'We used to party together, drink together, run around – like normal young people. But the difference was the sport: once you have sport in common you have this bond. Being in the same team, you are mates, no matter what,' she says. 'Deb also had this energy about her, she drew me in. I had this gut feeling – I just knew we were going to be mates for life. She had exactly the same values as a friend that I had, absolute loyalty. I would tell her anything. If I was in trouble, if my life was on the line and I could have chosen one person to help, it would have been her. It still is.'

Photographs from this time show the Kilroy family living an almost schizophrenic existence: shots of wild bikie parties, then a baby photo of Jody, then friends draped around each other in an alcoholic haze, then pictures of a child's birthday party. That was what life was like, Debbie says. 'It wasn't like having two different lives. You do this, like get drunk and fight, and then you do that, have fun with the kids. It was just normal to me. Party hard, run amok, have a blue, come home to my kids, have a birthday party, do the shopping, cook the meals. That was normal.'

More and more, though, the fights with Joe were ending in physical confrontations. They would push and shove each other against walls, slap each other hard, throw punches: 'It would be on for young and old on Friday nights, usually at the clubhouse, usually fuelled by grog,' she says. 'Then it would be calm again during the week and then on again at weekends. Joe would go away with the bike club and stay away for days on end. There would be screaming matches when he got back: where the fuck have you been? What have you been doing, running round with other sheilas? All that stuff. I wasn't going to put up with it.'

Jody recalls a family life that was 'very good when it was good, and very bad when it was bad: Mum used to get really drunk and she'd start on Joe, and he'd just flog her. I saw it, lots of times. I remember Josh waking up and I'd put him into bed with me; he was only one or two years old. But I could still hear them. It would go for an hour or so and then that would be it for a week or two. Then it would be perfect for a while. But I really grew to hate Joe for a bit; I used to think he was pretty putrid actually – horrible. He'd chop right into her, with his fists, he'd kick her in the head when she was on the ground. But she'd be down there saying, you're a black dog, a fuckin' black dog, she didn't care, she'd keep going. He'd be saying, *shut up!* And she'd keep going, so he'd start again. She wouldn't just take it. She couldn't beat him physically, but she beat him verbally every time.'

Gill's memories of the violence match Jody's, appalling images she still has in her head and can't erase. 'I thought one of them would kill the other, that's how bad it used to get,' she says. 'Many times I was between Joe and Deb, with Joe trying to get to her. When you have this incredibly fit, powerful footballer standing in front of you, wanting to beat and kick his wife, it's scary. Sometimes I wasn't sure if I was going to be hit as well. But Joe wasn't like that.'

Gill clearly remembers, however, at least one episode incited by Debbie. They were visiting Gill after she moved to Cairns, and had gone to a pub, where Debbie became gradually incensed with Joe as he talked to other people. 'Deb was drunk and lost it with him, abusing him. Joe punched her but it didn't fully connect, and next thing Deb's hit Joe over the back of the head from behind with a full stubbie of beer, and then ran,' she says.

'Deb always knew when to run, and I knew her well enough to quietly get into my car and slowly drive down the road, because I knew she'd spring out of nowhere – and sure enough she dived into my car and I drove her home. We had to keep Deb under our bed that night so Joe wouldn't find her. She stayed there until they'd both sobered up and cooled off. That's how it was with them. I knew Deb would push it to the limit but together they were both volatile and out of control towards each other – it wasn't a good idea for them to get on the drink together. When they were sober and not out clubbing together they were a lot better.'

The steady escalation of violence in the relationship, and the erosion of Debbie's trust, were accompanied by Joe's growing profile as a talented and marketable footballer, and by his increasing dependence on 'smoko' – marijuana. In 1987 Joe was still playing for Brothers, but as A-grade football clubs began the machinations which would see the creation of the Brisbane Broncos in 1988, and their entry into the Sydney Rugby League premiership, other eyes were on him too. Joe had the singular kind of talent that combined strength with speed. In 1983, the British football magazine *Open*

Rugby had named him the world's best rugby league fullback, but some of the most memorable games of his career were played on the wing. He was uniquely labelled 'explosive' and 'graceful' by commentators in the same breath.

But of course, football icons attract more than professional admiration. Debbie's reluctance to trust Joe was also tied inextricably to the silent code of private behaviour around high-profile football players. Joe and other A-grade and national stars were openly pursued by female fans who frequented the clubhouses after games and mixed with the players. The scrutiny of players' private lives was then generally restricted to social photographs of them with wives, girlfriends and new babies, but there was another, unspoken side to their off-field activities that involved willing 'groupies' and casual sex. Debbie had a bird's eye view of it: shortly after Joe joined Brothers, the club also employed her as a barmaid in the clubhouse.

'Women would throw themselves at Joe all the time, and at others, even at Brothers. These women would hang around the clubhouse, doing everything they could to hook up with someone famous, someone whose photo was in the paper,' she says. According to Debbie, it was 'common knowledge' around the clubs that many of the women were happy to grant sexual favours to the players after games and a few drinks. 'You'd go looking for X or Y and you'd be told they were down on the oval, getting a head job,' she says.

Gill Campbell also remembers women sidling up to Deb in pubs and intimating or claiming outright that they'd slept with Joe Kilroy. 'Deb wasn't the right person to say that stuff to – she was so volatile and jealous at the time. But Deb had never had one guy in her life she could trust or believe in – they'd all let her down in one way or another,' she says.

Joe's frequent disappearances on his bike – either with the Uhlans or on his own – and the rumours that constantly did the rounds of bars and football clubs only underlined for Debbie how unsafe this relationship was for her. Increasingly, her way of dealing with that, and with the escalation of drinking and chaos in their lives, was to prod and provoke Joe emotionally and physically until his temper frayed and broke, and he lashed out. The ensuing violence affirmed and validated her own suspicions and actions, and underlined her deeply buried belief in her own wickedness.

Debbie: Right back as far as the pain from the neck manipulation, my trust was blown, I think. Wilson made it worse, and it became a huge, huge issue, an incredibly hard pattern to break. I was always on the back foot, or going for someone's jugular, because straight up I wouldn't trust anyone, so I'd be testing them out, having a go. I was always coming from the premise that, whoever it is, that person is going to hurt me, so I was going to get in first.

I would come in hard and sharp, bang, and it must have been like a lead brick coming down on someone's head. They'd reel back, and then they'd run, and I'd think, see! They didn't really want a relationship or a friendship, so fuck them. You put yourself in a coffin, where no one is going to come and get you.

Joe would be so pissed off with me for having a go, having a go, because he's so laidback. But I knew no one could be trusted. They say they love you. Well, sure you do. So I'd press every button to see what they were going to do to me. Because I need to know what's coming, that's how I got control of it. By pushing the buttons and getting the reaction I would be in control of the violence, in a sense. But if I didn't see it coming it would freak me out, I wouldn't have control.

These days, Debbie can see connections between her father's death and the violence she invited from two men – Joe and, before him, John Parker – whom she describes as the most gentle, easygoing men she had ever met: 'Both men were like my father: he was laidback and easygoing too, nothing could ruffle his feathers. And what's he do? He drops dead – the ultimate revenge. So I've felt like I didn't deserve people who were nice, calm, patient, pleasant – they needed to be dishing out punishment instead.'

She has attracted criticism from domestic violence campaigners who have been appalled at her claims that she 'turned both men into raving lunatics'. But Debbie has never made excuses for any violence perpetrated by any man. Each has to take individual responsibility for his actions. What she has had to do for herself is to claim her own place in each incident, her own agency and her own needs, and the connections that reach back to her own childhood.

Like many young couples, Joe and Debbie also struggled with that most basic of marital tools: communication. Twenty years on, they can see how shackled they were by the barriers thrown up by race – his Aboriginal and South Sea Islander culture against her white European one – but then they were blind to the obvious. Unaware of the organic nature of the differences between them, they backed each other into emotional corners, building impenetrable walls as they did so. This was the kind of war they were both skilled at, after years of instruction within institutions where each child's own emotional corner was the only safe place. You only left your corner to guard it, and the only way to do that was to destroy the aggressor. 'That's what we did,' says Debbie. 'We tried to destroy each other.'

One of the crucial factors for them at the time was the absence of any leavening influence from parents or elders. Joe was rarely in contact with his father or other extended family, and the relationship between Pat and Debbie constantly seesawed. In Debbie's view it provided no source of advice or support. Joe regretted the lack of opportunity to seek help from someone outside the relationship, someone respected. He often felt lost and confused: 'But all we had were our own mistakes and each other. It's a terrible way to learn.'

When things were bad at home, Joe often turned to his mates at the Uhlans for company and support. 'A bike clubhouse – beauty, a lot of intellect there!' he jokes. 'But they were my family – most of those blokes came from fucked-up families or institutions, so we all had a lot of stuff in common. But that doesn't last forever.'

So he was delighted that his sister Kym – who he'd been separated from in the orphanage – began to visit the house more often after they returned from overseas, bringing the boyfriend who would soon become her husband, Sean Scott-Marlan. Joe had always been close to Kym and to his brother Bob, and the three had shared a house before Joe moved in with Debbie. Debbie says the siblings 'did everything together – they were like the Three Stooges, you couldn't separate them'.

Kym had a lot of control over Joe, Debbie believes, and did absolutely everything for him – the mother figure he'd been missing since leaving the nuns at St Joseph's.

Debbie didn't like Kym, and the feeling was mutual. 'She'd bring women around to meet Joe, she'd want to take him out with them, she'd constantly stir trouble,' Debbie says. 'She hated me and wanted Joe to hate me, and it caused huge dramas between us.' According to Debbie, Kym's friends were also very partial to dope and to ecstasy, then becoming a popular party drug around Brisbane.

Scott-Marlan, however, was different. Debbie liked him initially; he was pleasant and easygoing and, unlike Kym, he treated her with respect. He got on well with Joe, too, and quickly became Joe's supplier of smoko, setting him up with Debbie to on-sell heads and hash to others.

> **Debbie**: They were all big dope smokers, Scott-Marlan too. But he always had a lot of money to throw around and could always get the best dope. You'd never ask questions though. Everyone who came into the house smoked dope, it was social. And everyone who smokes dope wheels and deals, they sell ten bucks worth here, thirty there, to earn money to buy your own. That isn't trafficking in the way people assume it is – everyone does it, no matter how much you use or don't use.

But Scott-Marlan was different in other ways, too. Unbeknownst to the Kilroys – and to his wife – he was already heavily involved in supplying and trafficking heroin, with much of his activity protected by corrupt police within the then Queensland police force. Between 1987 and 1989, the Fitzgerald Inquiry into organised crime in the state would expose the sordid activities of a number of high-ranking police, including the then commissioner, Terry Lewis, and the extent of corruption in Queensland's institutions from the top down. It would also reveal how police were being paid off to protect prostitution, gambling and drug rings, and how the efforts of honest cops were stymied by entrenched and extensive networks of standover merchants and blackmail. In this murky and volatile world, Scott-Marlan was an experienced player.

Few people, even those firmly enmeshed in corrupt activities, could have predicted the extraordinary series of events the inquiry would kick off, and how the effects would ricochet through every layer of every criminal, political, legal and social network. Over the next few years, governments would topple, the highest ranking police officer in the state would be jailed along with several minis-ters of the Crown, and notorious crime bosses would close up shop. But much smaller fry would also be caught in the net as the crum-bling old order was replaced by the new. The personal would indeed become the political for bit players like the Kilroys when their lives intersected with Sean Scott-Marlan's, just as Tony Fitzgerald was taking up his historic commission.

Around the time he met Debbie and Joe, Scott-Marlan was operating at a high level in the national drug scene. He carried a loaded gun, even when he came to Emma Street, and wads of cash. He told them he was looking for a way to launder some of his earnings, and had decided on the manufacture and sale of leather goods through his own retail outlets.

One day in 1987, he put two ideas to the Kilroys that they received with enthusiasm. What about a partnership in a couple of leather stores? he asked Debbie, knowing she and Pat jointly owned the Emma Street house, and that its improved value could be borrowed against. And to Joe: what better way to promote the hip new stores than to front them with a familiar and admired sporting hero?

With a second mortgage of $30 000 on the house, Joe and Debbie had a big stake in the newly formed Kilroy Klothing Kompany. Together they organised to rent a warehouse in the nearby suburb of Albion, where they installed two friends of Joe's, expert machinists, to make jackets, suits, pants and dresses.

The first shop opened at the new Trinity Wharf development in Cairns, which they hoped would be a tourist magnet. The following year, a second store opened in Brisbane's giant new Myer Centre on the Queen Street Mall. Joe, dapper in suit and tie, presided over the Brisbane opening, along with footballers including Alan Langer.

Debbie busied herself with running the business in Brisbane. Scott-Marlan, meanwhile, spent a great deal of time interstate, buying leather for the warehouse – or so Debbie believed. Too late she discovered this was a cover for his drug deals, and the big-time buying and selling of heroin and high quality hashish. The hash she wouldn't have worried about, even if she'd known. Joe was smoking and selling dope and hash to his friends to cover his costs, and even though she wasn't a smoker ('I tried it but I didn't like it because it makes your brain slow; I hate anything that makes my brain slow'), she was also supplying, and didn't see it as a serious problem.

But heroin was a different matter. 'It was a big no-no to me and among all the people I ever mixed with. In any bike club I've ever been in the gear is the biggest no-no in the world. I've known blokes who have been busted in bike clubs for selling the gear and they get thrown out and their patches ripped off them and ostracised immediately and absolutely,' Debbie says. 'Besides, I hated hard drugs because of the way they were pumped into me at Wilson.' By the end of 1987, however, her steadfastness would waver. The stakes began to shoot up incredibly high.

Joe's football career hit the big time when, after a successful season which saw Brothers take the Brisbane premiership, he was signed in 1987 by the Brisbane Broncos to play in the national league for the 1988 season. With players like Wally Lewis, Alan Langer, Willie Carne and Peter Jackson, the Broncos were entering their debut season in the Sydney league on a huge wave of popularity and local support. Members of the team made up the bulk of Queensland's State of Origin teams that were regularly thrashing New South Wales, and premiership wins were in their sights from the first kick-off. They were coached by the brilliant but characteristically sober and unsmiling Wayne Bennett, known for his controlled and highly disciplined approach to training, and for his insistence that his players behave well, as good men, not just good players.

Broncos games at Lang Park always drew big crowds. Debbie and her friends would be there too, usually watching from the bar. Joe's first game with the team meant a bigger celebration than usual: after Lang Park she and Anita, Gill and another old friend – Batty Batterham – went on to the Hamilton Hotel, a regular watering hole, on their way to the Broncos clubhouse at Red Hill.

Debbie: I'd basically been drinking all day that day, and after the Hammo I went on to the Broncos. I was driving a station wagon, pissed as a parrot, with the music blaring really loud all the way there. I had no idea the coppers were behind me, sirens wailing – I didn't hear them. I go flying into the Broncos car park, which was all dirt then, police and sirens screaming up behind me, all the cars spitting up dirt all through the air. I got out of the car and when the dust settled there was Wayne Bennett, just standing there. It was the first time I'd met him.

The cops come over and say they're taking me into town for a breath test, so in we go and I'm sitting in the cells wondering what to do. Then I notice the antiseptic soap in the toilet. So I eat it. I'm not sure why, I remembered something about it helping, and it seemed like a good idea at the time. And it works. I don't register over the limit. After all that they have to put me back in their car and give me a lift back to the Broncos.

If the coaches, players and commentators were expecting the stereotypical footballer's wife – smiling, hair-flicking, little woman-behind-the-man ex-model – they were in for a surprise with Debbie Kilroy. She abhorred what she saw as the 'yuppie' side to football life, and the expectations about how she would look, behave and speak:

Debbie: All the other wives were yuppies. They didn't like me because I drank with the blokes. After games at the clubhouse, the others would have one drink and the blokes would send them home. Not me. They flew us all down to Sydney once for a State of Origin game. I got on the piss on the plane, and then when we get to the hotel they get all the wives in their flash dresses, makeup and high heels in front of this big mirror for a photo. That just isn't me.

Then they tell us we can't see our husbands before the game. Bullshit, I say, where's Joe's room? Off I went. I hate being told what to do. If they hadn't said that I wouldn't have worried. Then after the game all the wives go back to the hotel to bed, and all the blokes go to King's Cross. I went with them. In the morning they've got the blokes and the wives on different flights, so I ring up and change my flight to theirs, and go out to the airport on the bus with the team. All the other wives are saying, how did you do that? I told them: I just got on the phone.

Debbie was indifferent to celebrity, but there was one night when she really enjoyed being Joe Kilroy's wife. She was drinking with Gill in the city when an inebriated young man approached her, trying to chat her up. 'I'm Joe Kilroy, you know,' he told her. 'The famous footballer. Smokin' Joe.'

Debbie laughed, and tried to explain how she knew, 100 per cent, that he was not. The young man continued to insist he was Joe.

'You're hitting on the wrong girl. I'm Debbie Kilroy, Joe's wife,' she kept saying, unable to suppress her laughter. Finally, tired of him, she produced her driver's licence to prove it, but to little effect. She was the one making it up, he said. Eventually this young, short, pale-skinned, brash Joe Kilroy moved off to try his luck with someone else.

Scott-Marlan, on the other hand, saw big advantages in the celebrity of his friends, and went as far as suggesting that Joe should have his own personal cheer squad, complete with Kilroy Klothing Kompany logos on their shirts. The three dancers – two female, one male – duly took up their posts on the sidelines of every Broncos game, wearing high-cut gold leather shorts and KKK emblazoned across their chests and back. Smokin' Joe Kilroy – an ironic reference to his speed on the field – had made it.

But the pressure on the family was inexorably building: the routine Debbie felt safe within – weekday family life, weekend drinking – was being destroyed by Joe's new status, the leather business and the subtle demands from Scott-Marlan to keep up their sales of hash. Debbie was starting to resent Joe's high-flying lifestyle and his frequent absences with the Uhlans and regular outings with Kym; she felt she was being left to keep the household together, working the leather business, paying off the house, bringing up two children, making ends meet.

Typically, she retaliated with her own style of payback – hard drinking and some spirited provocation designed to push Joe's buttons. She saw the slaps and punches that followed as her due, but they still made her angry and unsettled. At least the customers Scott-Marlan was introducing to her were buying enough hash to put cash in her pocket.

A couple of them were coming to her more and more often to buy Scott-Marlan's high-quality, gold-stamped slabs of imported hash. She could sell a block for $30 or a bag of heads for $125 and make 'a bomb'. Steadily, she began to feel hooked by the buoyant feeling of having money. And Scott-Marlan, persuasive, charming, clever, encouraged her, making it easy for her with a seemingly endless supply of drugs.

Jody: I was only small, but one night I was watching 'Crimestoppers' on TV and they showed these bags of mari-juana – I realised for the first time what it was. I'd never known. Not long before I'd gone into a spare room upstairs. It was adjacent to the lounge room with the papasan chairs in it, and in there were all these big black bags of pot. I'd been looking for the bike I knew they'd bought me for my birthday, and there it was, in the middle of these bags. I thought, oh God, it's drugs. And drugs are bad. I wasn't worried though; I knew Mum always took care of everything.

Outside Emma Street, activity was accelerating throughout Brisbane towards the opening of World Expo 88, held on a transformed strip of old wharves and warehouses on the south bank of the city reach of the river. The expected influx of interstate and overseas visitors had already prompted the completion of a sophisticated arts precinct adjacent to Expo and the rejuvenation of the city centre.

With the gala opening of the world-class event, and the shocking and ongoing revelations from the witness box of the Fitzgerald Inquiry, the scales seemed to fall from the eyes of the good citizens of Brisbane, and they saw themselves and their city reinvented as finally grown-up, and mature. No longer would the city be denigrated as the capital of the 'deep north' by southerners. And the following year, when Queenslanders would elect their first Labor government in thirty-two years, integrity and accountability would become the new catchwords.

In this atmosphere of mounting consternation at the fallibility of their trusted institutions and officials, Debbie and Joe Kilroy were about to find out for themselves just how fallible those institutions were, along with certain trusted friendships. This was prompted by several events, but the most significant was the change in Scott-Marlan's approach to his supply of drugs to Debbie. The change was gradual, but by the beginning of 1988 he had begun to pressure her to sell heroin.

In certain quarters, the Emma Street house was already becoming known as a source of various illicit substances, but most people – friends, mates from the bike club, footballers – knew the Kilroys' antagonism to 'the gear'. It was completely off-limits. Scott-Marlan knew this too, but he kept asking. His persuasive and manipulative skills were 'amazing', according to Debbie. He hooked into her bubbling anger with Joe, her sense of alienation from his celebrity world, and her need to rebel against it – and her growing appreciation of money. And because he was already playing the role of conduit between the Kilroys and some of their customers, the networks were established and reliable.

Early in 1988, he introduced a new member to the network, a young man named Alex. In the world of illicit drugs, a first name was all you needed. Alex was personable and clean-cut and hungry for high-quality dope, hash and amphetamines. After his initial visit to Emma Street he returned several times with Scott-Marlan and then began to visit alone, buying bigger and bigger quantities and striking up a good friendship with Debbie. One day, he asked her if she could score him some gear.

Scott-Marlan was in the room that day when Alex asked the question. 'Oh yeah,' he said to Alex, 'I can get you that.' Debbie finds it hard to explain why she agreed later to ride with Scott-Marlan in his car while the deal was done. 'Intrinsically, I didn't like it,' she says, 'but I just went against that feeling. He was very convincing. He said, it's no big deal, you just come with me and I'll give it to him. And I had the shits with Joe, I had the shits with all the violence, and Scott-Marlan's this nice bloke who's taken me under his wing. So it was about, fuck you Joe. Fuck everything. I got sucked in.'

Joe knew nothing about Debbie's involvement in Scott-Marlan's drug runs to places like the local railway station at Eagle Junction, the Windmill Café and St Paul's Tavern in the city. Debbie knew that if Joe even suspected that heroin was going round he would 'hit the roof'. It wasn't so hard to keep quiet – Joe was away from the house a lot, training or on his bike. Besides, he had some other things on his mind.

Several months earlier, a poster had appeared on the wall of the Brisbane watch-house. Blatantly racist in tone, it superimposed a picture of a flagon of sherry and a photo of Joe over an Aboriginal flag. Civil libertarians were outraged, and threatened to take a complaint against police to the police complaints tribunal. The incident did nothing to improve Joe's well-established suspicion of white authority, and clearly indicated to everyone else that Queensland's police force was still home to rednecks and racists.

Over the next few months, as Joe enjoyed a wildly successful debut with the Broncos, Debbie rode several times with Scott-Marlan as he delivered parcels of heroin and, outside St Paul's Tavern on St Paul's Terrace, handed over thousands of dollars in protection money to police he believed were looking after him. At home, Alex was also appearing more frequently, with requests for various amounts of cannabis, amphetamines and heroin. Debbie was feeling increasingly uncomfortable with it all, and with the celebrity footballer lifestyle. The stress in the relationship was building to a crescendo.

It is a cool autumn evening in late May 1988. It's just on closing time, and patrons at the Hamilton Hotel are spilling out into the shock of a fresh wind off the river, laughing and calling to each other as they head towards parked cars and bikes. All full of booze and good humour – except a fierce blonde woman who is striding purposefully towards the car park as if she's got a date with danger and is determined not to miss it. Her young, pretty face is set and grim. Although Debbie Kilroy is very, very drunk, her direction doesn't waver. In one swift, steady movement she's unlocked the driver's door of her car, plunged the key into the ignition and planted her foot down. The car, a Chevrolet convertible, screeches off into the night.

She's got this one image repeating in her head as she drives fast through the quiet streets. It concerns her husband, and a rumour she has heard through the smoke and bullshit and bragging of the bar tonight. Her husband is a football star, ruggedly handsome, the target of lusty affection from unabashed female fans. Their own relationship is turbulent at the best of times, they are offhand and often brutal with each other. She has no proof that he is unfaithful, but she knows he has ample opportunity for it. Tonight, a sharp sliver of doubt has pierced her fuggy brain.

She pulls up hard in the driveway of the highset house, slams the door. Immediately regrets the slam: her two children will be asleep inside, and from the quiet and the darkened windows it seems her husband is too. But that's no barrier to her rage. She's up the stairs, through the door, into the bedroom and screaming before he knows what's happened. She's just standing there screaming something about him and some woman doing something on a wheelie bin. He yanks himself out of sleep. Vaguely, half dreaming, he thinks: a wheelie bin? She won't let up, so he's pulled a pillow over his head but that only inflames her, and the rant continues louder and more obscene by the minute.

Finally, he's had enough. He's out of bed and scooping her up, so fast she doesn't get a chance to fight, and carrying her in his arms out of the bedroom and down the hall towards the back door, intent on throwing her into the pool to shut her up. She's yelling even

louder; she's strong but he's stronger, unlatching the back door
without letting her go. She flails around, grabbing for some purchase
on something, anything, and grips the doorjamb. It halts him only
for a second, perhaps two, and as he pushes forward she's screaming
again: 'My hand! My hand's stuck!' He says, 'Sure it is!' and then he's
pushing and powering through the doorway and down the stairs
towards the pool.

At the edge he hesitates, and in that second she holds her left
hand up in the cold moonlight. Shock clutches at her stomach.
Her wedding finger is missing. Only a jagged piece of skin, hanging,
remains. And then she's screaming again, but it's different now.
'My finger, where's my fucking finger?' He looks at her face and
quickly puts her down and they both gaze at the appalling absence,
the sickening shred of skin. Then: 'Where is it?' she yells into the
night, the suddenly guilty night, and they both scramble back up
the stairs where she mutters alternately, 'Where is it?' and 'I'm going
to be sick.'

She slumps on top of a blanket box at the top of the stairs and he
thrusts a bin between her feet. From downstairs comes the voice of
their friend, Mal, who has been camping rough in a room under the
house; he comes running. Together the two men dash around in
their macabre search. 'Where is it?' she's crying feebly. 'Where's my
fucking finger, you bastard?'

Strangely, there is no blood, just two small drops on the floor –
and no pain. She might be imagining the whole catastrophe but for
the gap – and the tunnelling nausea. And, soon enough, the proof:
the finger is there, still hideously attached to the doorjamb where
her wedding ring has caught in the square steel tongue. The ring is
on the finger and the tendons are hanging, like a carefully moulded
exhibit in a chamber of horrors. One of the men says, 'Quick, get a
screwdriver, something, and some ice.' She is aware of an ambulance
siren wailing, a loud, insistent lament.

They roar towards the hospital. She is awake and still in shock,
looking wide-eyed at her transformed world. One of the ambulance
officers leans over her and smiles. 'Don't worry, love,' he says, 'we sew
men's dicks back on and they work just fine.' But in the emergency
department she finds her anger again. They want to cut her jeans and
shirt from her body but the jeans, at any rate, are her favourites, so
she yells the nurses away and, using both hands, reefs them off herself.

It's the last thing she remembers doing before they wheel her into surgery.

When she regains consciousness several hours later, there are white bandages tightly wound round her left hand and forearm, and a sorry-looking doctor tells her they could not save her finger. But the bandages cloak and numb the reality, and the loss barely registers. Nor does it seem to register with a constant queue of nurses, who appear only to ask if the famous footballer is here. After one day and night of this she's had enough, and checks herself out.

Several weeks later, she is back at the hospital's outpatients department with her husband to have her stitches removed. She is still in a kind of denial, which is rammed home by the sight of those around her here: people in wheelchairs with legs missing, faces held taut by elaborate braces, heads shaved and scarred. She's still thinking 'it's only a finger' when the doctors remove the bandages and she sees her left hand with its mangled stump for the first time. Nausea rolls up her throat. Back outside, she avoids the lift and heads for the stairs, where she suddenly slumps down and begins to cry. Even with her eyes shut all she can see is disfigurement. All she can feel is the violence of loss.

Her husband is behind her. 'What's your problem?' he asks. She is jolted by his insensitivity, reminded of all the cruelty she has had to bear by refusing – pretending – not to feel it. She rubs her face dry and stands up. 'Fuckin' nothin',' she says, and goes quickly down the stairs. But half an hour later, when she is buying coffee, she holds out her left hand for the change and it falls through the unfamiliar space between her fingers onto the shop counter. The shop assistant looks stricken, realising what has happened as the coins spin and clang too loudly, metal on metal. She ignores them and walks away, and lets the tears come.

The trauma of losing her finger – and the way in which it had been torn from her body – would haunt Debbie and inhabit her dreams. Although she would face seemingly greater tragedy and heartbreak in the coming years, the terrible symbolism of this loss would impact not just on her relationship with Joe but on her dealings with the world around her. She had only to look down at her palms, or hold an object in two hands, to be reminded of all the betrayal, all the cruelty, all the misery offered to her so far. If she was angry with the world before, the loss of her finger stoked a fury in her that had to be released physically. Now that she was so obviously marked, the world would be too.

Debbie: The following Friday night the Uhlans had this big party on a river boat. I got plastered, then went back to the clubhouse and drank and drank. My eyes felt like they'd been scratched with a pin. Then someone says I can't have any more to drink. Sorry, can't serve you any more alcohol. That did it. I stuck my boot under the table that was loaded up with all their drugs, and sent it flying, slammed it. Don't tell me when I can drink and when I can't. I want a drink now! So someone gives me one more drink, then they throw me out. 'Well, you can stick it, you maggots.' And I leave after I've thrown a few more things around.

Outside there's a security camera, and I walk up to it and stick my face right in it and say, you tell that fucking bastard to get outside now or I'll rip your fucking camera off the fucking wall. Joe was out in about two seconds. We get a cab home and all this stuff about my finger is pouring out, all this rage. I'm so sick of hearing how Joe's so wonderful, Debbie's out of control, she's a lunatic, look what she's done now got her finger ripped off, poor Joe. Well, fuck poor Joe. What about poor Debbie? It's never been poor Debbie, always poor someone else.

The following Wednesday night Joe was back at the Uhlans clubhouse at Buranda, attending the weekly meeting. There would be repercussions for Debbie's behaviour the previous Friday: she would be banned for life from the clubhouse for running amok, and Joe would be fined $20 for not keeping his wife under control. This only served to enrage Debbie even further. How dare they? But she had their measure.

The following week when several of the Uhlans (all of whom died within fifteen years) arrived at Emma Street to score their drugs, she was waiting for them. 'What do you want here?' she demanded, knowing exactly what they wanted. 'No way, you're banned from my house for life,' she told them. The bikies were bemused, shuffling their feet, muttering, 'Come on, Deb, don't be like that.' But Debbie was not moved. 'Fuck off,' she told them calmly but with deadly intent. She stood there until they'd gone.

6

D-Day

Joe Kilroy made his debut in State of Origin football in Brisbane on 17 May 1988, shortly after his wife lost her finger. It was just two months after the Broncos entered the Sydney competition with an explosive 44–10 win against Manly-Warringah in a game made more memorable by Kilroy's own try just minutes from full-time. His selection in the Origin team was no surprise, and when, in the third game of the series at Sydney Stadium on 21 June (coincidentally, his birthday) he duplicated history by scoring a try minutes from the siren, his name entered the pantheon of Queensland rugby league superstars. He had two weeks to enjoy the view from the pedestal.

On the weekend of 2–3 July 1988, two of the Kilroys' friends, Merv and Trish Gearing, were married at Ferny Hills. They'd left both Joshua and Jody with Nana for the evening, but Debbie called an unusually early night, and drove home via Nana's to pick up a sleepy Joshua around midnight. Jody wanted to stay. Back at home, she put Joshua to bed and went into the kitchen for a drink. She turned on the tap, and all hell let loose.

Their Doberman-cross watchdogs, Rocky and Clubber, suddenly erupted, shattering the midnight air with sharp barks and full-throated howls. Over the top of them came loud thumps and bangs on the back door. Debbie froze; it had to be police. She turned towards the door but before she had a chance to react or reply to the incessant thumping, the door crashed open as the smashed lock gave way and the timber splintered. A mass of police – more than twenty, she calculated later – stormed in.

Debbie: I was happy to let them in, because I knew there was nothing in the house, no drugs, nothing. But they couldn't wait, they have to big-note themselves and smash the door in. They start to tear the house apart. Joshua wakes up, of course, and he's freaked out by what's going on and crying, so I just sat quietly in the lounge room with him on my lap, trying to calm him down.

There's this one female copper – there's always one smart-arsed female – and she thinks I'm the yuppie wife of the foot-baller, and she's trying all the heavies with me. Come on, she's saying, where's all your drugs? They're ripping things out of cupboards and drawers, sweeping photos off the top of the TV, and then they start smashing things, but I won't give them a reaction. Go for it, I reckon. So they smash more and more, tipping things over the floor, throwing stuff around, their guns drawn.

Eventually, after failing to find any drugs or to get any kind of reaction from Debbie, the police seized some cash paid to Joe by the Broncos (and stored under the mattress) and demanded she accompany them to the station. 'What for?' she insisted. 'To be charged,' was the reply. 'What with?' There was little to say. 'You just have to come,' said one of the police.

Wearily, Debbie phoned Anita, apologising about the time – it was nearly two in the morning by this stage – and asked her to come and sit with Joshua, who was still distressed. With a child's intuition, the little boy understood something was very wrong, and when Anita arrived she had to peel him, crying, from his mother's side. Debbie climbed into a police car, assuring them she'd be home by morning.

Debbie: But down at the watch-house it's hours and hours of questioning. You want to tell us what you've been up to? 'There's nothing to tell, I'm not telling you dickheads anything.' The chair I'm on has these wheels and they're kicking it around the room. They're saying, come on, we've got your friends in the other room, Sean and Kym, and they're talking. I'm being really calm, really cool. 'Big deal, I don't know what you're talking about.' And we've got your other mate here too, Alex. 'I don't know any Alex.' You need to know he's a police officer.

In my head I think, oh shit, but I say, 'Don't know what the fuck you're talking about, I don't know any Alex, so either charge me with something or I'm off. I've had enough of you dogs. Charge me or I'm gone.' I get up, I'm walking out the door. They finally figure they're not getting anything out of me, I'm not talking, so they get out the typewriter and they charge me. In the meantime, Sean's next door, spilling his guts. They'd done the big scene with pointed guns with Sean and Kym, standing in front of their car like something out of Starsky and Hutch, or Mod Squad, because they knew he carried a gun.

Debbie was still in the watch-house on Sunday, and would be detained to appear in court. But there was no sign of Joe, despite extensive searches by police. He had in fact come home in the early hours of Sunday with Mal, parked the car behind the house as usual, and ambled up the back steps. Confronted by the smashed-in door, he stopped, peered into the house, saw that the television and video were still there and knew immediately he hadn't been visited by thieves, but by the police. He was back downstairs and on his bike before he even knew where he was going.

Later on Sunday, the lawyer who normally acted for members of the Black Uhlans, Stuart Bales, contacted the police about Debbie's whereabouts and the charges that might be pending against Joe. About the same time, a man Debbie describes as 'daggy, wearing ugh boots' came into her cell, sat down and began to talk to her, assuring her Joe was all right. 'Who are you?' she demanded, forever on guard. She needed bona fides. She soon had them: Myles Lewis was a lawyer in the same firm as Bales. Over the next sixteen months his face would become as familiar to her as her own.

By this time news of the arrest, and the police search for Joe, had been leaked to Brisbane radio stations. It was a big story: Joe was a local hero, especially among the young, who regarded the Harley-riding Origin player as 'cooler than cool'. It was inevitable the police would find him some time that day. After discussing the situation with his lawyers, Joe made an appointment to meet with drug squad detectives at the city watch-house the following morning. An expectant media crowd duly arrived, but Joe didn't. Then on Tuesday morning just after seven, with Bales at his side, Joe handed himself in. Debbie was still locked in her cell.

Five hours later, Joe was officially charged on one count of trafficking a dangerous drug, four counts of supplying a dangerous drug
and one of possession. Debbie had already been charged with two
counts of trafficking a dangerous drug, fifteen of supplying, possession of a car for the use of supplying and possession of the cash from
the sale of dangerous drugs.*

Three others were also charged with the Kilroys after a police raid
at Hamilton turned up $100 000 worth of cannabis resin hidden in
secret compartments in a suitcase and a briefcase brought into the
country by ship from Bombay. Sean Scott-Marlan, then thirty-two,
was charged on two counts of trafficking, six of supplying a dangerous drug, possession of drug scales and three pipes, two counts of
possessing a car used in trafficking. His wife, Joe's sister Kym, twenty-
nine, was charged with one count of trafficking, two of supplying,
five of possession of a dangerous drug and possession of a car used in
trafficking. The third, seaman Barry Hackett, fifty-one, of Ballina, was
charged with importing a dangerous drug, two counts of supplying,
two of trafficking, and possession of $500 from the sale of drugs.

Under the two-year-old Drugs Misuse Act, all faced mandatory
life sentences for trafficking. The much-criticised legislation introduced by the ailing National Party in Queensland gave judges no
discretionary powers in sentencing. The amounts specified in the Act
varied according to whether those convicted were dependent on
drugs or non-dependent, and a non-user like Debbie could face the
maximum penalty for trafficking as little as two ounces of heroin –
which was the exact amount cited in the charge against her.

Like their three co-accused, Debbie and Joe were remanded in
custody by the magistrate until a further hearing in October. The
police opposed any application for bail for Debbie, accusing her of
being the ringleader in a high-powered trafficking circle, but the
Kilroys' barrister argued hard. Bail was finally set at an extraordinarily high mark for the time, at least for Debbie: $150 000, in one
parcel of cash, and no property or house to be used as surety. The
amount and the conditions ensured her release was highly unlikely.
Bail was set at just $10 000 for Joe.

---

* The difference between trafficking and supplying is based on the amounts
  (i.e. the weight of the drug) sold; how frequently it was sold; and whether it
  was sold across state or territory borders.

Back in the watch-house, police gleefully taunted her with the prospect of jail. She knew what the odds for her bailout were – no one she'd ever known had even seen that much money. She was terrified, and anxious for her children. But there was no way the coppers were going to suspect that.

> **Debbie**: They're saying to me over and over, you're going to jail, first because they opposed bail and then because of the amount. I just stayed calm. Nope, I'll be free before you blink, you wankers. Just watch. But I thought I was gone. So I was pretty shocked when one of them came in on Wednesday and said, okay, you're free, you're on bail. All I could think was, how the hell? Jesus! But I grinned at them and said, see, I told you so, you dogs, and walked out.

In a stunning stroke of serendipity, Debbie's mother Pat and her husband Len had just finalised the sale of a block of units they had bought for investment. On the day Debbie and Joe were charged, they had banked a cheque for $309 000. Despite her troubled relationship with Debbie, Pat barely hesitated. She knew there was a risk that, faced with a life sentence in prison, Debbie might disappear before her trial. But she also knew what a fierce and loving mother her daughter was, and that Jody and Joshua were compelling reasons for her to stick around. On Wednesday morning she contacted Stuart Bales and offered to put up the bail.

Pat and Len's plans for retirement now hinged on Debbie's willingness to stick around and face a possible life sentence. All their funds were tied up in the term deposit – they knew they were gambling the lot. Three hundred thousand dollars is a tidy sum even now – in 1988, it was a very large amount of money for a middle-aged couple to lose. As Debbie said when she thanked Pat after her release from the watchhouse, 'Ronald Biggs would have got out for less.'

Apart from the children it was, in the end, Pat and Len's giant leap of faith that prevented Debbie from fleeing during the sixteen months leading to the trial, which would follow the committal trial in October. She knew she could physically do it – she'd checked out false passports for herself and the children – and a life on the run, even in exile, seemed a far more attractive option than life in a

Brisbane jail. But Pat and Len had risked everything for her, had taken the biggest financial punt of their lives for her. She knew that *they* knew the odds: Debbie could and might bolt. But she was never one to go with the odds. As always, she went against them, and stayed.

The Kilroys went their separate ways for some time after their arrest. Joe needed time to recover from the shock of the heroin charges against Debbie, and went to ground with his football and bikie mates. His lawyers, believing they had grounds to have him acquitted, organised a safe house in the inner city suburb of Red Hill. Debbie took the children to Pat's, angry that they were left to languish in full public view while Joe was protected. For months, she and the children slept on the floor or on the lounge at Pat's or sometimes at Anita's. She would take Jody to school in the mornings and then drive to the safe house so that Joshua could visit his father.

'I'd been painted in the media as the wicked witch of the west who led poor Joe astray,' she says, 'so of course they weren't thinking about protecting me.' But within days, word was out that some of the members of the old regime of police, peeved that they didn't actually find any drugs at Emma Street, were planning to return there to 'plant the place', and then raid it again. Both Debbie and Joe knew what they were capable of, and decided to stay away from the house.

> **Debbie**: But then we both just got tired of it, and decided to move back home. On our first night there, we're sitting watching television, trying to get some normality back in our lives, when we hear footsteps coming down the driveway and the dogs start to go off. It sounds just like the cops to me, and I freak out, and go and hide in this little room off the verandah. There's the bang, bang on the door, and Joe saying, 'Who is it?' Then a voice: 'It's Batty! Open the door!'
>
> When I heard his voice I just burst into tears. It was so stressful and I was out of my mind, waiting for these coppers to come and plant the heroin, because I knew that otherwise they had no evidence. I didn't traffic schedule one drugs [heroin], I did not. When they say they're going to stitch you up, you know they haven't got the evidence. I'd been in and out of the old World by

Night nightclub [a notorious strip club] in the city when the dirty
coppers were there, I'd seen the money pass hands, the drugs
pass hands, and there was no doubt in my mind they were going
to do it.

But the Kilroys' reprieve was short-lived. The next morning, a man
they knew as Mango was on the phone. He'd been to Emma Street
before and attached himself to Joe. He'd had the occasional smoke
with him, but now that Alex had blown his cover both Joe and
Debbie had doubts about Mango too. He'd jumped on Joe as soon
as Joe was released on bail, three months earlier, urging him to 'come
out and score'. When Joe told him he wanted nothing to do with it,
he'd tried Debbie. Of course, this morning he wanted drugs again,
more and more, and heroin. Debbie was adamant. 'Don't ever ring
here again,' she told him, 'there are no drugs here. I don't sell drugs.'

Debbie: It would've been ten minutes later that they arrive. All
these coppers in ten or fifteen cars – it's about eight in the
morning and Jody's about to go to school. And I've gone ballistic
this time, absolutely. I'm straight on the phone to Stu Bales:
'These arseholes are in my house and they're going to plant
something.' Stu is saying, calm down, Debbie, who's in charge?
Ask them who's in charge. And I'm yelling out, 'Who's in charge?
I've got my lawyer on the phone!' I'm going nuts and they're all
backing away from me.

Everyone outside can hear me because it's that time of the
morning when everyone's going to work. We've been in the
media nonstop, they've painted me as this manipulative bitch,
they've had pictures of the house, the kids' toys on the verandah
and destroyed our lives. All right, we've done what we've done
but not what they were saying we'd done and here they were to
plant drugs on us.

Finally, one of the police officers took the phone to speak to Bales.
There were more charges, he told him, so Bales advised Debbie to
go with them to the local station. Debbie was astounded. Unless
there were charges held over from before the arrest, there was
nothing they could get them on. She roundly abused them, knowing
the charges were mischievous. The police pressed them, nonetheless.

The following day, the local paper, the *Courier-Mail*, reported that the Kilroys had appeared in court once more, alleging they had continued to deal in drugs after their initial arrest. It was a whole new nightmare for both of them.

Gill Campbell, who travelled down from Cairns with her new baby to be with Debbie for the approaching committal hearing, was astonished at the harassment the family received from both police and the public. She'd been shocked herself at the seriousness of the charges faced by Debbie particularly: 'Deb was never into dope, never, and we couldn't understand it when we heard the heroin charges. We knew she'd sold marijuana and some speed, but someone had to bring in the money. Joe couldn't be relied on in those days, so in the end Deb took over. But we were all anti-heroin,' she says. Still, she wasn't prepared for the frequent police visits to the house, nor for the constant honking of car horns at the house and the expletives screamed at the family by passers-by.

In December, two months after the last raid, as Brisbane dismantled its spectacularly successful Expo and its citizens collectively slumped into anticlimax, Joe and Debbie Kilroy appeared once more in the Magistrates Court for their committal hearing, Joe on a total of fifteen charges and Debbie on twenty-eight. Neither was required to enter a plea. For Debbie there was no choice: she was not guilty of the charges, which carried a certain life sentence. Joe's lesser charges carried a much lower penalty. But when the magistrate committed them both for trial in the Supreme Court – to commence the following October – a cruel ten months later – a legal tussle began between them.

There were long discussions about a plea bargain which would trade a guilty plea from Joe on some of his counts for the police to drop the charges that would see Debbie go to jail for life. But the discussions were long and in Debbie's eyes, not definitive. Joe's prevarication over the plea bargain was, for her, yet another betrayal, and she felt angrier than she had ever been. That was the feeling she woke with every morning, a sick, churning feeling in the gut. For her, it was the last straw in the relationship. In the aftermath of the protracted negotiations, and throughout the tumultuous months leading up to the trial, their marriage faltered as they entered several bitter separations. Under the strain of the approaching trial, it would completely break down.

Joe and Debbie were united on one issue, though: the duplicity and betrayal perpetuated by Scott-Marlan. As the months progressed, they discovered more about the background and character of the man who, they believed, had been the catalyst for their catastrophic fall from grace. Before their arrest they had already found out that he was 'working with the police' after a drug bust which saw two Lebanese men sentenced to life imprisonment under the controversial and draconian Drugs Misuse Act introduced by the state's then premier, Joh Bjelke-Petersen, in 1986. Scott-Marlan walked free. He had been found with a quantity of heroin and a large sum of cash; the allegation was that Scott-Marlan had 'turned dog' on his suppliers for his freedom, and had been protected in his ongoing drug dealing by certain police officers.

But it wasn't until much later, in the weeks before the trial, that the Kilroys learned the full extent of Scott-Marlan's criminal history. He had a conviction for robbery with violence and, nearly ten years earlier, he had been sentenced to ten years jail with hard labour – later reduced to seven years with hard labour – for the manslaughter of a two-year-old child. The news sent shivers down Debbie's spine. She'd always felt an indistinct threat from Scott-Marlan that made her concerned for the safety of her children around him. While he appeared to get on with them, and bought them gifts with the wads of cash he carried in his wallet, she felt that, if things ever soured between them, he would be capable of anything. The news of the manslaughter conviction convinced her she was right.

She was also convinced that, because of his history and his connection with the police, the fresh new guard of post-Fitzgerald detectives assumed, when they began investigating his activities, that the Kilroys were in the same big league:

Debbie: They assumed they had big gangsters here, big drug dealers. They told us later they couldn't believe it when they didn't get frisked coming into the house. At first they didn't even wear a wire because they thought we might pat them down, even put a gun to their heads. I remember thinking, you've seen too many movies. That was hilarious, really; people thought we were these big-time drug dealers, it was so sensationalised. They made it look like a big hoo-ha, that they'd caught these big celebrity fish. But the amounts we were selling were nothing; only these undercover cops are pushing and pushing, harassing us to sell them more. For me it was never a big thing, but I guess I got caught up in the momentum of the greed and the money, and Marlan pressuring me, too.

Most of 1989 passes in a blur of alcohol, violent and distressing encounters with Joe, and partying. Faced with the prospect of losing her children, her home and her business, many of her friends and family, as well as her precious freedom, Debbie throws restraint to the winds. She goes out, she drinks, she tries hard to block it all out. Sometimes, she just sits around at home with Gill, Batty and Mal, or at Anita's, and they drink – alternately high spirited and appalled. Many days they go through a bottle of vodka on their own.

One day, after a long and bruising session with Joe, both of them hurling abuse fired with rage and frustration, Joe shoves her and she falls to the floor. Later, she won't remember the shove, or the screaming match that preceded it. She won't remember any pain. She will remember him on top of her, his hands around her neck, smacking her head against the concrete floor, saying over and over, 'Don't you realise I love you?' And the old memory of other hands on her neck, of other voices professing love, will arrive unannounced, like a haunting. But it will be years before all the violent ghosts give up their meanings.

The Kilroy Klothing Kompany was wound down. As the court would later hear, the Cairns outfit, at any rate, had been 'a lemon', and there was little profit from the Brisbane shop. The Emma Street house, too, was lost, sold at the bank's insistence. Joe went to live with friends and took work as a house removalist; he continued to train and play for the Broncos. Debbie moved to Nana's with the kids, giving Pat and Len a break from the noise and stress of three houseguests.

This was an inverted kind of positive for Joshua, at least. In the awkward negotiations around life *after* the trial, Len said that he and Pat could not cope with a pre-schooler, so it had been settled that Nana would take care of Joshua, and Jody would go to Pat, for the duration of Debbie's imprisonment. Looking back, Debbie and Pat can both see what an enormous error this was; that the children should never have been separated. But Debbie says now, 'You don't get many choices when you go to prison. What you'd like to happen and what you get are very far apart.' For the little boy, there would be some consistency in living arrangements. But the separation from her parents as well as from her brother would prove a major turning point in eleven-year-old Jody's life.

Even as they waited for the trial, Jody's emotional turmoil was starting to reveal itself at school. Her schoolmates at St Joseph's at Nundah were tormenting her about her parents: 'It was all in the news and they knew everything,' she says. 'They'd call them druggos and other names. I wasn't violent as a child – I'm still not – but I became very violent then. I'd just punch on, all day, boys, girls, teachers. I was in trouble a lot. I'd chat the teachers, try to bash them, I turned into a really wild little thing. I just couldn't cope with people running my parents down.'

In her alcoholic haze, Debbie wasn't aware of Jody's traumatic encounters at school, but she was determined that her daughter should not be around when she and Joe went to trial. That, she thought, would be too much. In the weeks preceding it, she spoke to her friend Gill, and arranged for Jody to join her in Cairns. The distance, she believed, would afford Jody some degree of protection from the rapacious media and her own preoccupations. But even that careful plan would backfire.

At the time, though, Debbie was relieved Jody would be away from the newspapers and grateful that afterwards, the children would be with people who loved and cared for them. Losing them was the great terror of her life. For Debbie, motherhood was some-thing quite apart from – and above – everything else she did. She loved her children with a fierceness that took her, and sometimes others, by surprise, and the thought of the imminent separation from them scoured her heart whenever she let it in.

These were the things that held her up in those harrowing months: Jody, Josh, and the mad release of alcohol. She'd take Jody to school, play around with Josh, and drink herself into oblivion in between. One awful day followed the next until October 1989 arrived in a cloud of mixed dread and relief.

On the morning their trial was due to commence, a plea bargain was finally struck with the Crown. Joe would plead guilty to traf-ficking in 'schedule two' drugs – cannabis and hashish – and the Crown would drop the trafficking in 'schedule one' drugs – heroin

– against Debbie. She would no longer face mandatory life in jail, but would plead guilty, like Joe, to trafficking in 'schedule two' drugs, to the four charges of supplying heroin, and to one charge of possessing money from the sale of drugs.

She was relieved, but the bitterness remained. She knew she could still face a heavy penalty on the remaining heroin charges, and Joe's acceptance of the plea bargain did nothing to ameliorate the resentment she felt towards him. Her anger would only intensify during the lengthy three days of sentencing that began in the Supreme Court on Monday, 23 October 1989.

> **Debbie**: I wasn't afraid of going to court, or of going to jail, never ever. That didn't worry me. But I was filthy with myself for being there. All I could think was, how did I get here? I don't even agree with drugs. What have I done? I was ready for a trial, I was going to fight it, I was going to prove I didn't traffic in heroin. I was ready for it to run its course; I wasn't pleading guilty.
>
> I was pissed off with Joe – I had no idea he was going to plead guilty until that first morning in court – but what I didn't realise was that I was pissed off with myself over the whole drug thing. We'd got involved in selling hash because Joe was smoking dope and it was about maintaining that; I was the little woman who kept it turning over, taking responsibility for everything.

Kym and Sean Scott-Marlan were dealt with first. In another plea bargain with the Crown, Sean pleaded guilty to trafficking in heroin and all charges against his wife were dropped. She was discharged from the dock, leaving Sean, Debbie and Joe sitting uneasily on the bench together, facing a full bar table of prosecutors and defence lawyers and the stern visage of Mr Justice Williams.

After a brief adjournment to finalise the pleas, the indictments were read and pleas taken. One by one, the three accused stood to hear their charges and to give their solemn replies: 'Guilty'. Convicted on their own pleas, they were then asked the same question: 'Have you anything to say why judgment should not be pronounced upon you according to law?' Each answered, 'No.'

The sentencing was then set down for the following morning, but before the final adjournment, Joe's barrister, Adrian Gundelach, got to his feet to explain clearly to the media representatives present that his client had pleaded guilty to trafficking marijuana, and nothing else. Wild rumours were doing the rounds, he said, about the type of drug Joe had dealt in, and he wanted no 'prejudicial misstatements or inaccuracies' made by the press.

Early in the proceedings on Tuesday, the Crown presented their evidence against Sean Scott-Marlan and, without the benefit of discretionary power, Mr Justice Williams had no choice in his sentencing: mandatory life. The court heard details of the two grams of heroin involved in the trafficking charges against him, each half gram sold to the undercover agent for $4000 by Debbie Kilroy. Details of the marijuana haul were also given: the suitcase and brief-case seized from Scott-Marlan had contained seven kilos of hashish, worth about $157 000 on the open market. The Crown prosecutor then moved on to the charges against Debbie and Joe.

The circumstances of the charges were read out: the various transactions involving heroin and hash, the visits by the undercover police officers, details of taped conversations between Joe and Debbie and the police. The next day the media would report on those conversations, quoting Debbie on the price of heroin as well as her reluctance to sell it. She had 'ounces of it for eight Gs', she had said, and then: 'I never sell it to any cunt because I don't like dealing in the shit. I'm just doing it as a favour for this other prick.' In another unrecorded conversation, Joe quotes the prices of mari-juana – '125 a half and 250 a whole' – and when he is asked if he makes a lot of money out of league he answers, 'No, it's just a front, mate. Drugs is where I make the money.'

Debbie was then called by her own counsel, Tim Matthews, to give evidence. He began with questions about her earliest contact with Scott-Marlan, a few occasions when they had met at the home of mutual acquaintances at Norman Park in 1986. When he asked her to talk about the Kilroy Klothing Kompany, she recalled that she had been 'stunned' that Scott-Marlan had set up the Cairns shop in under two weeks, taking it from a bare concrete floor to a fully fitted out, fully stocked leather shop with hourly fashion parades, commercials across the media and champagne for customers. She said he told her that she and Joe were 'family', and that he wanted to help them; also that he needed to launder some money.

Within weeks though, she said, he was hinting that his 'other business' – selling drugs – had been allowed to run down because of his involvement with the shop, and that he needed some payback from them. He was also hinting that, unless Debbie assisted him in his drug business, her children could be at risk. In April, he had pressed her to approach Alex, who was already buying marijuana from her, to also purchase 'hammer' – heroin. She was to offer him an ounce of 'good stuff' for $8000, or half ounces for $4000, but no less than ten-gram lots for $3000 a time. She was to assure him there was an 'unlimited supply'.

When Matthews asked her to tell the court why she had agreed to supply the heroin, Debbie said: 'Because Marlan wanted me to. I was worried for Josh more so than Jody and I was worried for myself. I knew who he worked for. He always carried a loaded gun and I had seen him do deals, walk around with electronic scales. I knew that he had been busted for heroin and he had never been taken to court for it. I was just terrified of him.' Joe, she said, had no idea about her heroin sales.

Under cross-examination by the Crown prosecutor, Debbie told the court that Scott-Marlan made her feel like 'a robot'. 'He pulled my strings; what to do, when to do it and I did. It's the personality and the person that he is.'

The following day, Scott-Marlan was called to give evidence. He claimed Debbie had pressed him to supply her with heroin to sell to Alex, not the other way around. He denied making any threats against the Kilroy children, and said he had a 'great' relationship with them. 'I am the sort of bloke that kids and animals tend to like,' he told the court. He said it was Debbie, not him, who had been worried about the Kilroys' debt to him.

At midday, counsel for Joe and Debbie gave their final submissions to Mr Justice Williams on the sentences he would shortly bring down. Tim Matthews gave a brief summary of Debbie's life, including the early death of her father but excluding her experiences in Wilson. There was no mention of the psychological effects that might have resulted from her early detention, or from the accusation that she killed her father, or from the horrendous violence she had suffered at the hands of Jody's father.

Although her interest in athletics and fitness was mentioned, along with her work teaching aerobics at two gyms and her involvement in touch football, no references from employers, coaches or friends were tendered. In her defence, Matthews said Debbie could be described as a 'small time trafficker when you look to see that over the four month, five month period, there is something less than a kilogram in total of green leaf material involved, and given the continued approaches by the undercover officers after the first few transactions'.

He spoke of the turmoil in the Kilroys' marriage since the arrest, and said that 'given Mr Kilroy's high profile in the community, the pressure exerted by [the] publicity has in this particular instance been more than one would usually expect'. Her instructions to him, he said, were that she realised she would go to jail, and that she would be away from her children for some time. 'The impact of it all upon her is that she has learned her lesson by all this, and hopes that some time in the future, upon her release from prison she can be able to lead as normal a life as possible, given the past, with her children in the community,' he said in finishing. His submission on Debbie's behalf would run to two pages of the final court transcript.

Joe's counsel, Adrian Gundelach, then rose to present his submission for Joe. With background information, references, and a lengthy psychologist's report, these would cover eleven pages of the transcript. By the time he was finished, Debbie's character would be effectively demolished, and so would any chance for a reconciliation between the two.

Gundelach began his submission by emphasising that the Crown had withdrawn the charges against Debbie carrying a mandatory prison sentence because Joe had pleaded guilty to trafficking in marijuana. Joe's actions had reflected, he said, his 'primary and paramount concern' for his wife and two children, 'whom he loves and cares for very much'. He went on to reiterate that Joe had sold only cannabis, or marijuana, and only when it was 'contrived' by the undercover police officer. There was no evidence Joe was supplying to the 'world at large', nor was there any suggestion he dealt in heroin or other drugs.

He then went on to draw a hard line between the actions and character of Joe and those of his wife. Debbie, he said, was 'obviously more involved in the trafficking scene' than Joe had been. She 'actively went out to sell the dangerous drugs'; Joe did not. The undercover agent had pursued Joe – never the reverse – and Debbie had actually introduced the agent to her husband. Joe had acted only as a party to at least four of the offences with Debbie, not as the principal offender. His boast that football was 'a front' for his real income from drugs was mere 'self promotion – making himself out to be a big fellow in front of the undercover agent'.

Gundelach then proceeded to his *pièce de résistance,* the reports prepared by clinical psychologist Michael Lannen after consultations with Joe. Joe, he said, had 'presented as a depressed man, overwhelmed with remorse and confused by his desire to conform to social norms, morals and expectations and the need to meet the demands made by persons around him who offer conditional love and acceptance'.

Joe had, he said, experienced early maternal deprivation as well as 'extreme rejection' from an early age. The results of this could account for his 'extremely low self concept and a pathological desire to please other people and be loved and accepted by them'. His Aboriginality, too, impacted on this, said Mr Gundelach. Experience showed that success for an Aboriginal sports star was frequently attended with very serious and tragic consequences, with many experiencing guilt over their success which led to behaviour that 'compensated for their success and guilt'.

Joe's 'profound sense of right and wrong' was overridden by a pathological need to please others: 'There exists within him an extreme fear of rejection. The consequence of this is that he sets himself up to be accepted by almost everyone he encounters and is then taken advantage of.' But it was clearly Debbie who was squarely in Gundelach's sights: 'Not having had a personal mother figure,' he said, 'he has been dominated and manipulated by his wife and has carried out her instructions almost in a way that a mother instructs a child.

'Mr Kilroy's wife organised all the family finances and business and she often went out socialising, leaving her husband at home to care for the children. It is his desire to accept total responsibility for their current predicament so that his children will not be deprived of a mother and shall not experience the orphanaged background that he himself did . . . [Mr Lannen] went on to say that Mr Kilroy's tests indicate that he has a lot of potential which he has not been able to utilise. This has been stifled and suppressed. He could be described as a gentle, peaceful, hard-working, easy-going man.'

He then tendered references from Wayne Bennett, coach of the Broncos and then of the Queensland rugby league team; from a teacher and long-time friend, Jonathon Jacks – who described 'Joey' as a 'person with a lot of love and loyalty, unselfish, obviously the kids of Brisbane respect him'; from Sister Christina White, who, at Nudgee orphanage, had seen 'the trauma he suffered after being deprived of his natural parents at a very early age'; and from Father Leo Wright, who had known Joe at Boystown and later at the hostel he moved into, and who had married Debbie and Joe at the Little Flower Church. In his reference, read to the court, the priest described Joe's dismay at 'bearing the Boystown mark' merely because he was an orphan, and at the violent treatment he received there. He said he refused to believe Joe had now entered a life of crime; his current situation had arisen through his 'friendliness and misplaced loyalty'.

Gundelach agreed: he had made the mistake of being loyal not only to the undercover police but also to his wife. Joe, he said, had done much for street children and Aboriginal children. Now he felt extreme remorse, shame and embarrassment. His achievements in life had been attained despite his poor start: 'He could well be considered a victim of our society. It certainly could be said of him that it was not an easy road for Joe Kilroy.'

Unsurprisingly, Debbie sat listening to the hymn of praise for Joe with mounting anger and resentment. It was an anger she could barely articulate: she was already well into the desensitisation mode that had got her through the horrors of Wilson. But beneath it, churning her up, was a profound feeling of hurt, betrayal and isolation. Where were the people to speak for *her?* Why did no one recite the litany of abuse and desperation that was the background to *her* life? Once more, she was the scapegoat. She was ready to acknowledge what she had done, the mistakes she had made, and pay her dues. But this recasting of her as the cruel, unfeeling, calculating shrew who had bewitched her good husband and destroyed him was grossly unfair, and untrue.

In the afternoon, Mr Justice Williams reconvened the court after a short adjournment and, without fanfare, delivered the sentences. He found Debbie had not been pressured to sell heroin by Scott-Marlan, was more active than Joe in dealing the drugs, and that 'her criminality was greater'. He found that Joe, while not the principal in the drug-selling business, was 'making as much money as he could from the supply of marijuana to his contacts'. But he conceded that

Joe had 'achieved a degree of eminence in the sporting arena . . . and a position of some eminence in society, notwithstanding the fact that he had a deprived background'. He had taken all the matters raised by Joe's counsel into account, he said.

In Debbie's case, there were no concessions. Nothing had been put before the court in her defence. The judge could only repeat what he had already said: her involvement had been deeper, her overall criminality greater.

Joe was sentenced to three years imprisonment for trafficking marijuana. Debbie was sentenced to six years imprisonment – four on the charges of trafficking marijuana, two on the heroin charges. The heroin sentences were concurrent with each other but cumulative with the four-year sentence. She was also given two years, concurrently, for the possession of $1600 from the sale of drugs. The court adjourned.

There are no familiar faces in the courtroom, no one Debbie can look to for verification of what has happened, to make meaning of it. There are none of Joe's friends, either. Of all his team-mates, only Peter Jackson – who will later take his own life after a long battle with depression – turns up to farewell him. Fans and well-wishers faithfully attended court, and one presses his hand, introduces himself and wishes him luck. Joe manages a half-smile. 'Just in the neighbourhood, were you?' he says, and then they are led away.

From the moment she walked into the courtroom, the reality of 'being on trial', of submitting herself to the will of the people, the Crown, the judge, whatever, was overtaken by something else. It was as if the real woman in the dock had separated from her body and flown to the ceiling, where she watched the proceedings with grim fascination. The detachment, however surreal, allowed her some kind of sanity in the midst of chaos, in the midst of lies and loss and her helplessness before it. But it didn't remove her from pain.

She had walked in the door expecting to confront a life sentence, expecting to fight hard to prove she was no heroin trafficker, even if it took weeks and every last cent at her disposal. But deep inside her, she had already begun to tread the endless path of life without liberty. When she had packed up her belongings, the clothes she loved, her children's toys, the whole household, she'd packed up her past and future and any shreds of faith she had left in anything.

But the news that it won't be a life sentence – merely a string of long years – does not restore that faith. There is a trade she wasn't warned of: for less time in jail, she must forfeit the truth. She must sit and listen to men in horsehair wigs describe a fiction which is meant to be her life, her self, to the judge. They paint a picture of her that is exaggerated and cruel, a distorted image in a house of mirrors. They make her, once more, the bad girl, the hard-nosed bitch, the receptacle of blame. She feels anger and betrayal but not surprise.

In the lift that drops them down through the Supreme Court building to the waiting cells, the silence is like a rock Debbie is trapped beneath. There are just two prisoners and a prison guard in the confined space, but a third presence – prison itself – hovers between them, keeping them quiet.

As they descend, looking straight ahead, Debbie feels the brush of Joe's hand and she snatches hers away as if she has been stung. Don't touch me, she wants to scream, but doesn't. She makes no noise at all, frightened of what will come out if she starts. Now that nearly everything is lost, she will not let anyone see what is left. The outrage and the pain will remain invisible. And mute, for now.

7

Prison

Women who were incarcerated at Brisbane's Boggo Road Women's Prison before it was decommissioned talk about 'The Beast' that lived within its red brick perimeter walls and watchtowers, breathing its animal breath among them day and night. The Beast had no physical incarnation. It was a presence, a sense, that represented the mood of the place and its occupants, a calibration of the level of threat or foreboding among them on any given day. They would wake each morning and feel for it, putting their ears to the ground in an almost literal way.

The Beast was unsettled the week Debbie arrived at Boggo Road, and for good reason. There was change in the wind; the reverberations of yet another inquiry into the prison system were starting to be felt. Although they hadn't yet reached the women's prison, the bureaucracy was bracing itself, and so was the staff. Tensions were building. Even without the apprehension that precedes reform, the arrival of a celebrity prisoner would have compounded the tensions and added a frisson of intrigue. Debbie Kilroy, however, was not the first woman whose case had electrified and scandalised the media to hit Boggo Road that week.

The entire nation had been spellbound through the previous days by a murder dubbed the 'Lesbian Vampire Killing'. A middle-aged man, Edward Baldock, had been found with his throat cut and more than twenty stab wounds in a park beside the Brisbane River at West End on the weekend before the Kilroys' court appearance. Four women had been arrested within forty-eight hours of the chilling discovery. Their swift apprehension was enabled by the discovery of a bankcard inside the dead man's shoe. It belonged to

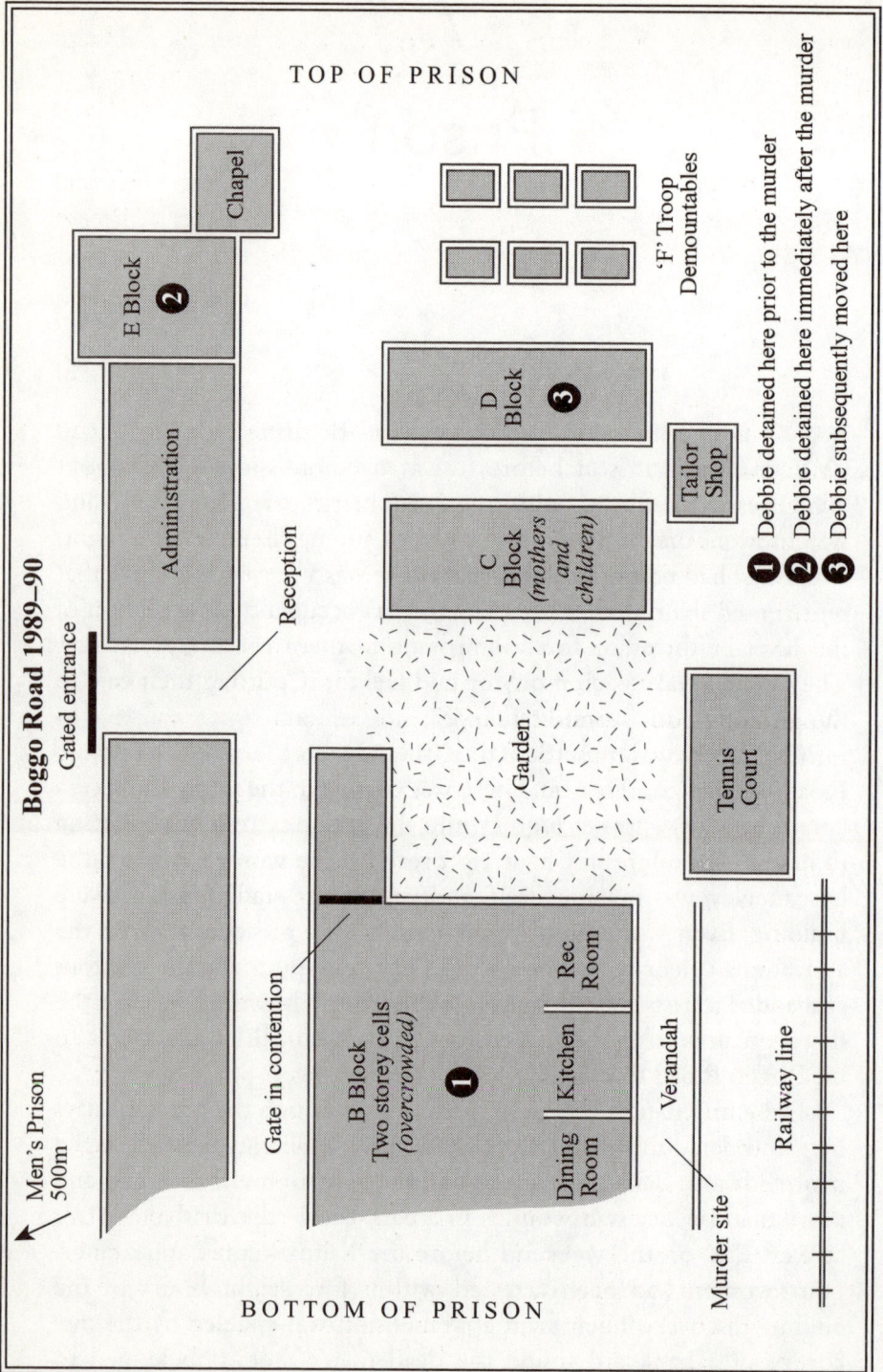

Boggo Road 1989–90

TOP OF PRISON

Gated entrance

Men's Prison 500m

Administration

E Block

Chapel

Reception

'F' Troop Demountables

D Block

C Block (mothers and children)

Tailor Shop

Garden

Gate in contention

B Block Two storey cells (overcrowded)

Dining Room

Kitchen

Rec Room

Verandah

Murder site

Tennis Court

Railway line

BOTTOM OF PRISON

❶ Debbie detained here prior to the murder
❷ Debbie detained here immediately after the murder
❸ Debbie subsequently moved here

Tracy Wigginton, whose lover and co-accused during police questioning referred laughingly to Wigginton's abhorrence of direct light and her 'need to drink blood', which had led to the horrific slaying. The legend and myth of the Lesbian Vampire Killer was born.

Wigginton, her then girlfriend Lisa Ptaschinski, Kim Jervis and Tracey Waugh were remanded in custody and arrived at Boggo Road on Monday, 23 October, the first day of the Kilroys' sentencing procedure and two days before Debbie's arrival at the jail. Wigginton was, and still is, a big, imposing woman, whose story precedes her into a room like the roar of an oncoming train. Other inmates – even the toughest lifers – were agog at the prospect of her joining them, although few would have admitted more than a passing interest.

Like most people in Brisbane – indeed, many around Australia and even overseas – they had seen the sensational television news reports which had detailed the murder plan, the frenzied stabbing, and the allegations that Wigginton had needed to 'feed'. The four women, but especially Wigginton and Ptaschinski, immediately assumed the status of feared top-dogs at Boggo Road, a role Wigginton both abhorred and enjoyed, and one which was entrenched by colourful and unrelenting media attention. Until Debbie Kilroy arrived.

Debbie: I got there in the late afternoon, just after five. I go to the induction area and the screws start to turn it up straight away, thinking they've got the prissy little footballer's wife here. I took no notice, just went through the motions. Take your clothes off, have a shower, wash yourself with the DDT stuff, put on your prison clothes. Then you get taken down to your cell. But a couple of the girls I'd known in Wilson were there, and I still knew them through the old networks, so I hooked up with them straight away.

We went in to watch the six o'clock news, and there's Fred (one of Wigginton's names in prison) and the others and they're all spewing because they're not on the news; I am. I couldn't believe it; I said, I'm going, you can have the news and the front page of the papers, I don't want it. But it was very funny, the way the whole Kilroy thing took over the Lesbian Vampire thing for a while, it was bizarre.

For Debbie, those first few days in prison were a process of desensitising, layer by layer, of stepping into the patterns of prison life and out of the patterns of life outside. This wasn't so hard for someone who had spent her formative years in a brutalising institution, much of it in isolation. She wasn't afraid. It was, at some level, like going home.

The highly structured routine of jail, the hierarchy of power among officers and among prisoners, the rules spoken and unspoken: these were all familiar, almost comfortingly so. The culture of prison was something she knew how to work with, and the relationships, unlike many of those outside, were negotiated on straight terms – respect, loyalty and keeping your mouth shut.

With a six-year sentence, Debbie was regarded as a long-termer. Then, and now, the majority of women in Australian prisons are on short-term sentences for crimes such as breaching an order, non-payment of fines, drug possession, prostitution and, for many Aboriginal women, the 'holy trinity': drunk, disorderly and abusing police. The average sentence was twenty-six months. One stay behind bars, however, virtually guaranteed a return – up to 60 per-cent of incarcerated women had been in prison before.

As a long-termer, and someone who had served time in Wilson and knew other inmates, Debbie became one of the more powerful prisoners as soon as she walked in the door. This would have meant little, however, if not for her strength in the face of taunting by prison officers, her reputation for staunchness with her mates, and for never, ever being a 'dog'. In the menacing prison culture, weakness and whingeing make you no friends and deliver you no power, but even the strongest woman who 'dogs' – tells tales, puts others in – is relegated to the lowest order, and is despised ferociously.

This is a culture in which trust is virtually nonexistent, in which women feel betrayed at many levels, so the code of being staunch, of never breaking a confidence, is the highest virtue. Debbie's alle-giance to the code was already known – in the past, even as a child, she had accepted punishment for others rather than dog – and it would become legendary over the months that followed.

Debbie's knowledge of how prison works, how to survive it and how to deal with both its overt and its covert violence, also gave her a powerful aura. She knew from experience that marks on the body are not the only manifestations of abuse. While the threat of physical

abuse and attack, from prison officers and other inmates, is insinu-
ated in every action and word in prisons, it is only one of the many
forms of brutality in the system. Violence in prison starts from the
first moment of incarceration, with the forced removal of liberty.
And it continues through the constant observation of prisoners
through every facet of their daily lives.

Prisoners are watched and scrutinised as they perform the most
basic functions, from personal hygiene to eating to standing in a line
– even sleeping – and they are forced to develop strong skills of
desensitisation to cope. This slow but certain erasure of privacy and
self is in itself a form of violence. The requirement to kowtow to the
arbitrary whims of prison officers – whether benign or malicious –
is another. Debbie Kilroy was an experienced and confident
combatant.

But there is always a patch of quicksand for any woman facing a
prison term, and for Debbie this time it was guilt about her
children, and the pain of missing them. She had to work hard not to
think about that, not to let it make her vulnerable. In prison,
emotions are a scarce commodity, and rarely seen. Tears or grief
might be shared with one or two others whose loyalty is beyond
question, but no one else, especially prison officers. That kind of
exposure opened a crack in a woman's defences that could easily be
prised apart and exploited. A woman in jail without defences would
not survive.

Like most of the other women, Debbie had to don a make-
shift but impenetrable mask when her children came to visit.
Any crack in the mask would open a floodgate of emotion, render-
ing her vulnerable for days in its wake. But Jody doesn't remember
her mother's distance – perhaps because she was distressed and angry
herself. The sojourn in Cairns that was supposed to protect her from
the distress of the trial had, ironically, left her more distressed and
confused than ever.

Gill had tried to organise a 'very ordinary two weeks' for the little
girl. She'd booked her into the local school, and teamed her up to
play with the children next door. More than anything, she tried to
keep news of the Kilroys' trial and imprisonment away from their
daughter. Her efforts, however, fell flat: 'It was hard to keep it all
away from Jody because every time you switched on a radio or TV
it was there. She started to say, I want to go home, I want to go

home. She really missed Deb, and she was frightened she'd never see
her again if she stayed with us,' Gill says. 'We'd thought coming here
would be the best thing for her, to get her away, protect her. But she
felt like she'd been sent away.'

> Jody: I think that was the real beginning of my resentment
> towards my mother. I was filthy about being sent to Cairns:
> palmed off again! I really missed her and worried about her.
> Even more so when I saw them on television and heard the
> sentences they'd been given. I would like to have been
> around. I thought, I get dragged around everywhere else –
> why can't I be there for the trial? I thought I might never see
> her again.

The first two months of her mother's imprisonment are the only
ones Jody can clearly remember; the rest have been blocked by the
events that followed. Back in Brisbane and living with Pat and Len,
she was taken regularly to see Debbie inside Boggo Road. In those
early weeks, she recalls going to the prison with Joshua: 'I was trying
to be strong for him, because he couldn't understand, and he'd lose
it every time,' she says. 'He'd been told she was at work. He was
thinking, well, everyone else's mother comes home from work, why
can't she? He'd yell his head off, and everyone would hear it – even
right up on the hill. So I tried to play it straight. But then she'd tune
me up about being bad or doing bad things and I'd just go, yeah,
yeah, bye now. Love you, see you later. I was desensitising myself,
I guess. I already knew how, after all the violence.'

As well as having her two buddies (from Wilson), Janelle
Scognomiglio and (Tracey-Rose) Taylor, Debbie quickly became
acquainted with Debbie Dick and Tracey Bromage. Bromage was
Taylor's co-accused in a series of armed robberies of post offices, and
'Scogs' was the girlfriend of a man she knew through the vague
network of crime and drugs, as well as a mate of Bromage. Bromage
lived in a different block, but the other four women became a
solid group. They would take their meals together at the same table
in the dining room, play cards at the same place on the covered
verandah.

According to Debbie, knowing who was 'staunch' was like a sixth
sense in prison – 'you know who's sweet and who isn't, you feel

safe with some people straight away'. She felt an immediate and mutual rapport with the other four women, and their common history and connections – and their apparent ease within the system – brought them reluctant admiration from newcomers, and envy and resentment from others – even some prison officers.

Debbie: The screws were always trying to gee me up. The ones down in reception would open my mail and read it and quote it back to me, verbatim. They'd go into my cell and tip my vitamin pills down the sink when I wasn't there, or turn on my radio to let the batteries run flat – there was no electricity in the cells. Most of them had no nous at all, they couldn't see I wasn't the little miss yuppie who'd get all upset and cry. They should have latched on to that straight away, even from the old tatts I had on my arm, and in my relationship to Scogs and Tracey-Rose, the women I knew and connected to. You wouldn't have to be Einstein to figure out where we knew each other from, or even to ask the question and be told. Wilson.

During the two remaining months of 1989, Debbie slipped easily into survival mode, 'sussing out' the routine and the other inmates. These included several doing the mandatory life sentences she had narrowly avoided, as well as more notorious figures like Fred and her co-accused; Wendy Lang (dubbed the Black Widow after buying a black funeral dress before allegedly organising her husband's murder, and subsequently nicknamed 'Spider' by Debbie) and Karen Tonkin, jailed for life for the murder of an aged pensioner in her home. She began to steel herself for the hard days.

She'd already had to face Joshua's third birthday – five days after she entered Boggo Road – without seeing him, and soon it would be Christmas. The women all moved towards that date through a numbing routine: woken at six in morning with a bang on the door; an hour to get showered in the cell, fold up the bed and mattress against the wall, then wait by the door for it to be unlocked. March down to breakfast in the dining room (cornflakes, white toast) then for the lucky ones, off to one of the rare jobs available – sewing or cooking. The absence of work opportunities within the jail then meant many women had nothing to occupy them, and spent the morning cleaning, playing cards, standing around.

At eleven thirty lunch was called, then prisoners were locked down from midday to 1 pm while the prison officers ate. More of the same in the afternoon, with recreation time between three and five before another hour's lockdown, dinner and television until lock-up at nine thirty. 'You'd do anything to keep your mind active, talk, scam, plan,' Debbie says. 'But you were bored shitless all day, really.'

In her first week, Debbie made an appointment with the education officer at the prison. She'd resolved before she got there to use the system to her own advantage this time, and wanted to pick up the threads of her education lost when she first went to Wilson at fourteen, and never regained. She told him she'd been given six years, enough time to do some serious study, but his reply was, 'What's your rush, then? You can wait. Come and see me another time.'

This had only deepened her feeling of hopelessness – on top of the lack of work and organised activities, it seemed there would be no education. If she had completed high school English, she might have described the situation the way others did at the time – Dickensian. The whole place was ripe for change – or for catastrophe.

In daylight, she could fool herself that everything was all right. In daylight, she dealt only with the visible, the immediate: the walls, the routine, the screws and their stupid attitude. She was on top of that. And sometimes, she could extend this fiction into the night. Those were the good nights, when she could put her head on the pillow and will herself to dreamless sleep, to a place where there was no guilt, no anger, and where the creeping feeling of foreboding hung as close to you as your clothes. She worked on having more of those: empty, blameless nights. They would get her through. The other nights, peopled by her children, her unlived life, all her unlived potential, were like shackles. When she woke from them she fought to shrug them off. Like the screws, like the walls, they were the enemy.

The women's prison at Boggo Road had been opened in 1982, and replaced an old Queenslander style wooden house on the hill adjacent to the men's prison. The house, hot and claustrophobic with its mesh-covered front verandah, held thirty women. The new compound was walled, and boxed in along its lower boundary by the city's main railway line running southeast towards Moreton Bay.

The buildings and the eighty-seven cells were white concrete, square, institutionally unimaginative. The complex was divided by gates into blocks – A (admin), B, C, D, E and F (the temporary huts). There was an outdoor garden area where approved prisoners could enjoy visits from their children, and a rough tennis court, but no other exercise yard. By the end of 1989, this open area had already been diminished by the erection of several freestanding demountable cells, made necessary by overcrowding in the main blocks. Up to one hundred and thirty women were trying to share a space designed for 40 fewer, and many short-term prisoners were 'doubling up', two to a cell, an arrangement that often led to squabbling and enmities.

Each cell – or slot – had one or two bunks bolted to the wall, a shower, toilet and washbasin, all visible from a glass panel in the door. Just one tap in the shower and basin – and it was either freezing or boiling, from all accounts. A desk, chair and minimal shelving completed the furnishings. Women were allowed some personal possessions: books, a battery-powered radio/stereo, writing equipment, photographs. There were no power points, no television: lights out meant *all* lights out. But then, women were out of their cells by seven in the morning and returned to them only briefly at lunchtime before night lockdown at nine thirty, in contrast to the current regime in Queensland jails which can see women locked in their cells for up to twelve hours a day.

Debbie's first cell was number 24, a single cell among other long-termers. She tried to personalise it with photos of the children. Nana sent in a kindergarten photograph of Joshua with a five-year calendar attached, which Debbie stared at hard before ripping the calendar off. She didn't need that kind of daily reminder of her sentence, didn't want to mark each day off with a hard black cross. Short-termers did that, she knew; she preferred to let the days roll into one another, without calculating their length.

If she had kept a calendar, though, it might have become a historical relic, recording some of the most momentous events not just in her own life, but in the lives of other women prisoners and their jailers.

Keith Hamburger had been the director-general of the prisons department for a year. His experience in prisons was already extensive: as a senior public servant he had been involved in his first prison inquiry in 1974, when men still used buckets for toilets and cells were stacked three storeys high along mesh-covered walkways. Hamburger saw the brutality of the men's prison at first hand – the regular bashings, overcrowding and lack of any meaningful activity – and helped to make recommendations about better programs and facilities, staff training, and the need to examine the causes of offending behaviour. The report was shelved.

Ten years later, he was again seconded to assist at another inquiry run by Sir David Longland, after serious riots at Boggo Road. More recommendations followed, about conditions for prisoners and prison officers and the need for rehabilitation, but despite positive encouragement in the media, the government once more buried the report.

Discouraged, Hamburger departed for the department of harbours and marine, but in 1988, barely two years after the Longland Report was completed, yet another inquiry, led by businessman Jim Kennedy, was conducted after revelations about horrific beatings by officers, an underground cell known as 'The Black Hole' where prisoners spent time in isolation without any natural light or air, and a cage at Townsville prison in which a man had been locked for thirteen years after multiple convictions for rape. This time Hamburger's role was limited to consultations, so he watched with interest as the failing Bjelke-Petersen government accepted Kennedy's proposals to make the prisons department a statutory authority, the Corrective Services Commission, and to create a community-run board to advise on management issues, rehabilitation and reform, effectively removing the political agenda from the prison system.

Shortly afterwards, he was approached to apply for the job of director-general of the new Corrective Services Commission. He initially declined, fearing there was no political will to enact real reform and that history would go on repeating itself. Prisons exacted a huge toll in human misery, and perpetrated the problems that created their inhabitants, but there were few votes in them, he believed. It would be too easy to leave the system as it was. But Jim Kennedy persuaded him otherwise. He was appointed director-general in December 1988.

Hamburger: On my first day in the job we had a hundred and
twenty people backed up in watch-houses, tremendous overcrowding in the jails, and unresolved issues over bashings by
prison officers. Through 1987, as the National Party government declined, Joh had appointed and then sacked four
prisons ministers. In the early years of my management I'd had
five ministers and seen a change in government, and eventually I had four former cabinet ministers, two CEOs, the police
commissioner and the former premier's chief adviser in jail. I'd
personally worked with the four ministers at different stages,
so those first couple of years were an amazing time in my life.

Hamburger set about his task with a reformer's zeal. In his vision,
prisons would give inmates the opportunity to revise their behaviour and attitudes and the encouragement to change. They would
provide work training skills, meaningful employment, and decent
counselling. The emphasis on punishment would give way to an
insistence on rehabilitation, and there would be increased access to
parole, work camps and community contact. He wanted to reverse
the shocking imprisonment levels of Aboriginal people, who made
up more than 20 percent of the prison population (and just
2 percent of the overall population), and work with Aboriginal
communities to help them establish work camps closer to home.

He also wanted to dramatically reduce the recidivism rate, which
saw more than 60 percent of prisoners return after their release. In
the six years he eventually spent in the job he would see much of
his ambitious plan implemented, including the closure of Boggo
Road jail. The men's section had become notorious as one of the
cruellest and most inhumane prisons in the country.

But while elements of reform had been effected in the men's
prison by the time the Kilroys were sentenced, little had happened
for those down the hill in the women's section. Industries for
women were limited to tailoring, nursery work and general cleaning, and release to outside work opportunities was rare. Young and
first-time offenders were incarcerated with older and more experienced offenders, and there was no low or open security facility for
women – everyone had to serve their time in the maximum security
setting of Boggo Road.

There were few educational opportunities, and few support

systems designed for women and mothers, despite the fact that the majority of women were the primary carers of children outside prison, and that 80 percent of all women prisoners had been the victims of sexual and/or physical abuse. Visiting times were restricted to three hours per week – male prisoners could have up to twelve hours per week.

Just six weeks after the Kilroys were sentenced, however, history was made in Queensland: the Goss Labor team won government in a landslide election that ended the thirty-two year rule of the National Party. The new government had a clear mandate for reform of the state's tired judicial, administrative and public institutions, all lacking the confidence of a community reeling from Fitzgerald's revelations of systemic corruption.

Almost every section of Queensland society felt buoyed by the new wave of optimism that followed the election. People who had felt stung and shamed by what they saw as the state's racist, misogynist and nepotistic policies and left for the south began to return, many of them taking jobs with the new administration. Reform and accountability became the buzz words. Keith Hamburger, however, worried by the fact that his appointment had been made under the previous regime, watched and waited.

Still, in the women's prison rumours of imminent change persisted. Inmates and staff were hearing about some of the positive outcomes for the men, who were beginning to enjoy rights and privileges like work release, weekend release and community release to hostels established in the suburbs and to work camps in rural areas. Rather than encouraging them, however, the news could only breed more resentment among the women who were living in crowded, substandard blocks, with no respite through release programs of any sort, and with the prospect of enduring Christmas and New Year without their children and loved ones.

Some time before the end of the year, bored and frustrated, Debbie Kilroy, Debbie Dick and Tracey Bromage approached the prison's then general manager and convinced her to address the women about their concerns, telling her how much they admired her way of working. She could win the rest of the women over, they told her, if she spoke with them directly. She agreed, and called a mass meeting of the prisoners.

It took only seconds for her to realise she'd been set up. The women launched at her, demanding to know why they were being denied privileges the men were getting, calling for her head. The meeting was halted immediately and the general manager stalked off, close to tears, leaving Bromage and the two Debbies clutching their stomachs with laughter.

Later, they would all be threatened with a charge of 'mutiny' over this incident, which carried a penalty of ten years in prison. But something had stirred in Debbie Kilroy that day, apart from the fun of seeing the general manager humiliated in the same way the prisoners were every day. She had seen an injustice and acted on it directly. The women themselves had taken their gripe right up to the general manager of the prison, and even though little was achieved, they'd learned to 'work smarter'. It was the very beginning of her politicisation, of her long road to effective activism.

In the meantime, outside the prison walls a new era in corrections was being quietly ushered in. Waving aside concerns that his director-general had been appointed by his predecessor, the new minister for corrective services, Glen Milliner, picked up the gauntlet of reform and decided to work in tandem with Keith Hamburger. It was the beginning of a professional partnership that would deliver unprecedented gains in Queensland prisons.

The two men found common ground almost immediately. With a shared vision for a more humane approach to justice, they embarked on a courageous program of change within Queensland prisons. The women inside the high walls of Boggo Road could not yet know it, but life as a female guest of Her Majesty was about to get a whole lot better.

It took very little time for a friendly bond to develop between Debbie and Fred. At first, Fred and her three co-accused were segregated from the rest of the prison population, but when they were allowed to mix it was obvious that many women were intimidated and even repulsed by Fred and the aura that accompanied her everywhere. Fred did little to dilute it, or to endear herself to anyone. But early in their acquaintance, Debbie saw something in Fred that no one else could at the time: that she was terrified herself.

Fred: When we walked in to the prison there was Kim, Tracey, Lisa (she indicates their heights with her hand) and holy fuck what's that? Everyone else removed those three and looked at this big one: she's it. But I remember Deb coming up to me and to all of us in the days after she got there and saying, I'm Debbie. You all okay? She already knew the ropes from Wilson and I think she protected us four in her own way. She'd say, leave them alone, they're new, they don't know the go yet.

She didn't like how they treated us when we first got there, like the used tampons I had served up inside my rice balls, or hanging on my cell door, or the screws walking in with strings of garlic around their necks. But she'd make light of all this bullshit; one day she walked in and said to me, hey, Drac, you're on telly again. The first time she called me that it nearly floored me. Nobody else would come anywhere near us, it was the fear factor, and that was good because they didn't realise we were more fearful of them than they were of us.

But it wasn't all plain sailing. Shortly after their arrival, Debbie was sitting at breakfast, showered and wearing fresh clothes, her hair teased up at the front in the style of the day, ready for a visit from her children that morning. Lisa and Fred came into the dining room, and Lisa walked over to Debbie, leaned across the table and said, 'You look like a toilet brush.' Debbie was seething, but held her temper. She looked steadily at Lisa, smiled and said, 'If I look like a toilet brush' – then she paused and gathered her voice into a roar – 'Then you look like the fuckin' S-bend!'

Lisa shuffled away, aware of all the eyes on her. 'Oh well,' she said quietly, 'I mean a *new* toilet brush, a *good* toilet brush.' It's an encounter Debbie remembers with glee. 'They thought they came in there with all this clout because they murdered someone, and we put them in their box in a split second,' she says. 'You're no one in here because you killed someone.'

Despite – or perhaps because of – the confrontation between management and prisoners over leave and other privileges, little was being done to take the pressure off in the hot and crowded women's cell blocks. The tension was especially high in B block, where lifers and long-termers were separated from those in other wings by a locked gate. In this 'bottom' section of the prison, the closed, hothouse atmosphere was intensified by the rub of factions that had developed, apparently with the tacit approval of prison officers. Some officers were seen to side with certain groups, encouraging the slow foment of aggression. Tracey-Rose Taylor says: 'I've done over ten years in jail now, but probably the eighteen months to two years around that time was the hardest time I've done. The tension was the worst I've experienced, and I blame the screws, because they stirred the pot so badly between the two groups. I don't think they realised how far out of hand it would get.'

The factional groupings were most visible in the dining room, where the women were all forced to come together several times a day. Storm Brooke, Amali Badenoch and a couple of other prisoners were known as the 'Plastic Gangsters' (try-hard thugs), and occupied their own table. Debbie Kilroy, Debbie Dick, Janelle Scognomiglio and Tracey-Rose Taylor sat together and were known as 'table seven'; Tracy Wigginton and her co-accused sat at another. Groups of unaligned women changed their composition constantly, and included the women seen as 'loners'. One of these women, Tracy McDougall, stoked the fire of factional unease by constantly running between the groups, listening, reporting back, exaggerating. That, according to Debbie, was 'the dangerous stuff, the treacherous stuff'. The 'runners', the women who ran between groups, inflamed any existing suspicions and rivalries, inciting hatred where there may have been merely dislike.

Fred: The Plastic Gangsters were the ones who would always pick on anybody and anything. They would pick on the ones who didn't run with the crowd, the loners. Deb and the others at table seven were always telling them to back off – they were always nice to the underdog. But you didn't step on their toes. At that time, leading up to Christmas, the place was as tight as a drum. It was like a POW camp as far as the screws were concerned. They were aware of the tensions. The whole place was evil, it was so thick you could cut it with a knife – you couldn't even say g'day to anyone without it starting a blue.

There were just so many people crammed into this little area, and the screws didn't give a shit. The Plastic Gangsters would always pick on us plebs, but mainly the tensions were between them and table seven. No one dared to sit in the row of tables between them. If they went off the screws would just lock the doors and go, and we'd all be stuck in there. Amali was the worst because she was a berserker, you could break her arm and she'd still keep on swinging. She was being manipulated by the others, and Storm, well she just seemed to want to fit in. There was this huge hostility in the air. Something was going to happen. Everyone knew it. Even the screws.

But just before Christmas, six weeks after Debbie arrived at Boggo Road, the women were treated to a piece of black comedy that momentarily broke the mood of cold and anguished anticipation. As they routinely did, a choir from the Salvation Army came into the prison, distributing gifts and treating the women to a rendition of Christmas carols in the chapel. The women had turned up to accept their Christmas gifts and were lounging around listening to the songs when an Aboriginal woman, Noreen Jumbo, went berserk.

Debbie: Poor old Noreen. She'd had a shocking life, full of terrible abuse and now she had syphilis, and was quite mad. She also had a particular smell about her, but of course, it was never mentioned. As we were standing around, one of the newer women put her nose in the air and said, 'What's that smell?' And oh God, it's on. Noreen grabbed a broomstick and started screaming, belting this woman about the body and chasing her around the room.

This woman can't get out, she can't escape from Noreen, and the screws have seen it and just pissed off. And the Salvos are singing away while Noreen's chasing this woman around, they didn't miss a beat. They just kept singing those carols. We're pissing ourselves laughing, and Noreen's chased her up these stairs and belting her about the legs with this broomstick – later she had the biggest black bruises on the legs, I'd never seen anything like it. And finally one of the screws has come back to stop old Nor. But the Salvos – you could have sworn nothing had happened at all.

8

Murder

Fred: It's after lunch, and everyone is waiting for lockdown. They're all up on the verandah, but I'm in the library. That was my project. When I walked into that place there were 1400 items, and that was it. Most of them were Mills & Boon, and there was a set of encyclopaedias that must have been printed in 1942. I was disgusted, so I started cataloguing books and lobbying to get more books in through the Prisoners' Legal Service, and taking orders. So I was in there, as usual.

Suddenly, there were the alarm bells, and then everything went really quiet, too quiet. To get back to the verandah I had to come out of the library, round past the office, up past the doors and round the corner. That's where I stopped. I could see Kim and Tracey sitting there, and they were looking straight ahead and their eyes were so wide they almost popped out of their scones. Then I looked the other way. And there was Storm standing over Deb. Amali had already bolted, Debbie Dick was already down, and it looked like Storm was stabbing Deb, but the look on Deb's face wasn't one of pain, it was: what? *What?*

And the look in Storm's eyes was madness, sheer madness, and everybody else around them was frozen in time – no one was moving, no one was saying anything. It was deathly quiet. And I looked, really briefly, and I saw, and much to my own disgust – it's something I will never, ever forgive myself for – I turned around and walked away. Out of everybody in the jail, there were two of us who could have stopped it, physically:

Amali, and she was a perpetrator, and me. Nobody else was big enough. I've always felt I could have stopped it. Instead, I turned around and walked back into the library, sat down and looked at the microfiche.

Tracy Wigginton – like anyone else who saw or witnessed any part of the murder in the women's prison on 7 January 1990 – is still unsettled by her memories fifteen years after the event. Despite the constant suggestion of danger inside prisons, and despite the violence that many inmates have seen in their own lives outside, the brutal murder of someone at close quarters – someone you forcibly work, eat and socialise with every day of your life – is a traumatic event.

The visual impact of stabbing, of great blood loss, of maniacal violence, also strikes vivid chords in the memories of people whose presence in prison might have been provoked by violence against them and/or their own involvement in a violent crime. For Wigginton, the flash of the forks invoked nightmare visions of her own crime. They froze her, forcing her to literally walk away from them. For weeks she was tumbled back into the dark recesses of the night of the Baldock murder, but with a new, dual guilt: now there were two deaths to deal with and, but for the tenacity of Debbie Kilroy, there might have been three.

That morning was as ordinary as any of the mornings that had preceded it for Debbie. After two full months in prison, she was settling into a kind of uneasy rhythm, her survival reliant on her mates, visits from her children, her fitness regime, and sleep. Sleep, she found, was easy. As a child in Wilson, she'd developed the knack of lying down and falling asleep instantly. As a defence mechanism it worked extremely well, and she called on it again in Boggo Road. Locked into her cell, she would put her head on the pillow and just drift off. Even now, if she needs to 'tune out, or get out of this world', she finds somewhere to lie down and switches the 'off' button. She's trained herself, she says.

And that is exactly what she planned to do in the dead hour after lunch when prisoners were locked up before the Sunday visits session. Without work, the morning had drifted on its cruel and slow way. The women in B block had spent it hanging around in the recreation room, watching television, flicking through magazines.

Deb and her mates had played cards. In the languid heat Tracy McDougall – known as Doodle – sloped from group to group with snippets of gossip, briefly inflaming passions between rivals. None of it was new, but in the pressure cooker of B block, where there was no release valve, none of it was forgotten, either.

Tracey-Rose Taylor remembers walking around the yard with Debbie Dick just before lunch. Debbie was crying, she recalls, and saying, 'I've got to get out of here; I can't cope.' She was due to be bailed the following morning.

Lunch came and went in the dining room – salad and processed meat – and the women milled around the verandah and recreation room, waiting to be escorted to their cells. A couple of groups of women slumped into chairs at the round plastic tables outside the dining room. At one of them, Debbie Kilroy, Debbie Dick and Janelle Scognomiglio mumbled together without purpose. It was that kind of day.

So they were all jolted when the scream of the alarm bells pierced the quiet, a signal that there was trouble in the top blocks – a punch-up, some kind of breach – sending all the prison officers from B block scurrying in a panic, relocking the gate behind them. A collective sigh went down among the women. A punch-up in the top blocks meant more waiting before lockdown, before they could close their eyes and obliterate life for a while. Debbie Dick, who seemed perennially tired and craved sleep more than anyone, crossed her arms on the table and put her head down. 'Jeez,' she moaned, 'I feel like I could sleep forever.'

Debbie: Next minute, Debbie and I are grabbed from behind, around the back and the neck. I've jumped up and spun away out of the hold. I don't remember being hit in the side. I've just swung out of it really quickly, out of the chair. My attacker, Amali Badenoch, dropped her fork and ran, and in the same motion I've picked up the chair. Storm still had Debbie by the throat and was in a frenzy, just stab, stab, stab with these barbecue forks, stabbing Debbie in the heart, in the chest.

She'd blanked out, I could see, and she just kept going. I had the chair in the air and I just smashed it over her head. She snapped out of it then. She looked at me and took the forks and ran through the side door and into the kitchen. There was someone waiting there, and she took the forks from Storm, watching me watching her through the window. This other woman knew I could see, she was just looking steadily at me, as she wiped the fingerprints off the forks and threw them under the sink. Then she walked out.

It happened so quickly that people didn't even realise until I started yelling. I'm screaming out for them to get a doctor, over and over. I'm holding Debbie and she's bleeding, losing a lot of blood. The nurse finally comes down and lays Debbie on her side. I was still holding on to her, and freaking out because they've laid her on the side where most of the stab wounds are, and I'm worried that she shouldn't be on her sore side. Then all these screws are running around, they're freaked out and I'm yelling at them to fuck off – *fuck off, you dogs!* – and calling for doctors, an ambulance. *Now!* I'm sitting there watching Debbie's face go grey, it's draining of blood, I'm watching the blood drain out of her. And I knew, then, that she was gone, no hope.

The two women were taken away in separate ambulances to the emergency section of nearby Princess Alexandra Hospital. By now Debbie Kilroy realised that she had been wounded too, but superficially, she thought, looking down at the puncture marks on her ribs. So when, in emergency, doctors attempted to administer oxygen to her, and warned her she would need exploratory surgery, she angrily shrugged them off. 'I don't need oxygen, you idiots,' she said. 'I'm fine, I just want to know how my mate is. And you're not opening me up.'

The emergency room was alive with medical staff and prison officers. But no one would answer her question: *where is my mate?* Debbie was becoming hysterical, her intuition reading the worst into their silence. Even in this state of high anxiety, however, she managed a joke. Nancy Bailey, the prison officer who had been designated as her escort, was standing solidly beside Debbie's trolley, holding her hand. She looked down at the tears streaming down Debbie's face, and seemed stricken, helpless. 'It's all right, it's all right,' she said, squeezing Debbie's arm. Debbie managed a laugh. 'I know, but it's your hand, Bailes,' she said, indicating the drip beneath Bailey's firm hold. 'You're shoving this needle halfway up my arm!'

Debbie would not be officially told of Debbie Dick's death until later that night. Despite her obvious distress, her feelings would not be spared. The news was delivered by police as she lay in an open ward, surrounded by other patients and prison officers. The cold approach would only hasten her flip back into impervious defensiveness:

Debbie: I don't remember being sore, because as soon as they said Debbie was dead I just totally desensitised. I just wanted to go back to prison and see my mates. And the screws guarding me were so embarrassing – I couldn't eat a thing, but they were taking the stuff off my tray and putting it in their bags, they even took the cellophane wrapping from the flowers Mum had brought up. I was there for two nights, but I just wanted to go back. I wanted to find out what the fuck was going on, who else was involved. I wasn't afraid – not of scumbags who run at you from behind. I wanted to say to them, here, come this way, from the front – but no, you run from behind, you gutless piece of shit.

Days later, Debbie would be devastated to find out that Debbie Dick had fallen from a trolley or X-ray table just before her death at the Princess Alexandra Hospital. The *Courier-Mail* reported that Dick had 'rolled off an X-ray table during an episode of respiratory arrest'. Debbie was told her friend had fallen because the side of the trolley had not been lifted. The news filled her with anxiety: what did Debbie really die of?

A nurse finally explained that several blood clots had formed around Dick's heart from the stabbing. One had probably burst when she fell, killing her instantly. But, the nurse explained, the clot would have burst in surgery anyway, as soon as doctors began their incisions. The information filled in the gaps for Debbie, at least, but did not reassure her entirely. Whatever had happened at the hospital, she suspected, there would have been little sorrow for Debbie Dick from anyone.

Two days after her release from hospital, Debbie – still in considerable pain from her shallow puncture wounds and bruising – and Tracey Bromage attended Debbie Dick's funeral at the Albany Creek Crematorium under heavy guard:

Debbie: The place was full of screws and crims. All the screws
were in a state of shock because we didn't shed a tear, either of
us. We were in absolute desensitisation mode now, and thinking
of payback. They let us walk up to the front of the chapel and
stand beside her coffin. I remember looking at her body – they'd
put this blue eye shadow and red lipstick on her – and I'm saying,
she didn't wear that shit, you should take it off. But it was good to
know it was really her in there. And the screws were on tenter-
hooks. They knew they'd fucked it by allowing the murder to
happen. But they weren't afraid of us doing a bolt. They knew the
culture, they knew paybacks were coming.

'Payback' is the prison version of 'an eye for an eye', and it was
firmly in Debbie's head from the moment she was offhandedly
informed her friend had died as a result of her stab wounds that
terrible afternoon. Through the shock and the anger, it seemed
simple to her: Debbie was dead, now her killer had to die. In the
days that followed her release from hospital, and the days around the
funeral, she was single-minded, sure as steel. Storm Brooke would
die. Not because she had come to hate her for what she had done –
hate had little to do with it. It was process, prison process.

Deeply immersed in prison culture, this was 'normal' for Debbie.
This was the way it worked. It might look outrageous and even
ridiculous from the outside, but the outside had receded. There had
to be payback. The repercussions – another death, and a certain life
sentence for murder – did not enter her thoughts. Concern for
herself, her children, her mother, evaporated in the heat of this pure,
hard conviction. Nothing else existed outside this morbid trans-
action: Storm had taken Debbie's life, and now Storm would pay.

But not for a while. While Debbie was in hospital, Storm had
been taken from the women's prison to the men's, just up the hill,
where she was locked in isolation in a cell without a bed or a
shower. Between that cell and the one she subsequently occupied
back in the women's section, she was to spend fourteen months in
total isolation.

Taylor, Bromage and McDougall were separated out, too: 'We'd
lost the plot a bit,' Taylor admits. 'We'd started throwing rocks and
stuff. So they got rid of everyone who'd been emotionally involved
in it and stuck us in a dirty old disused library in the men's jail – a

place that had been declared uninhabitable for men. We were there for ten days, and it would have been longer if people hadn't been protesting outside the prison about our treatment.'

The murder was a baptism of fire for the new Goss Labor government, especially for his new prisons minister, Glen Milliner, but it was also, of course, an enormous incentive to instigate long overdue change. Action had to be immediate: the murder had done nothing to defuse the deadly tension inside the women's prison and it was obvious to all that further violence would be inevitable. Criticism was already flowing from community groups claiming the government had been warned how volatile the women's jail had been before the murder. Now they'd been proved right, and Milliner, along with Keith Hamburger, was of a mind to listen.

One of the first actions they took was to remove the serving prison manager, installing an interim manager, David Hayden, whose brief was simple: create a release valve. Hayden read the situation clearly, and his early initiatives proved vital in preventing certain and immediate bloodshed.

He acted decisively when Debbie returned from hospital to ensure the two parties most likely to be involved were kept well apart, dispatching Debbie, along with Tracey-Rose and Janelle Scognomiglio, out of B block and into an unused wing in a block outside the locked lower gate. Storm and Amali Badenoch were locked up in a detention cell in the men's prison, well away from the women. He also organised work sessions for Debbie and her mates in the tailor shop, where their informal sewing work was overseen by a sympathetic prison officer, Nancy Burrows.

She prowls around her new, more spacious cell, under no obligation to work or to move at all because of her wounds. The marks left by the murderous prongs – the bruising, the dark marks like spider bites – are distinctive tattoos, but they cause her little pain. For now she will use them, though, to garner some time for herself, hours in which she can plan her revenge. She and her mates talk of little else: the knives and where to stow them, the time, the position. They go endlessly over the variations. The one thing that is not negotiable is the act itself, the necessity of it. This is assumed. For days and weeks they have only this. They have no children, no partners, no parents, no country. They are not mothers, daughters, wives, sisters; they are only who they are in this cell, the makers of this deal.

It never leaves her. She eats, breathes and sleeps it. At night, her dreams are not metaphors but extensions of her daylight thoughts, and in them, the deal is done. In them, she raises the knife, she brings it down hard, she raises it again. Storm drops to the floor. She raises the knife again. The dreams are vivid, in reassuring colour. Blood – a rich red – runs freely over the concrete, just as it did before. Storm's face pales to grey, just as Debbie's did. And just like before, no one intervenes: there is no need to. They understand what has happened here. The payback has been achieved. Storm is dead. Now she can let go.

Investigations into the murder began immediately at all levels. Police and Corrective Services needed answers. They weren't going to get many from the prisoners, though – anyone cooperating with their inquiries was seen as dogging. Nevertheless, a team of police was installed in an interview room at the prison and the women were led off, one by one, for questioning. Fred took one of the prison officers with her as a witness. 'It was a five-minute conversation,' she says. 'Who are you? There's my name. When were you born? There's my name. What did you see? Nothing. See you later. And that was it, that was it for everybody.'

Everybody included Debbie Kilroy. The more inexperienced police were astounded, but prison authorities were not surprised when Debbie refused to utter a word about the murder. Still, they kept summonsing her, over and over, asking the question, always getting the same answer: 'I'm not interested; ring my solicitor.' They knew she wouldn't dog; they also knew she would try to balance up the scales herself. Somehow, she would get her payback. But it wouldn't be by helping coppers or screws.

Faced with this lack of cooperation, prison management made their next decision: to diffuse the tension and partly alleviate the overcrowding by allowing many of the women access to weekend leaves of absence (LOA). In an unprecedented move – and one which has never been repeated – weekend leave was extended to prisoners on mandatory life sentences, those inside for drug offences and robberies, and even murderers. Debbie was among them. Over several weekends, she was picked up by a friend, driven to her mother's to pick up Jody, and then on to Nana's, where Joshua was waiting.

This early initiative didn't last long; there was general unease about 'murderers, armed robbers and drug traffickers' loose in the community, and an incident on Debbie's third weekend leave, in February, put an end to everyone's leave in the short term. Once again she had been picked up on Friday by Sheena, who had a daughter around the same age as Jody. Sheena and another friend, Graham, had already picked up Joshua, and the three drove to Pat's house to wait for the two young girls, who were at a school function. At seven o'clock, the three adults and three children piled back into Sheena's car to return to Nana's at Kedron, where Debbie had agreed to spend the two days of weekend leave. With the car full, Debbie sat in the back with Joshua on her lap.

> **Debbie**: Suddenly, on the way back to Nana's, the coppers pull us over. They're carrying on and yelling for us to get out of the car and then they start to pull the car apart. Jody and Joshua are freaking out, they're both screaming on the footpath. The whole thing for them is re-traumatising – these dog coppers doing it to them again. They find nothing of course, and then they tell us we can go.

Police and prison files record a very different version of events. Officially, the car was pulled over after the driver made 'an illegal turn' and the officers noticed an 'unrestrained minor' on a passenger's lap. According to the files, police merely wanted to ensure the driver was not inebriated, which they apparently did without taking a breath test. They noted Debbie's name and checked if she was legally out of prison on leave. Then they let them go.

> **Debbie**: Back at the prison on Monday, I get called to the office. I asked Burrey [Nancy Burrows] to come with me; the coppers had been harassing and harassing me and I thought it was them again. Burrey was still on her way when they get me in this room and close the door and it's these management screws and they say, 'Did you have a nice weekend at home, no trouble? Oh no, the police didn't pull you up, did they?' And then I just knew they'd set it up, and I went off my nut. Burrey could hear me going

ballistic as she walked over – 'You fuckin' dogs, you can stick your LOA and your parole up your arse, I'll do my whole six years and you can all get fucked because you're *not* getting your statement out of me, you maggots.'

Then I walked out and went straight into the next office where this temporary manager was and I nearly leapt across the table. I wanted to smash him for setting it all up – 'You tell those coppers to get the fuck off my back' – and by now Burrey's got me by the shirt and she's pulling me out the door, but she's going off at them too, sticking up for me – 'How dare you do this?' I was livid. They could have a piece of me, bring it on, but stay away from my kids.

With all leave cancelled, tensions that had dissipated slightly began to rise once more. Debbie's murderous thoughts came to the fore again, aided by the return to the women's prison of Brooke and Badenoch. In her time in detention inside the men's prison, Brooke had confessed to Debbie Dick's murder and claimed total responsibility, earning a life sentence. Back inside with the women, she was kept separated, totally alone except for a short time sharing the cell with Badenoch. For a while she barely glimpsed daylight. Left with no other voices except the ones in her head, Brooke quickly lost control, and all the demons from her own scarred past crept into the cell with her.

Bent over their sewing machines in the tailor shop nearby, Debbie and the others could hear her constantly screaming and moaning from the depths of some dark, writhing pit into which she had fallen. The noise could not be drowned out, not by the machines, not by loud conversation nor any act of will. Brooke was a trapped animal, willing herself to die. Debbie was unmoved.

Debbie: She would keep trying to kill herself, all the time. She'd slash herself up and be carried out, blood everywhere, and I would say, here's a razor blade, do it properly, slit yourself under the tongue or I'll do it for you. I was serious too. One day they carried her out on a stretcher with a ballpoint pen jammed into her veins. It was still sticking out and the blood was spurting. I watched as they took her. 'Why don't you kill yourself properly, you maggot?' I yelled out. There was no other feeling. We just kept planning and scamming about how we were going to knock her.

Tracey-Rose Taylor recalls: 'This is what it was like: I'm going to have to kill her, or she'll kill me. I really believed that, in my heart of hearts. So everywhere I went I went armed up. The defence in my head was, *me or her*. I was even envisioning down the track to court cases.'

In the course of those jittery weeks, the interim prison management agreed to allow several community groups access to the jail. Members of these groups had had some contact with the women months earlier, and had warned management about the extreme volatility among them prior to the murder. Now, in its aftermath, the visitors were keen to help restore some kind of equilibrium.

Over two days representatives from groups like the Women's Legal Service and Catholic Prisons Ministry met with women prisoners to thrash out solutions to the tensions and problems within Boggo Road. There were two groups: one met in the chapel, the other in rooms beyond the heavy steel gate that divided the prison. Debbie didn't get a chance to attend: she was still isolated from the others in another block, and was barely aware of the momentous meetings taking place. But as she remembers it, good intentions almost led to disaster several weeks later.

Trying to gauge the emotions that were still running high between the factions, one of the community representatives decided the obvious solution to the hostilities was an open mediation session in the chapel, where all sides could come together, voice their anger and work it through. In Debbie's view, this only proved how little many of the outsiders knew about them and about the system. Anyone who knew how prisons worked would never have dreamed of organising such a meeting: it was an open invitation for mayhem. The women in Debbie's camp smiled grimly and planned their approach. To them it was like manna from heaven: a sanctioned meeting, where retribution would be firmly on the agenda. They couldn't believe their luck.

Debbie: The shivs [knives] had disappeared from the kitchen and we had them stowed, three of them. We knew we'd be able to go in loaded. It was all too good to be true. It was all set up for us, these people coming in to 'help' us, but having no idea what prison culture is, and they think they're just going to do a little bit of mediation. They just assumed, without asking.

But when they told us about it we said, yeah, we'll come. We loaded ourselves up. And off we went, walking down towards the chapel. Everyone was invited, so it was pretty packed in there. Next thing, Ninja comes flying towards us. He was a security officer, we'd named him after the Ninja Turtles. He says, what the fuck are you lot doing? And we all say, we're having a meeting, Ninj! Sorting it all out! And he says, the fuck you are, get out of here!

And he closed it all down. He knew what was likely to happen, he wasn't stupid. He was probably one of the only ones I've ever met among prison officers and security who had any brains in his head and knew how the world worked inside a prison. The rest were hopeless. It would have been on, it would have been a bloodbath. Because there would have been a couple of them go down, if not four of them.

Ninja locked us down and took Storm back. Damn! But we thought, *next time*. It really was all too good to be true. A little mediation in a prison just after a murder's happened? As if. Good intentions, for sure, but it was very short-sighted.

Later, Debbie would remember this close encounter and its lessons, which would help to inform the principles of Sisters Inside, the advocacy group she now heads as director. The 'power over' rather than 'power with' approach of many 'Good Samaritans', she believed, meant they could only help women in prison from a position of superiority over them. Women who are in prison or who have served time can smell this approach a mile away, and see it as patronising and unauthentic. Most of them have had experiences with 'helpers' who can only remain in the role while the prisoner is struggling to regain her feet; once there is a relationship resembling equality between the two, the helper disappears.

Debbie: Later, some of those sorts of people got to know us and attached themselves to us as friends, but with many it only lasted while we followed their line. Once we got on our feet and began to challenge them and some of their actions, we were dropped,

or accused of 'going back to our old ways'. We quickly found out
that once you step outside the do-gooder's vision for you, that's
it, they ditch you. It is a relationship built on their power over you.
Once you start to get your own power, and walk in the same
arena, they're off. It happens again and again.

Debbie and her mates went back to biding their time, but they
didn't get another chance to unsheathe their knives. The opportunity simply did not present itself, certainly not in the fortuitous form
of the planned mediation in the chapel. And in the meantime,
another vital change occurred in the women's prison, a change that
would have major implications for the women for years. It came in
the shape of George Brand, who was appointed the new general
manager of the prison after a long search that had begun in the
aftermath of the murder.

George Brand had been manager at Rockhampton prison before
moving on to Sir David Longland (SDL) at Wacol ('where all the
rogues were') as its inaugural operations manager in 1988. He'd
found the first couple of years at SDL 'very, very stressful', with half
the staff brand new to corrections and many of the prisoners the
hard-core recidivists from Boggo Road men's prison, which had
been gradually phased out. Despite that, Brand was developing
his own challenging views about prison management based on his
observations that the better prisoners were treated, the more respon-
sive they were. By the time he arrived at Boggo Road he had a
reputation as an 'interactive' manager whose style was non-
confrontational and based on fairness and respect.

Brand: I guess I brought a certain attitude with me to Brisbane
Women's, but it grew while I was there. I'd always thought
that generally, we did things wrongly in prisons by treating
prisoners as prisoners and not as human beings. In my
previous jobs I'd used a fairly open management style, sitting
down with prisoners and talking with them, and making sure
they had immediate access to staff when they needed it. When
I got to Boggo Road I found a lot of stuff I didn't like. The
staff members were all separated from the prisoners – few staff
actually mingled in the prisoners' areas. It was like, this is ours
and this is theirs. Them and us.

There was a very draconian management style – they were still lining up on musters, taking a pace forwards and answering, 'Here, ma'am', they weren't allowed to wear makeup or to wear their hair loose below the level of their collar in case they could secrete something there. It had to be tied up or cut off, instead. They weren't allowed anything that allowed them to be an individual, they weren't allowed to exercise any initiative. The excuse was security; you can't have lipstick because that might impinge on security somehow and you might hide something under your hair. It was just total nonsense as far as I was concerned, a real throwback, and far behind the times of any male prison I'd ever worked in.

Brand immediately set about diffusing the simmering anger in the prison by reinstating leaves of absence, trimming a top-heavy staff, and getting to know the women. Although the rivalries were obvious, he liked the women straight off: 'Some of the staff, including those at management level, were quite frightened of these people. There was a lot of fear in the place, and I don't think it was for good reason. They'd just never bothered to get to know them, never tried to. I remember another manager looking at one of the girls and saying, "When I look at her my hair stands up on the back of my neck". I can honestly say I never experienced that kind of feeling at all.'

These days George Brand is retired, and runs a dog kennel on Brisbane's outskirts with his wife, Scotty. He is a gentle, avuncular man with a slow smile; he considers his words before speaking. It doesn't seem surprising that he was seen by Debbie and her contemporaries inside the women's prison in 1990 as a man they could communicate with, someone who would listen, someone who was firm but fair.

Even before the official reports were completed, Brand reviewed all the available information about the conditions in the prison when the murder occurred, and began to make changes of his own. His first and probably most significant action was to order that the gate separating the bottom B block from the others be left unlocked. It was obvious to Brand that, with factionalism still rife among the women, and the tensions surrounding the murder still high, nothing would improve while members of the warring parties were trapped together in one section of the jail.

Brand: The atmosphere was getting tighter and tighter. All these people locked in together – there were some girls who'd done nothing more than have a bit of dope in their handbags and they were on life sentences; there were people like Tracy Wigginton and her friends, and there were women who, when they were on downers, were quite dangerous. You can imagine all these people in one room. There was no work for them. It was like a cauldron. They had nothing in common and they all hated the world and hated one another. It was almost like the murder was set up to happen.

There was just no freedom of movement, they couldn't walk away from it. It was all right for the staff who could go home. But the gate chopped those women off from anything, any support from friends in other blocks. If they had to see the dentist they had to wait until there was an escort, and if there wasn't one available, then they'd just have to wait.

So I ordered that gate remain unlocked, and I gave them freedom of movement – if they wanted to leave a section they were only required to tell an officer where they were going. If they wanted to hit a tennis ball around the court, they could, or they could go and visit someone else in another block. But every time I walked in there for a month that bloody gate was locked, and I'd yell out, 'Who's got the key to this door? Did it blow closed again or what? I want the tongue out and I want it open – if I see it locked like that again you're in trouble.' But the staff just didn't want to leave it open.

Brand's view that 'it was almost as if the murder was set up to happen' is interesting, given that it was one also formed independently by both Debbie and Tracy Wigginton at the time. While none of them point the finger at any one person – blaming the explosive confluence of factors inside the jail – their opinion might be a telling indicator of attitudes among prison officers before the reform era.

Debbie recalls that, in the weeks leading up to the murder, when officers were entering her cell in her absence, emptying her vitamin pills into the sink and running her stereo batteries down, they could have looked across the narrow corridor into Storm's cell and seen the sharpening stone lying on her desk. She maintains officers were told that a murder would be committed in the women's prison. 'They knew. And did nothing,' she says now. According to Wigginton, prison officers promoted the murderous tensions inside the crowded block, running it 'like a POW concentration camp'. She takes the theory further by suggesting prison officers fortuitously left the barbecue forks lying in the dining room, to be spirited away by one faction or another.

Whatever the circumstances were in the lead-up, it took months after the murder before the anxiety and apprehension among prison officers settled; many simply took extended stress leave, others made ample use of sick leave. Brand can recall one particular day just after he began when not one prison officer turned up for work. 'They were all just "sick",' he recalls. 'They were scared. It took a lot of effort to get them onside.'

There was no sympathy for them from the women. 'They were all off on stress leave,' Debbie recalls, 'all off seeing psychs. They could walk out the door. But we had to survive in that prison, we had to do it all ourselves, and all we had was each other, we supported each other. We just had to get on with it and survive. Kill or be killed. People wonder why we can do desensitisation so well – because we had to become experts in showing no emotion.'

Gill Campbell remembers this time well. She and Deb had been corresponding and occasionally speaking by phone up until the time of the murder. When news of the murder reached her, she had tried desperately to make phone contact through the hospital. No calls were put through to Debbie, but after her discharge, Debbie managed to call Gill. That was when Gill noticed a change: 'Deb was really bitter and angry at the time. The change in her was frightening. Her letters were so full of hatred towards everything – I felt I didn't know her anymore,' she says. 'She'd always sworn a lot but it was nothing compared to the sort of language she wrote in her letters to me. It frightened me – I wasn't sure how she'd be when she came out of jail.'

But gradually, survival for Debbie meant more than biding her time, more than just the intense planning and fever for payback, more than vengeance. As the weeks melted into one another after the aborted mediation meeting, and the warring factions were kept apart, she felt something inside her slip, and give. One day, sitting inside the tailor shop, listening to Storm howl and cry in isolation, Debbie looked up from her machine:

Debbie: For some reason her screams just hit me that day, they were screams of absolute despair, and they hit something in me that brought back all the trauma of being locked up as a kid in Wilson. Suddenly it felt like me screaming, it was coming from a place I knew. She'd been locked up for months by then on her own, and I just looked at Burrey and said, 'Why don't they just let her out of there? Just let her out.' I'd lost my intense feelings about her by then, I wasn't constantly thinking and dreaming up how to kill her. It kind of flowed away.

And slowly they did start letting her out for a few hours. I just knew that was a turning point for me, I recognised it. She's done it, it's over, you can't just keep locking her up in there. To me it was about the mistreatment of someone. Just knowing the prison system and how fucked it is. Okay, she's fucked up and killed someone and she's in prison, but you're torturing her. Let her out. This is the punishment, being in prison. Not being tortured.

When Storm was permitted to leave her cell for short periods – George Brand was horrified about her extended isolation and changed her routine immediately – Debbie had more demons to face. Had she let her friends down by not executing the payback? Was she weak because she hadn't killed Storm? The internal conflict continued, even though the powerful drive to kill had disappeared. Getting past that, she says now, was a matter of answering her own questions: do I want to spend the rest of my life in prison? Or do I want to get out and give my kids a go?

She eventually answered them in a compelling way. Around this time, just after George Brand's appointment, some of the women were asked to stand up in front of a group of community representatives and other prisoners to talk about their experiences of incarceration. Debbie was one of them. The timing was good: it coincided with her own internal battle over how she should proceed with her life. Perhaps she might see a way forward by looking back. She agreed to do it, and sat down to write.

She wrote down everything she could remember, from her first taste of a lock-up as a fourteen-year-old at Wilson, through the abuse and violence that followed. She included her shock and trauma around the circumstances of her father's death, and the litany of violent relationships and alcohol-fuelled rages that characterised her younger life. It was a simple narrative, with no attempt at analysis. She wrote and wrote, and rehearsed bits of it with Scogs and Taylor, testing her strength.

But on the day the papers were to be delivered to the large gathering in the prison gymnasium, something fractured and broke in Debbie Kilroy. As she recited the bare facts of her own story, meaning began to swell between the lines. She began to understand where she had been, why she was here. The effect was visceral, as if the blades had found their mark after all, slicing through her hard-won numbness:

Debbie: When I stood up in front of the group and read it out, I began to realise what I was saying. I was saying that I had taken responsibility for Dad's death. I was twenty-nine, and for fifteen years I'd believed that I'd killed my father.

For the first time I really confronted it. I broke down completely, sobbing. Tracey-Rose came up to me and offered to finish reading for me but I said no. I had to do it. I had to go through this realisation that I was not a bad person. That I did not need punishment for killing my father. And that I was the victim of a system that had betrayed me and betrayed many others and shoehorned us all into a life of imprisonment, grief, marginalisation.

It was a speech that took perhaps ten minutes to deliver. Its effects, however, would endure, lighting a way forward for Debbie that had previously been dark and unsure. Freed from the need to attract punishment to atone for her father's death, she could see it was possible to live a different life. It was possible to do so even while she was still inside. It was not a matter of changing. That wasn't part of her thoughts. It was about behaving in a way that would deliver her that other life. She set about it with the extraordinary energy that was – and still is – her singular trademark.

9

Reform

Everyone, apparently, was expecting Lazarus. Some kind of miraculous transformation, at least; someone who could be held up as a model – or a warning – to others. But Lazarus wasn't the person who emerged when Debbie Kilroy stepped out of the shadow of her friend's murder inside Boggo Road jail. That person was the same Debbie Kilroy – clever, tough, uncompromising, unafraid – and now a woman steeled by an awareness of her own potential. People began to watch with interest.

> Fred: They expected her, I think, to come back after the murder either broken or re-made. Amali came back broken, Storm should have been broken. But Deb came back quiet for a time. It was almost like she was sitting there thinking, and then all of a sudden she stood up saying, 'You can't do this to me. You can't systematically or personally take my life; you can't do this.' And then instead of putting her anger into the perpetrators, she put it into the system. The system allowed this to happen. Oh my God. I actually think that was the moment Sisters Inside was born.

Earlier, in the days after Debbie returned from hospital and had been moved out of B block with her friends, Wigginton had been amazed at Debbie's apparent equilibrium. For Fred, this was important: in the short time they had been imprisoned together, she had already begun to look to Debbie as a guide in how to behave. Debbie had 'an aura and a presence', Fred recalls, and it meant one thing: 'no matter how frightened I am, I will always show that I am confident'.

It was just how Fred aspired to be. 'It didn't matter how bad things got, I would put myself forward as confident. Knees knocking, pissing myself,' she says. 'And that was Deb all the way through.'

She recalls the feeling of relief when she initially realised that Debbie was back from hospital – or back from the dead, as she saw it at one stage, because for a while, no one at Boggo Road knew which 'Deborah' had survived. Fred saw that Debbie was fine, was virtually unscathed physically, and within minutes realised she had survived mentally too: 'She was hanging over the railing (at E block, where they'd put her) when she came back. And she just said, how you doin', Drac?' Wigginton recalls. 'And I thought, man, you've been stabbed, and you're still asking me how *I'm* doing? But there had been all this movement, all this upheaval with the murder, people being moved. Nothing was stagnant. And when we saw Deb hanging over the railing we knew some semblance of order was coming back into our lives.

'We felt that Deb's mob were the head of the matriarchy in there, we looked to her to see what she was doing or what her frame of mind was, and we'd think, okay, we'll follow that. After the murder it all felt like chaos, and then there she was, and it seemed to us that she'd come out of it better than we had. She was the one walking tall, and we were falling apart. So we followed her example.'

Debbie's emergence as a leadership figure for many of the women came, fortuitously, at the same time that Keith Hamburger and George Brand were drawing up their blueprint for the reform process. An integral part of all their plans from the outset was the involvement of the women in as many of the decision-making processes as possible. They needed them onside.

Like Wigginton, Brand remembers how, initially, Debbie was reluctant to say or do anything, and kept her distance from him and from everyone else. Once she had broken her silence, however, and asked why Storm shouldn't be released from solitary, he realised something had been triggered in her. She was looking, he could see, outside herself, was leaving behind whatever intense internal monologue she'd been conducting since her return. It was a relief for all kinds of reasons, not least because Brand suspected that where Kilroy led, others might follow. He hoped it might mean that she would get involved in what would become one of the bravest experiments in prison reform ever seen in Queensland.

It would be easy, given the conditions that govern crime and punishment in this new millennium, to forget that there were times when prisons really were a place of last resort for sentencing judges and magistrates, and that there was a time when these original 'gated communities' did not proliferate over the landscape like an angry rash. Although the prison population throughout Australia soared during the nineteenth century as places to detain wayward convicts, vagrants and drunkards, numbers gradually began to decline after Federation. Between 1900 and the late 1920s, the number of prisoners in Queensland jails more than halved, from 554 males and 50 females in 1900, to around 240 and 15 in the 1920s. But with the post-war period came the beginning of the rush to create and fill jails. The number of women prisoners rose from 17 in 1958–59, to 25 in 1973–74, and 43 within the next five years (according to Wilson, McCartney & Lincoln, *Justice in the Deep North*).

But the next twenty years saw numbers skyrocket: by 1996–97 there were 189 women in Queensland prisons. In January 2004, the Australian Bureau of Statistics (ABS) confirmed what many had suspected – that we are locking people up, particularly Indigenous people – at an extraordinary and frightening rate. The Australian prison population, the ABS reported, had risen nearly 50 percent in the ten years from 1993 to 2003 (15 866 to 23 555 inmates). The Australian adult population in that time had grown just 15 percent. But the truly alarming figures were those for women. In the same period, the number of women in prison had leapt by 110 percent.

Conditions within prisons have really only improved in the past fifteen years, and then only after repeated inquiries into ongoing problems and a belated capitulation by government to the trends and policies that were revolutionising prisons elsewhere in the world. By the time the Kilroys hit the prison system in late 1989, these overseas trends and influences were only just being noticed by Queensland authorities, and it would take several years to implement any significant change. But politicians have always relied on the suspicion that there are no votes in prisons, and have easily dismissed protests raised in defence of those behind bars. Attempts to improve conditions are decried as the work of bleeding hearts and are frequently hijacked by the law and order debate: we need tougher sentences to protect the community against crime/we need sentences that are deterrents; why should prisons be air-conditioned? Familiar arguments to anyone who reads a daily newspaper.

So when Debbie Dick was brutally murdered inside the women's prison in 1990, revealing the culture of intimidation, frustration and cruel despair that still flourished among prisoners, officers and management, the new Goss government might have been expected to back carefully away from the reform agenda and make some kind of political capital out of the incident. These days, that is exactly what happens: successive governments have taken violence inside prisons as a springboard for tightening already stringent security controls. Murders, even those inside prisons, are horrific and unsettling events; it's a natural reaction to want to hunker down, batten down the hatches. Astonishingly, in 1990 Hamburger and Brand were able to do the opposite of what would be expected in the same circumstances today: instead of locking the prison up and screwing everything down tighter, they loosened everything up. Effectively, they opened up the women's prison.

It is true that in Queensland in 1990, the ground for reform had already been prepared in response to the findings of the 1988 Kennedy Inquiry. The prisons department had been replaced by a statutory authority, the Corrective Services Commission, and a community board had been established to allow public input into rehabilitation and management issues inside all the state's jails.

To the delight of incoming director Keith Hamburger, the focus of the new commission swung away from punishment towards rehabilitation (within a 'safe and secure' environment) and there was real interest in investigating and addressing the underlying causes of offending behaviour. Better working conditions for staff and improved physical facilities were also being examined.

Hamburger had already endured a tumultuous year exacerbated by industrial unrest over Kennedy's report. After the government changed in December 1989, he and the new prisons minister, Glen Milliner, spent a couple of months sizing each other up and then plunged forward with the reform agenda. Hamburger believes Milliner showed 'great political courage' to persevere in the early days of change: the prison officers' union did not spare either man, but it was Milliner as the elected official who had to bear the brunt of public and media criticism over their plans.

But Hamburger had to show courage too. He drew a great deal

of ire after explaining the essence of his approach in an annual report, in which he'd tried to appeal to the public's compassion:

> Hamburger: I'd spent years coming to the understanding I had about the prison system. If you spend time in prisons, and you talk to prisoners, if you look at them as people and think about yourself, you have to ask yourself: if those had been my circumstances, what would I have been like? I also spent a lot of time on parole boards and interviewing prisoners, and I can tell you from the evidence that over 80 percent of prisoners serving more than five years, the serious offenders – armed robbers, rapists – have come from severely dysfunctional backgrounds as young children.
>
> And that's what I wrote in my annual report that year. They were the kids who didn't get toys at Christmas, who came home from school and got abused and beaten, who then struggled with the education system – because it's hard enough for people from loving families, who come home to their support, to work hard at school and get good results.
>
> But if you come home to some drunken abusive family . . . so I painted a picture of that. I didn't try to justify the crimes they'd committed, but I tried to explain it. If you take that demographic and think you can punish crime away by punishing those people further, by beating them up or locking them away, if you think that's going to make society safer, well that's just illogical and stupid.

When the annual report was published and sections quoted in the media, all hell broke loose. A previous prisons minister in the conservative government, Russell Cooper, attacked Hamburger, accusing him of being a bleeding heart. Then the two talkback shock-jocks, John Laws and Alan Jones, joined the chorus. Hamburger remembers it vividly: 'They were savage. "What kind of fool have they got in charge of corrections in Queensland?" and "These grubs should be dealt with" – that sort of nonsense,' he says. At the height of the outcry, however, Laws was also roundly criticised by some listeners. Eventually, Hamburger received a letter of apology from the broadcaster, which he regarded as a rare prize.

Keith Hamburger believes prisons are an essential evil to protect the community from certain offenders, but his views about the treatment of prisoners still sound radical in some quarters. He shakes his head at the notion that, in 1988, he had the power as director general to punish prisoners with seven days bread and water, and that prison officers then were not permitted to speak to a prisoner unless it was to give them an order. 'How we deal with people in jail is a measure of our civilisation, of the sort of people we are,' he says. 'I see jails as places where we can stabilise someone's behaviour, do a thorough assessment of their needs, capture their attention. And then focus on the underlying causes that have got them into that situation. That's what jails are about. They're not about punishment as such, they're about containing people for the protection of society and then trying to change those people.'

The appointment of George Brand was an important plank in the raft of reforms Hamburger drew up. Hamburger knew Brand shared a similar philosophy about prisons and that he had a confident, 'firm but fair' management style. In the aftermath of the murder, the prison needed someone like Brand, someone who wouldn't be intimidated either by the event or by community and political expectations. Crucially, though, Hamburger also had enough faith in Brand to let him come to grips with the situation inside the women's prison on his own terms, and then get on with the job. Brand seized the opportunity with both hands.

In the first months of his appointment in early 1990, he began to investigate the possibility of legal 'special status' for women in prison. These days, looking back, he believes the departmental heads and bureaucrats he met and argued with had no real understanding of the breadth of the proposal, which was approved and granted soon afterwards. Brand's sales pitch at the time was that women in prison had greater needs than men, and different needs, especially given their roles as primary carers of children and other relatives outside jail. But his intention was to divert women from the harsh security requirements that applied to male prisoners so that he could get women from all security classifications out of prison for weekend leave and certain other activities he had planned.

A prisoner's security status was and is determined by a number of factors, including the length of their sentence, the nature of their crime, their criminal record and their behaviour inside prison. The kinds of activities Brand had in mind would have been impossible to organise for most prisoners under the classification as it stood: 'Until then, if they didn't have low security status they couldn't go anywhere. There were guidelines about security ratings so just because someone was a nice person or you thought they could be trusted, you couldn't just lower their levels. You couldn't rig it,' he says.

As soon as the 'special needs' status was established for women, however, Brand threw away the old rule book. There were still guidelines about who could do what, but Brand was able to use his own discretion in a much more flexible way. Soon there were monthly excursions like the one on which he took seven high-security prisoners, among others, on a canoeing trip on nearby Moogerah Dam. One of them was Tracy Wigginton. 'She nearly drowned me that day, trying to up-end my canoe,' Brand recalls fondly.

Before that trip, however, the groundwork was laid with escorted leaves of absence for some prisoners, and the inclusion of community volunteers who escorted prisoners outside the prison to the dentist, to education programs, or shopping. Many of them were 'religious visitors', mainly nuns, all registered with the Community Corrections board, or parole board. It was a radical initiative, unheard of anywhere else, and it worked. 'All they had to do was ring up and report it if the prisoner ran away,' Brand says. 'It never happened.'

Brand gave the women the freedom to suggest various activities that interested them, but one that he put forward was probably the biggest success. It involved an experiential learning centre at The Outlook, at Boonah, southwest of Brisbane, which specialised in high and low ropes courses, mainly for children. But Brand could see how women desensitised to fear might benefit from the challenges of the programs, which were based on participation, safety, respect, trust and justice – many of the notions these women had given up on completely.

Beginning with low and medium security prisoners only – which helped appease some prison officers still averse to what they saw as management 'going soft' – groups of women attended the courses, coming back with positive feedback about what they encountered. Facilitators at The Outlook focused on building self-esteem, developing trust, challenging entrenched behaviours, encouraging women to own their own decisions and processes and to take responsibility for change.

> Brand: I knew the value of that kind of training because of my own early army training. All that outdoor stuff, adventure training, orienteering, ropes, it gives you a lot of personal satisfaction, and teaches you to work in teams. The effect of it was immediate: they came back walking a foot off the ground. And it helped to change staff attitudes too, because they could see it was working, they knew it couldn't be wrong.
>
> At first with The Outlook and the other activities I had to coerce staff to go; I'd go myself and take some with me. They weren't paid, it was out of hours. At the time it went right against their thinking. But it went from staff saying, 'No, I'm not going,' to 'When is it my turn?' They were having fun, and having their thinking changed too. I reckon we could have gone on those outings with no staff at all eventually, and all the prisoners would have come back safe and sound. That level of trust had built up. It was extraordinary.

Brand and Hamburger also laid the groundwork for another highly successful initiative that the women took over and made their own. As part of a community advisory committee – made up of some of the fiercest critics of the old prison management, along with staff members and prisoners – a series of subcommittees was formed inside the prison led by some of the more high-profile prisoners.

Brand and Hamburger reasoned that they were dealing with women who had rarely, if ever, had any power or control in their outside lives, women who had not made their own decisions and felt overwhelmed when confronted by responsibility. This would be their first taste of involvement in something resembling a democratic process, and of authority figures who might actually listen to them and talk. Brand asked for suggestions from the women, and for volunteers to act as convenors for each committee, who would all come together regularly and enjoy equal places at the table.

Many of the ideas had their origins in those early meetings held with community agencies directly after the murder: health and education issues, sport and recreation, families, Indigenous issues, food, complaints and community work. Some of them came from

the women's areas of interest: Debbie volunteered and was
appointed convenor of the Street Kids Committee, and began work
on plans to raise money for young people whose experiences she
understood so well.

Brand remembers another high profile prisoner, Wendy Lang,
coming to him with a proposal for a particular committee's activities, a proposal he turned down because 'it was really just about
getting Wendy out, on leave of absence. When Brand turned down
her proposal, Lang was nonplussed. 'What do you mean, "no"?' she
asked him. Brand repeated his decision. She looked at him squarely
and said, 'You know what happened to the last bloke who said no
to me, don't you?'

Brand still enjoys the memory. 'That's the way we interacted with
those committees,' he says. 'But they knew if I said "no" I meant
"no". I didn't ever say anything I didn't mean. I'd say to them, tell
me how we could make that work, rather than a straight "no", or
"it's against the rules". It was up to them to come back with something.'

This unequivocal stance also won approval from the women.
'He called a spade a spade, and didn't string anyone along,'
Debbie remembers. 'I admired him for that. When he said yes he
meant yes, and no meant no. He even avoided saying, "I'll look into
it", because that was another way of saying, "I'm not going to even
think about it".'

The admiration was mutual: 'Deb was a tearaway, but she was a
good prisoner,' Brand says. 'She didn't break the rules for the sake of
breaking the rules. She behaved as she was expected to behave. She
would be very outspoken, but generally in the right way. When
she was given the forum she'd speak out. Eventually she set a very
good example for other prisoners.' Keith Hamburger agrees:

Hamburger: She was a very strong-willed young woman, very
determined, but I always found her very respectful and easy to
talk to. She was tough, there was no doubt about that – she
had no hesitation in telling me very directly what the
problems were in there, but never in a way that I took offence.

I would always make a point of introducing myself to prisoners, and saying hello when I was there, but there weren't
that many who would just rock up to me, as the director

general, and say, 'Hello, Keith'. And then she'd tell me. I always felt she was open and honest. What you saw was what you got. And she obviously had influence with the others. On the committee she had the respect of other prisoners because of her power to articulate. Many of them couldn't, but Deb always could.

During the next two years, the committees organised several large functions that brought prisoners into close contact with members of the public. Media representatives were sometimes invited, but the universal reaction from prison staff was hesitation and mistrust, according to Brand. One such function was a dinner at the upmarket Crest Hotel in the centre of town, attended by all the committee convenors, managerial staff and representatives of community groups like Second Chance, which enlisted businesses willing to employ ex-prisoners.

Brand: I know there were some executive managers who were dead against it, and I know that some of them went to the function armed. They were sure all these girls were going to run away – of course, none of them did. There was a report that Wendy Lang returned to the prison without her knickers. I still don't know if that was true, if she arrived without knickers or lost them at the dinner. I'm not sure how anything could have happened – there was at least one staff member at each table, and only one prisoner among the rest.

The media didn't know about the dinner. They didn't know about the canoeing trips or the ropes courses either. Sometimes I wouldn't even tell Keith about an activity until we'd done it. Then I'd ring him up and tell him we'd had a successful outing that day. There were many things the bureaucracy didn't know about.

There were at least two other memorable committee activities Brand is proud of. One involved taking the committee convenors and community escorts to visit Townsville prison to introduce the notion of more interactive management there. 'It was a goodwill visit, the prisoners' idea,' Brand says. 'They were getting it a bit easier by then and they were saying, what about the poor buggers in

Townsville? So we thought, well, let's go up and have a look.'

The group (which once again included Tracy Wigginton, and an escort named Anna Bligh, who, some years later, would become a state government minister) flew north on a commercial jet, and the visit proceeded without a hitch. But Brand remembers it for another reason: 'On the way up, it was quite obvious that while the staff and others all got metal cutlery, the prisoners got plastic. Mysteriously, it was the other way round on the way back. I've never worked out who organised that, but I think it was Anna.'

The other function was a 'Sportsmen's Dinner' inside the prison organised by Debbie in her role as Street Kids Committee convenor. High-profile sports personalities including swimmer Tracey Wickham, cricketer Greg Ritchie, Broncos coach Wayne Bennett and footballers Alan Langer and Willie Carne, joined Premier Wayne Goss, journalists, prison staff, their friends and prisoners – one hundred and eighty in all – to raise money for street kids.

Denise Foley, who had just begun working with Catholic Prisons Ministry and helped organise food donations and waitresses (and whose mother and sister helped cook in the kitchen that night), remembers it well. There were exquisite silver bain-maries from the upmarket Heritage Hotel, where her sister was working as apprentice chef, prisoners were allowed to dress up, some waited tables, and sports memorabilia, including autographed football jerseys, were auctioned. It was a huge night, and Debbie's original enthusiasm – and her contacts inside the world of professional football – paid off: there was positive media coverage and a few more stereotypes about prisoners were demolished.

Debbie: The committees worked on all kinds of levels. Because we had a say in what was happening, we took ownership of it. When you start seeing the outside world again, and it isn't just this closed environment, not just kill or be killed – you could leave that behind. You could make your own decisions, instead of all your decisions being taken away from you.

You could go to George with an idea and instead of saying no, he'd say, tell me how that would work. Even if he eventually said no to something, I'd go away and think about that. If he said no because of x and y, I'd come up with answers to x and y, and then take it back to him again. That really began to develop my mind

around thinking strategically, thinking around corners and finding
the side doors we didn't know existed.

Throughout all the cell blocks, including D block, where Debbie
was now established, life began to settle into a new rhythm. With
more work, education and training opportunities, and a less strained,
more collegiate atmosphere, the women were busy and more
positive. A new education officer, Gabrielle Spencer, was appointed
in 1990 and immediately began investigating pathways for prisoners
to further their studies at TAFE and university.

Outreach programs were formed like the one led by Catholic
Prisons Ministry, which took prisoners, including Debbie and
Tracey Bromage, out to schools and other venues to talk about their
experiences. Activities like gym work and aerobics classes were
extended, hairdressers were invited in regularly and women were
encouraged to wear their hair and makeup in their own way. Brand
even arranged for a masseur to visit periodically. A plant nursery was
established just outside the prison gates to extend employment
hours.

Meals were no longer mass prepared in one kitchen. Each section
would choose its own menu for the week and be allocated the
appropriate provisions. Women either took turns to cook or they
identified the best cooks in the section and relieved them of other
duties so that they could do the job. 'You'd order in what you
wanted – flour, bread, rice, potatoes, bananas, sugar. You could cook
what you liked with it, a pie, a cake. There was a limited range of
fresh fruits and vegies, so we ate quite well,' Debbie remembers. 'But
there were no treats as such. We didn't get pineapple, for instance,
and I loved pineapple, so once when we had an outside buy-up I
bought three, and had mouth ulcers for weeks. A woman we called
Mother had gone to cooking classes and she'd make the flashest
cakes in town.'

In Debbie's block, however, a Singaporean prisoner named Anna
Loh (but nicknamed 'The Slope') was worried that Debbie's food
might become contaminated. Just prior to the kitchen arrangements
changing, meals had been deliberately contaminated with Ajax
cleaning powder, and Anna didn't trust anyone. She began to cook
solely for Debbie, serving her up her own homespun dishes of
steamed rice, chilli and vegetables. She even took to baking cakes

just for her, always making up two batches of mix – Debbie would eat one bowl of cake mix raw.

Later, when Debbie was moved to F block around the beginning of 1992, Anna moved with her. The two women became very close before Anna was deported back to Singapore after serving two years. (She had been arrested at Brisbane Airport with a package of heroin she had agreed to carry in exchange for enough money to clear a gambling debt.) After the tragic death of Anna's son at home in Singapore, Debbie barely left her side, successfully applying to take her on weekend leave with her to Nana's. She called Debbie 'Cow' and was fiercely protective of her, even restraining prison officers from waking her from her afternoon naps. She would massage Debbie's head every night. The two women worked together daily in the tailor shop, and Debbie remembers Anna sending off every cent of her tiny wage to her family at home. After Debbie was released and Anna returned to Singapore, they spoke by telephone a couple of times. Anna told Debbie she was struggling to look after her elderly parents. Then they lost contact.

The warm friendship between the two women helped both of them to deal with the loss of other important relationships. Anna was separated geographically from her entire family and, while Debbie was able to see her children, she felt her marriage to Joe was over. The hurt she felt from what she saw as his betrayal over the plea bargain would not go away, and she was in no mood to negotiate with him.

Joe had other ideas. Even during their separation before the trial, he had gone to the Emma Street house regularly before it was sold and, if Debbie was out, he would spend hours doing the housework, leaving a trademark bunch of flowers on the front steps as he departed. From his cell in the men's prison at Wacol, he wrote to her every week, sometimes twice. Debbie studiously ignored each letter, and never replied.

Even when, after the murder, prison authorities allowed inter-prison visits for families as another way to relieve tension, Debbie thought long and hard about boarding the bus which regularly took women from Boggo Road to visit husbands or boyfriends at Wacol. She had absolutely no desire to see Joe then, but figured the bus ride would at least be a way of escaping the prison for a few hours. On the first few visits, she sat across the table from him in the visiting area, steadfastly refusing to speak. 'Don't talk to me,' she'd warn him when she walked in. But Joe would talk anyway, determined that one day he'd get through.

Debbie was just as determined to remain aloof, using up all her energy to stay busy, to pass the time.

She began to apply for a variety of courses as a lead-up to university studies. She enrolled in a landscaping course inside the prison and was given weekly leave to attend a fitness course at Kangaroo Point TAFE. Her prison escort also accompanied her to a gym at Toowong, where she completed the practical component.

Remarkably, she also agitated successfully for a group of women to be released twice a week for running sessions along a nearby river path after convincing several prison officers to accompany them as volunteers. Months later, members of this 'running club' were part of a group that participated in a celebrated 'Cops'n'Robbers' race from Cairns to Brisbane between police and serving prisoners. Ironically, given her level of fitness, Debbie wasn't among them: she was considered too 'high profile' and her security classification had not yet been reduced.

There were consolations, though. She was given leave of absence to attend her brother Michael's wedding, where she watched proudly as Jody played flower girl and Josh played page boy. Another came when she was chosen by the Convenors' Committee to undertake an instructor accreditation program at The Outlook. The process was highly competitive: everyone wanted the instructor's job. But Debbie sensed there was an important learning curve in there for her, something more than the transitory feeling of satisfaction that came with confronting the high ropes. Later, she would say the process of becoming an Outlook accredited trainer was life-changing, and challenged her 'whole thought process', showing her plainly for the first time that there were consequences from all actions.

Inside the prison, the women used their new landscaping skills to revamp the small exercise and visiting area at the back of the cell blocks (and Debbie went on to work-release landscaping at the local Police Youth Club). They dug gardens, reshaped and replanted, built a fish pond and organised a children's climbing frame. Once Joshua was accustomed to the notion that this was where his mother lived, he would play out here with Debbie on weekend visiting days.

Sometimes he would run around the rough tennis court and play with the children of other prisoners before the trauma of leaving his mother again. But there was never any doubt that Joshua missed Debbie terribly. Although he became very close to Nana, he could not understand why his mother wasn't coming home.

> **Debbie**: In the early days, the kids were both really upset when they came up. Jody would be distressed and flip around the place. But Joshua didn't have so many verbal skills. He'd either hide under the table, or sit on top of the table and grab me by the hair, and force my head down, or just spit in my face for an hour. That's how he was dealing with it, with me abandoning him. He'd just tear my hair out, or spit at me, that's all he did.

After one of her weekend leaves, Josh drove with Debbie's friend Batty when he dropped her back at Boggo Road. Outside the gates, she cuddled the little boy and he held on tight. And held on, and held on. When she whispered that she had to go, and that he had to go home with Batty, Josh began to scream. He held her as hard as he could with his little three-year-old arms, as if that would keep her there, as if they were really one person.

Finally, in desperation, Debbie signalled to Batty and he peeled the little boy's body from his mother's. The pain of that separation would stay with Debbie for years. At that moment, though, she had to turn and walk briskly away, willing herself back to numbness, back to survival mode. She walked through the gate without turning around, the crash of the heavy lock sounding another brutal farewell.

With the new regime in place, a more optimistic air permeated the sour corridors of Boggo Road. The women began to look forward and out, rather than stewing in the miseries of the present. Somehow, they even managed to find some amusements within their cages, to create humour where there was precious little to laugh at.

> **Debbie**: Once, we managed to do some topless sunbathing out the back of the tailor shop, but were caught. Our punishment was to wash the windows along the whole block from the chapel

down. But they didn't tell us *how* to wash them. So I just turned on the fire hose and, unfortunately, all the windows were open at the time. Water sprayed through every one of them. I just said, you told us to wash the windows, you didn't say close them first. It was a minor breach, but Spider was crying and crying. I've got an impeccable record, she was saying. Oh God – you've got a life sentence for fuckin' murder, you idiot, I said. Get over it.

Spider always managed to get alcohol in somehow, usually a Popper in her boyfriend's pocket that was full of straight vodka. We had a clothes line out the back and every fortnight you'd see all these expensive G-strings and fancy bras hung up, all Spider's.

At first she used to always insist she was innocent, that she didn't organise her husband's murder. I'd say, sure you are, Spider, we're all innocent here. You're bullshitting. I was the only one who ever said that to her. But she'd told me about all the violence he'd inflicted on her, it was horrific, years of it. I'd say, you're bullshitting, come on, you've got to stop that and tell the truth, because you're seen as this nasty criminal, the Black Widow. And eventually she did stop and started telling the story.

There were lots of practical jokes. A couple involved a prison officer who was keen to enter the police service and who, as Debbie recalls, was constantly 'investigating' possible scams or breaches inside the prison. For his benefit, the women wrapped talcum powder in plastic wrap and pressed it between the leaves of a pot plant. Just hours later, he discovered and seized the tiny parcel and, with a delighted smile, presented it to a senior officer, announcing he'd found a 'big score'.

They tricked the same officer into believing the amber liquid in a plastic bottle he'd found stashed was a 'brew'. Once again he'd passed it to the senior, suggesting it was a brew and that she should smell it. The senior laughed and suggested *he* smell it. She'd been around long enough to know it was urine.

One day, a couple of the women discovered a disused telephone and, in true cloak–and–dagger fashion, would cover each other while they rewired it and plugged it into a spare socket to make illicit calls. They managed to keep the scam going for several months before the phone was found and seized by officers.

Because there was so little room for sport or recreation at Boggo Road, George Brand arranged for the women to be bussed once a week to the men's prison at Wacol, where they could play softball on the oval. Male prisoners, including Joe, could often interact with the women if they were on mowing duty on the other side of a low fence. It was this contact that allowed Joe to get a special present to Debbie one day: a tiny black kitten concealed in a cardboard box. He didn't give it to her personally. She still refused to speak with him, so he'd decided on other strategies to get her attention. Debbie had always loved black cats, so when a litter of black kittens was found abandoned near the oval he pounced on one, knowing she would find the gift irresistible. Taking advantage of some lax security, he managed to pass the package with its mewling contents to one of the women playing in the outfield, close to the fence, who gave it to Debbie as they were leaving.

> **Debbie**: All the way back from Wacol in the bus this kitten's making this *eeeeee!* noise so we're all going *eeeeee!* as if we're singing. When we walked into reception I gave the box to someone else, went in, got searched and took the box back. They were hopeless back then. Often after LOA we'd smuggle food in, prawns or mangoes, in the same way. Put the bag down, get searched, pick it back up. They had no idea.
>
> So we took this kitten in and it was great therapy for The Slope after her son died. We were all worried about her because she'd set up this shrine in her cell with photos of her son in his coffin. But she just played with this kitten all afternoon. The next day it was busted. It jumped out the door and some screw saw it. 'There's a kitten!' she announced. I said, 'No, it can't be a kitten, it must have been a rat.' But it was gone.

From George Brand's point of view, the harbouring of the kitten was a betrayal of the trust that he'd invested in 'the girls'. But apart from that, and a couple of other small hiccups (like the attempt made by one woman to escape by jumping the prison wall from the nursery, only to be hauled back by Wendy Lang, who admonished her with 'You don't do that kind of thing here') Brand felt the new regime was a resounding success, both for the women and for him personally.

Brand: I don't remember how it happened but eventually I felt like the father figure and all the girls were my kids. Whatever I'd do for my own kids, I'd do for them, if I could. I'd often do the outside escorts with them myself, not because I wanted to be a martyr but because, with the limitations on staff numbers, I couldn't always afford for staff to go. I'd take them out to see their babies or kids, whatever. Once it was Tracey Bromage for a radio interview about the committees, and my wife came too. I'd always have somebody else with me. Another time it was one of the girls who had little twins. There were some problems and my wife and I took her to the hospital.

I knew most of them individually, but I didn't always know their stories. I didn't try to find out. But if we were sitting down chatting about something and they started to talk about things in their childhoods, or whatever, I'd listen. I didn't go looking in their files for the crimes they'd committed. After a while you'd develop an understanding of how they ended up where they did. Most of them were pussycats, really. That didn't surprise me. Prisoners are people. When my wife and I lost our son to cancer, I wasn't in the prison for about six weeks or so, and there was not one incident. Not one. They knew what was happening.

Twelve months after I first went in there, there were lots of changed people. They had confidence. They weren't sitting in a corner, looking downtrodden. They were strutting around the place, which I thought was great.

Some people [in bureaucracies] won't take a chance. When you take a chance you have to expect a certain failure rate. And what happens these days is that if you take a chance with a hundred people and one fails, that's it. You don't get that chance again. That's crazy. In prisons these days nobody focuses on the cup half full, it's always the cup half empty.

If it wasn't for Keith, though, I probably wouldn't have tried to the extent that I did. Keith had done all the research and passed on all the ideas he wanted to try, and I'd try them out for him. But people outside couldn't even conceptualise what we were trying to do. You will hear these people on the street. They'll say, 'That person should go to jail for that,' but never 'That person should be trained not to do that.'

The women did get one of the great last laughs on Brand, though: 'They put on a play, with external help, and invited their friends and family and it was great. One of them had asked me if they could have the ride-on mower to use as a prop and I said no, you bloody well can't. And would you believe it, there we were, in one of the scenes of the play, George Brand and Keith Hamburger – done up pretty well in likeness, too – riding the ride-on mower across the stage. I laughed and laughed. And Keith nearly fell off his chair laughing too.'

One of the most important relationships Debbie formed in her two years at Boggo Road was with Tracy Wigginton. Although their memories of its origins differ, both acknowledge it now as a very close and sustaining friendship, one that has weathered hard times and the seemingly endless years of Fred's incarceration. But the seeds of it were sewn in the relatively brief time they spent together as fellow prisoners.

Such friendships, Debbie says, have a different quality to those she has with people outside: 'People in the outside world won't understand the friendship, because three months in prison is like six years or more of friendship on the outside. Out here you could know someone for three months and not really know them at all. But in prison you're in each other's pockets, you know everything about a person,' she says. 'That's why Fred and I are friends – we probably know each other better than anybody else. And also because of all the shit you live through, and you've got to work through it.'

Fred: The first time she called me 'Drac' it nearly floored me. Nobody else would come near me because of the fear factor. And that was good because then they couldn't see we were more fearful of them than they were of us. But this is what got me through the trial and all the media shit – it was Deb and Scogs and a few others making jokes of it, not bad jokes, but it bolstered me. 'Hey, Drac, you're on telly again.' Or she'd walk past me and say, 'Hey, don't let it get to you.' And then one night, when it was all on, she just got up and turned off the television. She'd had enough. And that small action meant more to me than words can say. It said to me, it's all shit and

I don't believe it, fun time is over, this is crap. That seriously kept me alive.

But it was several years later, when Debbie renamed Drac yet again, that the friendship became an unconditional one, bound by love and the fiercest loyalty. A friendship that did prove to be life-changing, as Fred believed it would be. In the meantime the lives of both women would be changed substantially by other events, would be fired at length in the crucible, reemerging in shapes that would surprise them both.

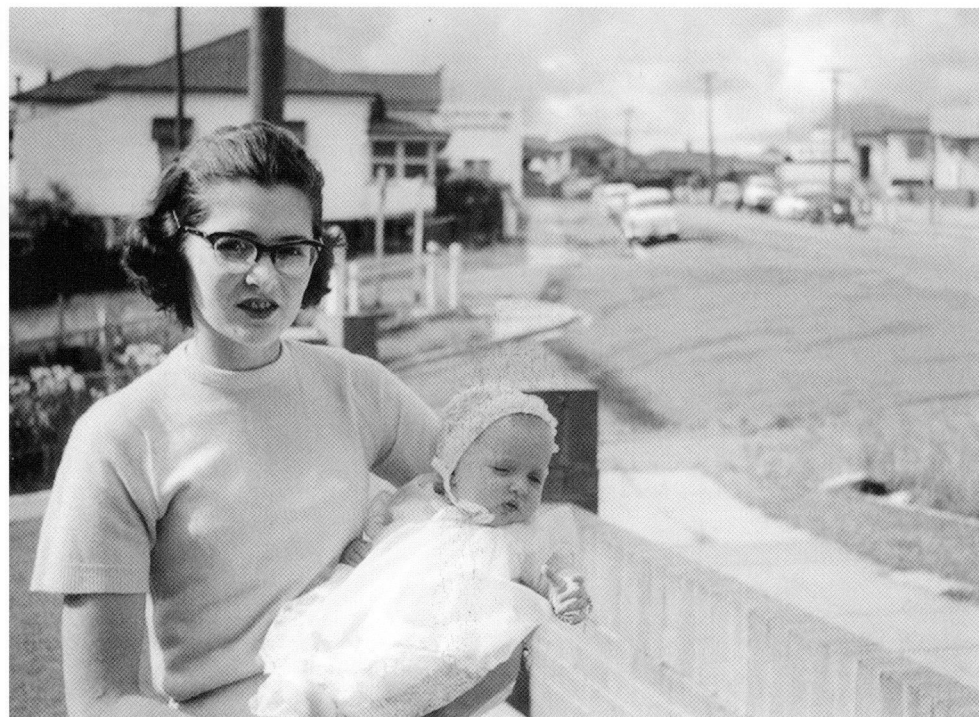

Pat holds Debbie in her christening gown, 1961. She was unimpressed, even then, by lacy white dresses

Nana with Deb, at 9 months. They were kindred spirits and Nana would have given her 'anything'

Deb and Michael, 1964. The ball is in Michael's court, for once . . .

Kevin and Deb, aged 3½,
at Lone Pine Koala Sanctuary

Deb's first day at school, aged 5. From the beginning she was on a collision course with the nuns

Grade 6 at St Anthony's. Deb was a 'bright but underachieving' tomboy, who'd already learnt to hate authority

Deb and Jody, 1979: not flinching, not expecting much

Deb with John Parker, at her 21st birthday celebration

Deb (left) and friends, show their form for an aerobics video at the local gym, 1981

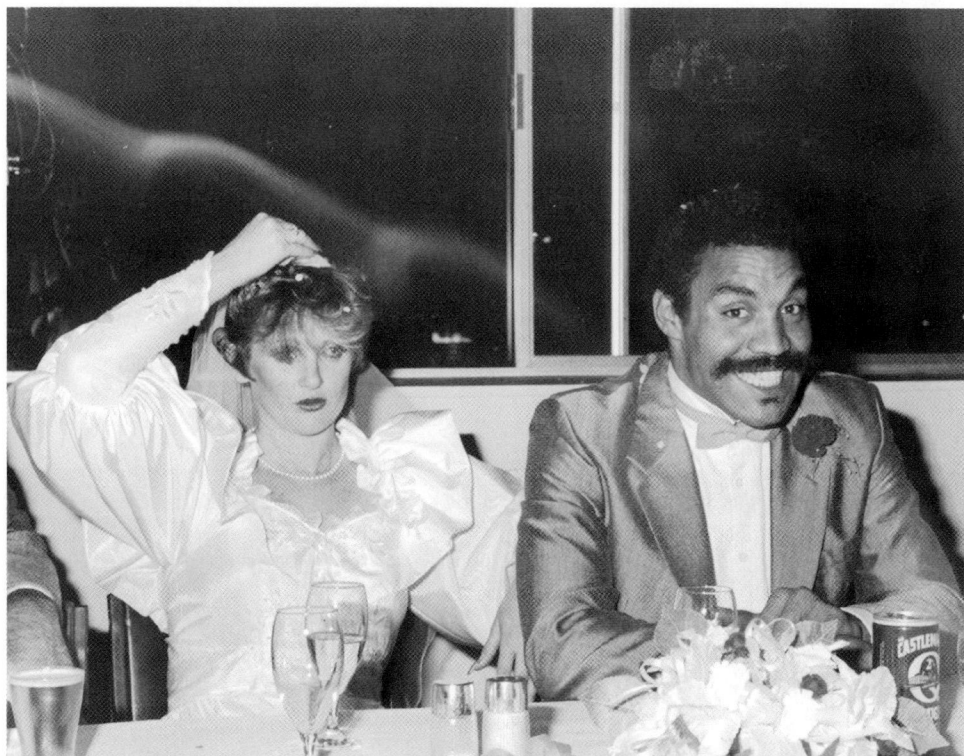

Wedding day, 1986: 'I just wanted to get it over and get the dress off'

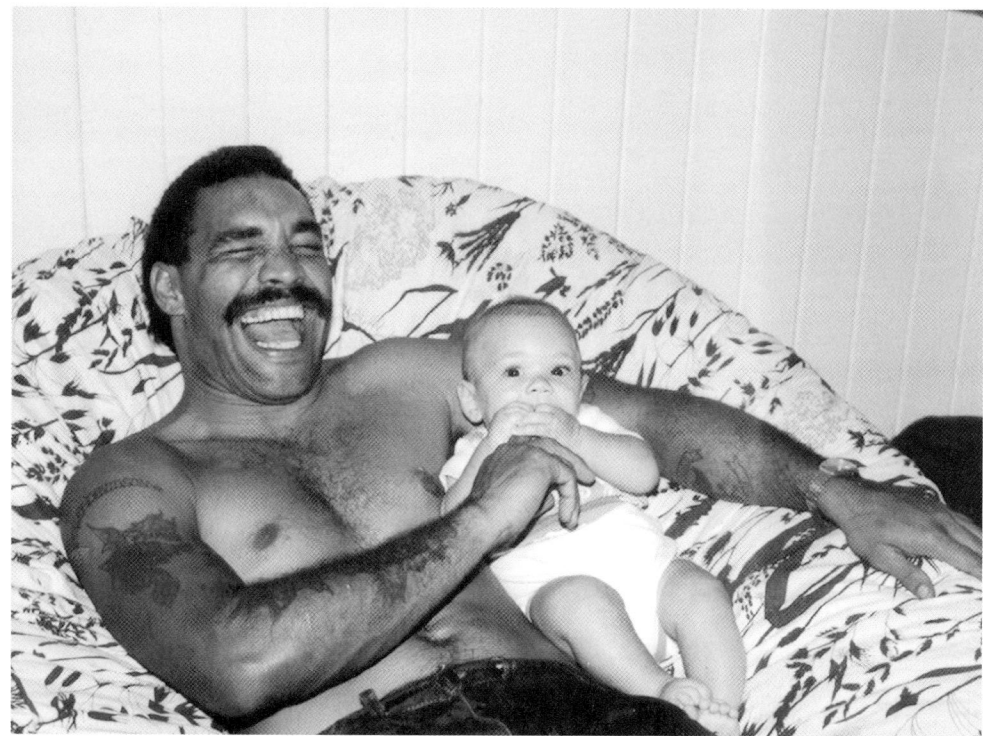

Joe and Joshua, 1986: Joe adored his son and Joshua thrived on Nana's recipe for healthy babies

Jody and Joshua, 1987: traumatic times had made Joe and Deb fiercely protective parents

Debbie Dick. 'I watched the blood drain out of her'

Family Day, Boggo Road, 1991. The pain of separation from her children would stay with Deb for years

Joshua, aged 5, his father's son.
An autographed modelling
photo his parents had done for
him

Jody in 2000, at 22, in
Brisbane's Correctional Centre.
Still 5 years from release

Christmas 2003 at Deb's mother Pat's. Joe loves getting together with Deb's family

Joshua, aged 18, off to university

The management committee of Sisters Inside at their AGM in 2003. Left to right: Paulette Dupuy, Janice Walker, Kris Olsson, Anne Warner (Mary Phillips is absent)

Surrounded by a staunch band of fellow activists and supporters in New York in 2003, when Deb was still allowed into the US. From left: Gina Dent, from the University of California; Canadian prisons activist Kim Pate; Queensland prisoners' advocate Karen Fletcher; and celebrated international activist, author and UCL professor, Angela Davis

Deb with proud mother Pat at her graduation ceremony, having received her degree in social work from the University of Queensland

Recognition by the establishment: Deb, celebrating her Community and Government Award at the Telstra Businesswoman of the Year Awards 2003, with Natalie Bell, her friend and colleague from Sisters Inside

Deb and Joe with Tash Engwirda and friend Tia Mitchell, celebrating Tash's 21st. The Kilroys took Tash under their wing and into their home in 2003 when she was released from prison with nowhere to go

Deb is honoured with the Human Rights Medal for her work with Sisters Inside, December 2004. Celebrating with her is Anne Warner (top), the former Labor minister of Family Services and Aboriginal Affairs, a constant source of inspiration and guidance to Deb in her post-prison life; and one of her oldest mates, Tanya Sale, whose loyalty earned her the nickname 'Sticky' from Deb

10

Swings and Roundabouts

June 1991 would prove to be a big month for Debbie. She had been involved for some time in a range of activities that devoured her days and allowed her to see beyond prison to the possibilities of life outside. She'd done the landscaping course and had been released over several days to reshape the old tennis court at the Police Youth Club in Fortitude Valley. The fitness course at the Kangaroo Point college of TAFE took her out one evening a week, and the running club two afternoons a week.

Through TAFE she also completed two sports coaching units, a personal grooming course and an elementary hairdressing course. And there was still the Street Kids Committee, which was bringing her into increasing contact with an innovative educational facility in Logan City, on Brisbane's southern outskirts. The Centre Education Program provided an alternative learning experience for young people who, for various reasons, did not fit into mainstream schools in the area, but that description belies the extraordinary role it played – and still plays – in young lives already affected by poverty, violence and racism, and by the particular ostracism that goes with them.

The venture had grown out of the concerns of a couple of Christian Brothers in the mid-1980s about chronic truancy in Logan and the accompanying risks for those young people who were already falling foul of the law. Staffed at various times by teachers, youth workers, arts workers, family counsellors and volunteers, the Centre serviced the educational needs of a shifting number of boys and girls through a mixture of programs and activities that included some curriculum-based subjects like English, maths and science, practical training in areas like welding or computers, as well as camping and excursions.

But its philosophy was what really set the place apart: young people were accepted as they were, warts and all, but had to take responsibility for the decisions and choices they made, and answer to the group – adults and other young people – for their actions. Above all, no young person was left in any doubt: he or she was cared about in this place. There was always a listening ear.

Debbie recognised the faces as soon as she walked in the door early in 1991 as a guest speaker, along with George Brand. There she was, a small piece of her in every one of them, and every one of them a mirror of the kids she'd run with and been locked up with inside Wilson. But these kids weren't locked up, not yet.

The Centre was offering them all the things she never had at their age, and operated on principles she surely would have responded to: acceptance, gentleness, acknowledgement of difference. After she addressed the group that night – detailing her own experiences, and all the reasons they should *not* follow her example – she was asked if she would attend the centre one day a week as part of her community work. Brand agreed, setting in motion a long and transforming relationship between Debbie and 'Centre Ed'.

Debbie revelled in her contact with the Centre from the beginning. She loved being with the kids and found she had a natural aptitude for communicating with them. But her regular contact with them, and increasing knowledge of their issues and confrontation with these issues, was double-edged: it brought her hard up against the patterns she shared with them – violence, hurt, failure, rejection. She could see that, in order to work effectively with troubled young people, she would have to face some old demons herself.

One of those demons presented itself in a place she was least expecting it. At Boggo Road, the women had organised a forty-hour 'aerobics-a-thon' to raise money for charity. As the aerobics instructor, Debbie wanted to participate – and so did Storm. On the day, Storm was already inside the gym when Debbie and her friends approached the metal louvre walls outside. Storm remembers another prisoner, a friend of both women, asked her to 'come over to the louvres – Debbie's over there'.

Storm: I didn't want to – I thought, are we going to start arguing? Is she going to be angry? I accepted that she might, but I didn't want to ruin anything. But Sue put her arm around me and said, 'It's all right, come on. It's all right.' So I went over and listened. Sue said, 'Okay, we want Debbie in here, is that all right, Storm? Is that all right, Debbie?' We looked at each other. Sue said, 'Well, are you going to make a truce? Yeah? Good.'

But it didn't end there. If there was going to be a truce, the others wanted a visible sign of it. The two women were still standing there, on either side of the louvres, silent. Sue intervened again. 'Shake on it,' she instructed. Storm and Debbie looked hard at each other. Then they both lifted their right arm, and shook hands through the louvres and bars. The women on both sides of the wall breathed out in unison.

Storm: That really changed things; it shifted the energy. I know that afterwards, when people could see that we weren't at each other's throats, it shifted a lot of things around the whole jail. People could breathe again. People could talk to each other again.

The phone call Debbie had been waiting for came on 24 June. Her move to Albion – a low-security halfway house for prisoners moving closer to parole – had been approved, almost twenty months to the day since she entered prison. Debbie was ready for this. She was already spending more time out of Boggo Road than inside it, and felt her life had a new momentum that she needed to keep up. The move to Albion would provide the necessary push.

There was an enormous feeling of relief to be leaving the dingy, sad old prison behind, together with the daily reminders of tragedy. But she was relieved on another count, too: the move to the low-security house would help stabilise her relationship with her children. Months earlier, Joe – who had served twenty months in prison and a halfway house and had now been released – had intimated to her that he was planning to take Joshua away from Nana to live with him. He might even take him out of Brisbane. Debbie panicked. Already racked with guilt over her absence from her children, she strongly believed her little boy needed the stability and love offered by his relationship with his great-grandmother – and by regular contact with his mother.

> **Debbie**: I flipped. I wanted Joshua to stay at Nana's. There was a big blow-up, and I spoke to George and he said okay, we'll make sure it doesn't happen, and he let me use the prison phone. So Joe and I sorted it out. But it was that stuff about having no power, it freaked me out; because he could have done it. He was on the outside, he could have just taken him.

Life changed immediately when she left Boggo Road. The day after Debbie packed up and left for Albion, Greer White, a Presentation nun working at Centre Ed, arranged for Debbie to increase her contact with the centre to four days a week. She was officially appointed assistant to the youth workers, a role she found extremely rewarding. She told friends she had found her 'true niche' in life at last.

Those who saw her at work already knew. 'Deb had something that connected with the young people straight away, the moment she got there,' says James Finn, a youth health worker attached to the nearby Youth and Family Service in Woodridge. 'She had no pretences, no middle class values, she didn't play games with the young people, she called a spade a spade. If they were being stupid, she'd tell them they were being stupid. As soon as she got there, she was doing good work with them.'

Around this time Debbie also met Suzi Quixley, a youth worker and human services worker who would become a major influence in her life. Quixley was running a workshop on working with young women, and was surprised when Debbie, 'just out of Boggo Road and pretty scary', insisted the agenda focus on 'professional, philosophical stuff, feminist theory and how it applied to prison and poverty and race': 'I suggested we go through what I called the bullshit stuff in the workshop, and that she and I should have a drink afterwards and continue to talk,' Quixley says. 'I think we kept drinking and talking for several nights, and haven't really stopped.'

Quixley immediately admired the way Debbie could engage in the 'minutiae of academic debate as well as communicate in the language of people around her at the time'. 'She had that street readiness, and she brought that into her communication as well as her assessment of people,' she says.

Debbie's days were filled up: she was also teaching aerobics voluntarily at the Fortitude Valley Police Youth Club, and was still running regularly. Staying physically busy kept the days rolling, but she was beginning to crave some intellectual stimulation as well. Just before her move to Albion, she had decided she would apply to be accepted as a mature age student in the faculty of social work at the University of Queensland. In reality, this was what she had been moving towards since her sentencing.

Even then, on her first day in prison, she had decided to use her time productively – the way she had done it at Wilson obviously hadn't worked, so this time she would use imprisonment to her own advantage, preferably by getting an education. The murder and its aftermath had presented a temporary derailment, but now that she had jettisoned her need for payback – and with it, her vision of herself as a creature of the system – she was free to pursue the person she might become on the outside. Gabrielle Spencer, the education officer at Boggo Road, took up Debbie's cause.

Debbie: Gabrielle really believed in education. She'd already had us doing a lot of stuff. I'd already done every TAFE course you possibly think of, so it was time to move on to uni. I chose social work because I wanted to work with other people, like I had on the Street Kids Committee, and especially with kids, stopping them ending up where we had ended up. So I wrote to the faculty at UQ and Gabrielle started to advocate on my behalf. I wasn't allowed to attend the interview myself because I was regarded as high profile, so Gabrielle went for me.

Before the end of the year, the decision was made: Debbie was in. She would take up her studies in first semester, 1992. In the meantime, she kept up her routine, which intensified when, in November, she was given release to work by the Board of Community Corrections, and was immediately appointed a full-time, paid youth worker at Centre Ed, with permission to use her own car for transport to work and for her regular weekend leave at Nana's.

Crucially, she was also attending weekly counselling sessions with Greer, who had watched Debbie struggling with her own demons in her dealings with the young people at Centre Ed. They went back over Debbie's very troubled youth and frankly examined the destructive patterns that had developed and intensified as she grew older. They talked about the difficulty of breaking those and establishing new ones in the new life Debbie was carving out for herself. For Debbie, this was enormously confrontational. Although she felt she had resolved and left behind the self-hatred and blame that accompanied her father's death, clearly there were deeply entrenched habits and ways of reacting to the world that she needed to challenge. As 1991 ended, with the prospect of freedom by the end of 1992, two frightening experiences drove this home.

> **Debbie**: I had this momentum up: I was out at the halfway house, I had uni to think about, and I was going to work at Centre Ed, where I loved working with the young people. I was going home on weekends to my kids, to Nana's. Then on my way out to Nana's one day this woman at Albion says as I'm going out the door, 'I've got a key [of marijuana] to get rid of,' and I went straight into automatic and said, 'I'll get back to you.' That's what I said, without even being aware.
>
> That night I'm lying in bed at Nana's, I've got Joshua sleeping beside me, a baby still, a little boy, and my teenage daughter sleeping on the floor and the house is quiet, and it hit me. *Fuck – I said, I'll get back to you.* It scared the shit out of me. And then I got really angry with her because she knew how hard it was trying to flip my life, so when I got back to Albion on Sunday night I said to her, 'You fuck off out of my life, I want nothing to do with you ever again, you nearly set me up a beauty.' It was lucky I only had ties with her in prison, because if I had historical ties and I'd said, I'll get back to you, the contract would have been made. Because I didn't I could walk away.

The second incident involved another woman at the halfway house who was giving Debbie a hard time, constantly insulting her and trying for a reaction. One day, Debbie lost the composure that had allowed her to ignore the woman. She chased her up a set of stairs, threatening to 'punch her through a wall', while the woman screamed and prison officers chased them both. When she finally cornered the woman, Debbie stopped. Then turned and went slowly back downstairs.

Debbie: I thought to myself, I've got to get out of here, soon, because I can feel myself going backwards. I could see I could turn violent again, belt the fuck out of someone for being a smart-arse. I had to get out of the prison system if I was going to keep going forwards. You lose the whole momentum of getting back on track. You just lose heart. I could physically and emotionally feel myself going back to my old ways, because that's who I'd been for thirty-something years.

By early 1992, she had another reason to worry: Jody, now an angry fourteen-year-old, was starting to act out her resentment at her mother's absence by repeating some of Debbie's childhood history, with truanting and temper tantrums and petty theft. Greer had included Jody, along with Debbie's mother, stepfather and grand-mother, in some family therapy sessions that appeared to have helped everyone relate better to one another. But Jody's anger remained simmering below the surface, and Debbie could feel it with each encounter they had. Jody's anger with her, with the world, was a mirror of her own at the same age. Debbie didn't like what she saw in the reflection. But Jody, of course, saw it differently:

Jody: I didn't want to live with Pat and Len. They seemed such bad stiffs to me then. My life went from party, party, party to this stiff life, and I just rebelled. That's when I first started getting into trouble, running off, stealing money from the next door neighbour. I just hated it, and wanted to be out of there. I wanted to be with Nana, and with Joshua; we should have been together. I hated him for it; because I thought he had the good life – and he did, with Nana. So my resentment was building up and up. I think keeping us apart was one of the biggest mistakes they made.

Unbeknownst to her mother, her grandmother or anyone else at the time, there was another reason for Jody's anger and displacement. She would hang on to the secret for years, ashamed and without any real understanding of its effects on her. According to Jody, Arthur, the same relative Debbie had come to despise after he delivered her back into custody as a teenager, had been sexually abusing her while Debbie was in prison. At first she had been terrified, unable to escape him, but after a while she began to fight. It was then, she says, that he threatened to turn his attentions to her little brother. She knew he was serious. To protect Joshua, she would be silent while Arthur continued to rape her, she told her mother much later, for years.

Debbie wasn't eligible for parole until October 1992. She knew she had little chance of being considered for earlier release, despite her spotless record as a prisoner and her reputation for hard work and honesty. Nevertheless, as her terror for both her children and herself mounted, she sat down in January and wrote an application for special parole. There was no way she could use her fear of regressing as an argument, but there were authentic and pressing issues about the children that could, with a lot of luck, sway the panel of community representatives and the head of the Community Corrections Board, Jim Kennedy. The most obvious was Nana's advancing age and infirmity, along with the increasing responsibilities of looking after a child who was now school-aged. Joe had been paroled and had left Brisbane on his motorbike without contacting her, so the board would be able to see she had real concerns about her children's welfare. Debbie talked it over with Greer, who was soon to leave Centre Ed to travel and study in South America and Boston, and who was also keen to see Debbie resettled before her departure.

The two letters – one from Greer and one from Debbie – that arrived at the office of the Board were powerfully written and persuasive. Greer wrote of the 'consistency and great courage' Debbie had shown during the process of confronting her own destructive patterns and the dark places in her past. She had identified her own strengths and weaknesses, she said, and decided what she wanted from life. 'As a result she is determined not to return to her old ways but to shape a new future for herself and her two children. I am under no illusions that this will not prove diffcult for Deborah but she is a woman of action not just words and has a courage and determination far above the ordinary', she wrote.

Greer also backed up Debbie's concern about 'her grandmother's health and her son's care', explaining she had witnessed Nana's care of Joshua and 'I assure you she does have grounds for concern'. Jody too, she said, had been hurt by her mother's past behaviour but was yearning to live with her mother again. 'Deborah will not have an easy time taking up again after two years absence the nurturing of her two children. She is determined however to do this to the best of her ability and has named this as her first priority. She is very aware of the damage and hurt her past behaviour has caused her children. The children will both benefit by an early return of Deborah to the role of full time mother.'

Debbie's letter is not as polished but is no less compelling. Over four pages, she tells the story of her life to date with powerful simplicity. Looking at the document fourteen years later, the reader can see the varied talents of an intelligent, street-wise woman who might lack formal education but who is familiar with the strategic art of persuasion. Using a deft mixture of starkness and low-key emotion, it is a letter written by a person in the midst of discovery – of who she is, where she has been, the direction her new road might take her. A person not entirely able to disguise how desperate she is to continue down that road.

She speaks of her troubled childhood, her incarceration in Wilson, how she was blamed for the death of her father. 'I have carried this guilt . . . for many years and it has only been because of recent counselling . . . that I have come to terms with his death and realise that I should never [have] carried this guilt. Due to this guilt as a child I continued to commit offences and was in and out of institutions', she writes. On the matter of drug trafficking: 'I started to sell marijuana to pay for his [Joe's] habit. The situation of selling drugs snowballed and I lost sight of everything that I believed in . . . After my arrest I was so glad because it gave me an out of a situation that I thought I had no control of.'

She goes on: 'During my incarceration I witnessed a death of another inmate. The impact of how a life was taken so quickly and violently made me realise what was happening to my life and that I have to change for myself, my children and my family. I sought support from many people, one was George Brand . . . He gave me the courage, support and strength to begin this change.'

After detailing her involvement with Centre Ed and her work with the Police Youth Club, the courses she had completed and the counselling she was undergoing, Debbie came to the point of the letter:

'I am applying for early parole because of the health of my grand-mother. She is 71 years of age and has been caring for my son Joshua since my incarceration in 1989. Joshua is now 5 years old and begins primary school this year.

My grandmother has emphysema and doctors have told her that it cannot be cured as it is in an advanced stage. She is finding difficulty in caring for my son. The distance that she will have to walk to and from school is over many hills and this causes her great pain in the chest . . . My daughter is in the care of my mother and stepfather [and] they are also getting on in age. My stepfather is 70 years old and my mother is in her late 50s and find it difficult in bringing up a teenager.

My husband, Joe Kilroy has not been in contact with the children or myself for many months . . . Since he was paroled he has made minimal contact with our children and does not support them in any way. I realise that our relationship is over and I will be applying for a divorce once released.

I feel that I am at a stage of suspension and not able to progress any further. I am carrying great stress because of my grandmother's health and worry for my children. I have spoken to Mrs Fraser [manager, Albion] regarding my progress in my sentence and she also feels that I can not make an advancement whilst here . . .

Even in the context of sentence management at the time, the last paragraph of Debbie's letter is audacious and risky. Read by an unsympathetic board, it could easily be written off as a cheeky scam by a prisoner who, with an original sentence of six years, was already progressing swiftly through the system. But – not for the first time in her life – luck was on her side. Astonishingly, the Community Corrections Board believed the arguments for releasing Debbie were sound. On 9 March 1992, a full seven months before she would even become eligible to apply, Debbie was granted parole.

Debbie: No one had ever got early parole, and I was thinking, I'm not going to get this. But one day, about seven in the morning – I was dressed to go to Centre Ed to work, and I was going to uni that afternoon – the chair of the board rang up. I picked up the phone and he said, 'How are you going? What are you doing today?' And I was playing it real cool because I wasn't getting my hopes up, so I said, 'I'm going to work, going to uni, going to the gym.' He said, 'So you're fairly busy? You probably won't have time to pack your bags then, will you? Do you want to pack your bags?' I said, 'Well, that's up to you, isn't it?' And then it came: 'Well, if you want to pack your bags you can leave this afternoon.'

I turned around and walked down the stairs and these women were standing there, supposedly staunch women, and I said, 'I've got fuckin' parole.' I think the tears must have been rolling down my face. But most of them just ignored me, they were pissed that I got parole. Only one of them said, 'Well, I'm not going to help you pack because I'm fuckin' jealous,' and I said, fine, and one of the screws helped me pack. That's how the system works. You're loved when you're in the shit. Everyone's so individualised, they don't see that if someone gets something, it could be to their advantage down the line. So I packed my car and drove to Nana's.

But the elation was short-lived. Several days later, the phone rang at Nana's during the quiet of early evening. Debbie was getting Joshua ready for bed. The caller was one of the prison officers from Albion, leaking information about a meeting during which a parole officer had announced she was going to get Debbie's parole 'pulled'. The parole officer, apparently, believed Debbie had no right to early release, and was going to do everything in her power to have it revoked.

Debbie flew into a rage. How dare she? Next morning, after phoning Greer, the two women drove directly into the city and headed for the office of the board of community corrections:

Debbie: I got into the lift to Jim Kennedy's office, and – it was so funny – this same parole officer got into the lift at the same time. I said to her, 'Hey, you fuckin' dog, you better come with me and talk about the little meeting you had last night in the prison.' She asked me what I was talking about. 'Well, you're going to get my parole pulled, are you? Let's go and talk to the parole board now.' She just said calm down, calm down, but I was irate, I was flippin' out.

We get out of the lift and I walk straight into Kennedy's office – there was no security then, nothing – and off I go. And

Kennedy's saying, calm down, but I'm going ballistic. He listens and says to this officer, 'Is this true?' She said, 'Yes, we did have a meeting –' and Kennedy cuts in and says, 'The parole board makes the decision about who gets parole, not you. Now you can go.' When she leaves, he says, 'Debbie, if anyone's going to be pulling parole it's us, not her.' Going back down in the lift she's apologising. But I just wanted her out of my face.

With that last hurdle cleared up, Debbie was finally able to set her sights on surviving the next few years. Although she was elated to be free, she knew the seriously hard work was now about to begin. She had to start living the life she had promised herself: one without the old support networks of drugs, criminal contacts, violence and heavy drinking. From now on, life would consist of work, fitness, caring for her children, counselling, and staying as far away from all her old friends and haunts as possible. All that, with the responsibilities of single parenthood thrown in, and two children who were confused, needy, and uncertain of her and of each other.

Debbie had always known that as soon as she was released, she would need to make a new home for herself and her children away from Nana. She had flagged this in her parole application. Despite – and because of – the love Nana had lavished on Josh, Debbie believed she had to physically remove her family to re-establish her role as the mother figure. This was very important to her.

In her counselling sessions, she had realised how divisive Nana's influence had been in her own childhood, how it had eroded her own mother's efforts at discipline along with any need for Debbie to face the consequences of her own actions. She adored Nana, and was aware of the enormous efforts her grandmother had made while she was in prison. But she had to get away.

She also needed to disprove Nana's theory that although men were useless, women couldn't make it without them. According to Debbie, this was Nana's mantra: 'blokes are bastards, blokes are useless', then, in the next breath: 'but you need a bloke to look after you, you can't live without a man in your life'.

'It was that double standard,' Debbie says, looking back. 'And I actually swallowed that for a long time, that I needed a bloke to survive. I don't know why I did, considering how strong I was. But when I got out of prison it was about making it by myself. Proving to myself that I could do it without a man, because I'd always had a man in my life. Proving that I could hold down a job, raise these children, pay the rent, get an education – and do it all legally. Without doing crime. I figured I could get into a routine like all the other vegies [straight people] in the world. If those vegies could do it, I could do it too.'

By the time Debbie was released on parole, she had decided her marriage to Joe was over. She had told him as much. For a while he insisted that it would all be fine, that he wanted them back together, but Debbie stood firm. She needed time on her own to sort through her emotions, through the feelings of hate she still harboured about the trial and the sentence and the violence that had preceded it.

'You have to remember,' she says now, 'that none of my primary relationships at that stage were ever going to be "normal". Whatever "normal" is, institutions and violence don't breed it in relationships. Joe and I were so damaged by life by then, and there was this big gulf between us.'

So Joe would come to pick up Joshua and would be greeted with grunts from Debbie, and they would have the kind of short, staccato conversations familiar to anyone who has ever endured the process of handing children over between access visits.

Joe had been getting on with his own life. He'd set some goals too, the highest of which was a return to A-grade football. He achieved that in 1991. At season's end – and with Debbie's rejection still ringing in his ears – he walked off the field at Lang Park, climbed onto his Harley, and drove out of Brisbane. Over the next few months he would ride the country's back roads, looking for somewhere that felt like home. Eventually, his search brought him to Gladstone, in central Queensland. There were family connections there, and he liked the vibe.

Within weeks of being paroled, Debbie found a house to rent in Greenslopes, in Brisbane's inner south. It was close to Jody's school and to Pat's house in nearby Ekibin, and a fifteen-minute drive to Centre Ed. She arranged for Nana and Josh to spend a couple of nights together every week, either at Greenslopes or at Kedron. There was another small hiccup when her parole officer told her that a condition of her release was that she continued to live with Nana, resulting in a flurry of letters to and from the board about the best interests of Debbie and her children.

Eventually, in early April, the board approved the move, and with great excitement Debbie, Jody and Joshua set up house together in Dunellan Street.

The excitement didn't last long. Despite Debbie's efforts and some intense counselling, Jody's unresolved anger at her mother boiled over soon after the move. She began to act it out in small ways at first, provoking fights with her mother and little brother, swearing, refusing to go to school. Debbie tried not to react – the situation was fragile enough – but a reaction was what Jody wanted.

Debbie: I'd be lying on a mattress on the floor – we had no furniture – with Josh lying on top of me, reading a book, and she'd come in and spit at me. Or she'd call Josh out of the room, and he'd innocently go to his sister, and she'd pour chilli down his throat. That time I did react. Joshua was screaming and I said, get out of the house. She was screaming abuse at me and I said, just get out until you've calmed down. So out she went and smashed all the windows at the front of the house as she went. Screaming, 'Bitch!' Everyone must have thought we were raving lunatics, because that was just ongoing.

One day, she was standing outside the Police Youth Club where I was taking an aerobics class, and she's screaming at me from the footpath. So I came out and said, 'Get in the car, we're going home.' But she just kept screaming and screaming so I backhanded her. Then she ran into a car yard nearby and yelled, 'That woman's trying to murder me!' I said, 'I'm her mother,' but she's going on, 'She's trying to murder me!' Oh God. I said, 'Just get in the car or I *will* kill you.'

By this time, Greer White was overseas, leaving Debbie with the option of seeing a male counsellor at the Sunnybank Family Support Centre, Mac Hamilton. Mac was (and is) a Gestalt therapist, but at the time Debbie had no idea what kind of therapy he used and didn't particularly care. Greer had recommended him, so she was willing to give him a go.

Mac clearly recalls their first meeting: 'Deb sat in one of the three armchairs in my counselling room and looked expectantly at me. I can't remember who spoke first, probably I did, but I started to establish from the outset whether she wanted to come to see me or whether she was there under duress. In her own inimitable way she told me that she trusted Greer and "if she says you're okay, then you're okay",' he says.

One of the central tenets in Gestalt therapy, in Mac's view, is that people change because they want to change: perhaps their lifestyle, or a 'less than useful' learned behaviour that they carry with them from their past. A person needs to know what they want to change and to believe they have choices that will allow them to make life-altering decisions. Above all, he says, Gestalt therapy is about taking personal responsibility for decisions, and understanding that past decisions were based on the best information available at the time, along with support or lack of it.

Mac isn't sure what made Gestalt appealing to Debbie at the time, only that, in the next six months, she came to trust and embrace the therapy and entered her own process of change. He knew, though, that this process had begun earlier, when she broke down during her speech inside Boggo Road: 'That was her first big breakthrough. She had begun to reconnect with her emotions again, and broke down in tears, something which was unacceptable in the prison culture of denial and violence. I was – and continue to be – touched by this incident. I believe one of the reasons Deb was able to work as well as she did in therapy was her ability to express her feelings about her past and present situation. She could confront her own issues with ease.'

Not so Jody, however. Although all the family attended sessions with Mac (including Joe, when he visited the children) Jody was obviously not responding. She'd begun to refuse to attend school, communicated with her mother only through abusive references to her as a 'slut' or a 'fuckin' cunt', and finally began to make allegations that Debbie was violent.

Jody: I was really acting out then. I used to call her terrible names. I was taking off from home, drinking, abusing her, going nightclubbing, driving cars, stealing handbags and even claiming domestic violence with the coppers. I just wanted her to pay, to punish her. Looking back now, if I could turn one thing back, it would be the way I treated my mother then.

But at the time, she was hell-bent on revenge. She took her claims of physical abuse to the state department for families, where a case was opened. Despite Debbie's protestations, and representations from Mac, who, as Jody's counsellor, believed the claims were imagined, the department decided to remove Jody to a foster home. 'They said they wouldn't take the word of a drug trafficker. Jody had said I assaulted her, and they believed her,' Debbie says. 'But a week after she was placed, she told them she wanted to go home. They said she couldn't, because her mother assaulted her, and she told them she'd lied.

'I was so pissed off that no one would believe that I hadn't bashed her, except those close to me. The department assumed that because I'd been to prison, I'd been a bad mother. I'd never been a bad mother. But I was on parole, and I had to be very careful about what I was doing. Jody would come home with stuff that was obviously stolen – car keys for instance – that I just couldn't have in the house. And there was still Josh to look after.'

Two alternative placements followed, both of which Jody fled. The first was with Joe, who by then had moved from Gladstone to Caloundra, on the Sunshine Coast, where he had a contract to play club football, and back to Brisbane. Again, Jody refused to go to school, preferring to borrow cars that she drove without a licence or any knowledge of driving. Debbie received at least one call from a friend who reported she'd been following Jody as she careered around the streets. You better stop her, before she kills someone, Debbie was told. If she wasn't driving she was showing up constantly at the Black Uhlans clubhouse.

The second placement followed a year later, and would prove far more disastrous. Despite a total absence from her life, Jody's natural father, Matthew, applied for her custody. Debbie was outraged. The idea that the courts would allow Matthew – virtually unknown to her, and a heroin addict – to take responsibility for a wayward fifteen-year-old was beyond belief. 'I sat there in the courtroom, livid. I wanted to kill him. But they did it, they handed her over. And the very first morning she's with him she catches him with a needle in his arm,' she says.

With that, something tipped over in Jody's troubled mind. She'd been living on the wild side, regularly being picked up by police and arrested, and had already spent one stint inside John Oxley

Detention Centre, a new youth centre at Wacol, built to cope with increasing numbers of incarcerated children. But now, her anger etched up a notch. She packed up and ran, heading for the Gold Coast and ports south, leaving a trail of fraudulent credit card transactions that were the beginnings of her first successful scam. Debbie had no idea where she was at any given time. 'She wouldn't call me because she knew she was in deep trouble about the lies she'd told about being abused by me,' she says. 'But she'd often call Nana.'

Mac remembers this time in terms of Debbie's own growing awareness of the reality of relationships. Jody's behaviour was a catalyst, he believes, for Debbie's realisation that 'she could not live up to the expectations of others and that they would not live up to hers'. That didn't, however, prevent her ongoing concern as a mother for what was happening to her child, he says – or stifle her still ebullient sense of humour. 'She's got more talent than I ever had,' she told him wryly when the credit card scam was uncovered.

While Jody was challenging her maternal love and commitment, Debbie was also struggling hard with her own sense of self, of who this new Debbie Kilroy might be now that the chrysalis was falling away. In her old life, she had defined herself by the blame she had taken for her father's death, and by the friends whose behaviour and attitudes mirrored and validated her own. But now that she had begun to separate herself from both, who might she be?

Apart from Mac and the friends she was slowly making at Centre Ed – all 'straight', all 'vegies' – there was no one she could measure herself against, no one she trusted. All her trust had been in the mates she had been told to stay away from, to leave behind, if she was to make a clean break from crime and drugs. She'd lost all her reference points, all the ordinary, daily things that subliminally remind us who we are.

Debbie: The importance of severing ties when I got out was tied to survival. I knew that if I kept one link in that vulnerable time, and then if something happened, I would have to go with my loyalty to those old links. So it was about staying strong, and it's the most isolating, lonely place I've ever been in my whole life. I had to get strong and stand on my own two feet, and then I could reconnect with those relationships, but on my terms, not on the terms of the culture. So I was told to make new friends – what, friends with vegies? I'd never had friends like that, I thought there was no way in a million years I could even have a conversation with vegies, with stiffs. Or that they would relate to me, or like me.

People said, you have to be different, you have to change. Well, change to what? Have I got to be wimpish, say nothing, sit in a corner and have no mates? I started to think I couldn't do it. I was getting these massive headaches because, with every conversation I had, I was thinking, what will I say, how will I say it so I don't freak them out? I'd always been upfront, honest, straight, so I'd be thinking, if I said it this way or that, is that going to freak them out? Or is there another way? It was driving me insane. Every time I met someone I'd think, should I dress differently, interact differently? I started to think, fuck this, I'm going back to my mates, at least I can communicate with them.

It would take some time to figure it all out, and she can still remember the day, a year or so later, that it all came together in her head:

Debbie: I was talking to Greer, saying, I don't know who the fuck I am, I feel like this empty person, I'm trying to be someone I'm not and it doesn't feel comfortable. It's not working. And Greer just said, well, you don't have to change *everything*. And I thought, oh my God, you mean to say I can keep some of me? I can keep myself, my inner self, I don't have to sell it? Oh, great! So that's what I did, I kept everything – all I didn't keep was doing crime.

And I also had to calm down, because people would always say I was quite abrupt – I'd just say things, smack bang, and they'd have a bad reaction. I had to reframe that, think of the kind of impact something would have, whether it needed to be said or not. This was all tied up with trusting people, too. That was a problem. I didn't trust anyone so I'd just throw something out there to test them, to see whether they were going to run out the door or not. And most of them did, of course.

Trust was part of the huge task of relearning emotion that Debbie had to face now. The culture of prison dictates that trust and love are unconditional only for those in the inner circle, that is, those who have proved they are staunch, inside prison or out. You are either 'sweet', or you're not. There is no middle ground. People who have never experienced this, either first hand or by association, find its black and white nature difficult to understand, and the approach hard-line and extreme. But prison is an extreme experience, and women who are bound by it are *always* bound by it. It is a link between friends, says Debbie, that will never be severed, 'no matter where we are on earth, we've been there and experienced it, and we know we'll look after each other till our last breath, because it's about loyalty and commitment'.

And while that would never change, Debbie's challenge now was to find that middle ground with people on the outside. She had to take the gigantic step of offering tentative trust and friendship straight up, and giving others the chance to prove themselves 'sweet'. This would be more difficult than she could ever have imagined. Even Mac was kept at a distance for a while, though she liked him very much from the beginning. But liking someone was a far cry from trusting. And what she was just starting to acknowledge was that for her, trust was all tied up with love.

But not the love of children. She was clear on that even then: 'That's different. I loved my children first. I've always loved them because they were in my body, and when they come from your body, they're part of your life, your blood, your breath, your being. But relationships . . . For me, anyone who even said the word "love" was suspect. I would have said "I love you" to someone without any real awareness, because I didn't know what it meant, except that I'm going to get done over. If someone said they loved you, you'd know they were going to hurt you really, really badly,' she says.

The major task, then, was to reconnect to 'normal' emotion, something she knew she had never felt. It would take a long time: 'I had to un-learn all the things I'd learned from childhood, all the violence, all the desensitisation. And it was like taking off a bullet-proof vest, taking off my protection. In the group training sessions with Mac, people couldn't believe that for most of my life I'd barely shed a tear about anything. I'd look at them crying and think, *sooks*. And then one day I had this one tear, maybe two, and for me that was like sixty-five bucket loads.'

Down at Centre Ed, meanwhile, Debbie was having no trouble connecting with the kids. They loved her. Unlike some of the 'vegies' in her life, they liked her straight-talking approach and her easy way of dealing with issues and problems. According to James Finn, the young people felt they could trust her – no small thing for those who had been let down badly by the system, by families, by schools and even friends. They felt comfortable in her company, enough to play along with her own adolescent sense of humour and fun, which often came out on the frequent camps held throughout the year.

On one of these, a bike ride from Stanthorpe to Boonah, Debbie 'laughed till she cried' when one of the boys fell off his bike and into a big, fresh cow pat. Inevitably, cow pats became the weapon of choice for the expedition, appearing on bike seats and helmets or hurled from the back of the pack. Debbie copped her fair share, but kept her counsel until an awards ceremony after the camp, when all the kids received a gift. Two of the boys were thrilled to receive a 'beautifully iced round cake' from Debbie, which they came within centimetres of eating before she revealed what the main ingredient was.

But they saw the other side of Debbie, too. At the end of 1992, the girls decided to make themselves dresses to wear to the annual Christmas party. They carefully chose designs and fabrics and laboured for weeks cutting, sewing and fitting, and helped and advised each other without the usual signs of rancour and rage. On the afternoon of the 'graduation' (as the girls were now calling it) Debbie arranged with them to meet up to get dressed together and to do their hair and makeup. There was lots of 'loud music, lipstick and laughing', lots of mutual compliments and no comments about boyfriends, another staff member, Lorraine Brown, recalls in a short history of Centre Ed, *One Step Beyond*:

It is hard to explain but something very deep and significant was happening. Debbie had chilled some bottles of non-alcoholic wine, and when everyone was ready she produced the long-stemmed wine glasses. They toasted each other, and Debbie toasted them and told them what I think they already realised: that they looked beautiful because they felt beautiful because they were beautiful deep down inside, and that they were never to forget the feeling of that moment because this was the truth of themselves.

Getting to the end of the year was cause for celebration for Debbie, too. She had survived her first nine months as a free woman and had completed her first year of part-time social work studies. Although she was blissfully unaware that the following year would bring the heartbreak of Jody's flight from Brisbane and her crime spree, Debbie was still hoping, in December 1992, that her daughter would settle, and that the ongoing counselling with Mac would help resolve things.

The most exciting prospect of the year rose out of a conversation with a youth worker with the Youth and Family Service, Gabe Scattini, who Debbie had met at the Beenleigh courthouse when they were both supporting young people on charges. They were bemoaning the absence of support for young women in prison, and together decided to approach the youth detention centres about establishing a support group. But the obstacles thrown up by the system were huge and, angry and disappointed, they abandoned the plan.

Then the comic-book light bulb flashed on in Debbie's head. Like many other women had done in the past, on her release from prison she had promised those left behind that she would be back to support them, to make noise if it was necessary, from the outside. She knew that the door slammed shut by those in charge of youth detention might just be opened by the man still in charge at Brisbane Women's, George Brand. He had, after all, been pivotal in her own move to remake her life, and there was no reason to think he wouldn't now help her to help others. Here was the chance to fulfil her promise of going back into Boggo Road.

> **Debbie**: I said to the women, I'll be back. And one thing I really believe is that the one thing you've got in this world is your word, and nothing else. And if I can't keep my word, I'm fuckin' nobody. I'm really strong about that. When I say I'm not giving up on someone, I don't give up on them, and when I say I'm going to do something, I do it. I said *I'll be back.*

The embryonic cells of Sisters Inside were about to be formed.

11

Just Another Mob of
Ex-druggies and Prostitutes

George Brand: It wasn't a very popular move, letting Deb and her friends come into the prison to have meetings. The staff said, they're just another mob of ex-druggies and prostitutes. They didn't want them there. But to my mind, that's what we were about, helping people. I said, if it just does a little bit of good, it's worth having. They're not going to create a major break-out or anything. I had a lot of heart-to-hearts with the staff about it, but they thought it was just a group of trouble-makers.

George Brand's faith in Debbie had not diminished. When she and Gabe Scattini first approached him about forming an advocacy group inside the prison, he saw it could be the logical extension to the work he had been trying to do, and was willing to face down sceptical staff to give it a try. He told Debbie, if you've got a reasonable message to deliver, you're welcome. At that stage, Debbie was unsure what the message might be. She didn't really know what they might achieve. She just knew she was fulfilling a promise.

When they first went into Boggo Road as a group, Debbie, Gabe and another woman, Kate Harrison, joined some long-termers and lifers who had been meeting inside for some time. Kate Harrison, who worked on a prisoners' show on the university-based radio station 4ZZZ, had been visiting the prison over the previous five years, running music workshops and guitar lessons, and knew the system well. She had also been involved with the Combined Community Agencies – a loose grouping of agencies that had worked inside the prison – in the aftermath of the murder. She and Debbie had an established, but separate, relationship with the long-termers, which eased the way for others from the outside, although mutual trust within the group was by no means immediate.

Scattini remembers an early meeting in the courtyard outside the chapel at Boggo Road when the outsiders were inducted in a kind of bizarre ritual. 'Everyone smoked and we laughed a lot, but they were clearly trying to work out whether we could be trusted,' she says. 'One of the things they made us do was play bum coin. It sounds silly, but it was quite bonding. They'd put an empty can on the ground. And we had to insert a one dollar coin, tuck it inside our cheeks and then squat over the can and release it. It was a very humiliating sort of bond but it really broke the ice. We were on their turf, after all.'

Muscles and commitment tested, they then got down to talking. From the outset, it was clear that the new group wanted to provide services, to raise awareness of prison issues, and to advocate for the human rights of women prisoners. But what kinds of services were needed? And what kind of organisation was it going to be? In those first meetings, identifying the gaps in the system seemed a priority, along with establishing women on the inside as part of the management of the new organisation, with an equal place at the table. Debbie and the women on the outside wanted the whole experience to be empowering for women inside. They were all just as insistent that the new group would operate strictly outside the Corrective Services Commission, and thus keep its credibility among all prisoners.

Credibility was one thing, however, and faith was another. Although there was enthusiasm among the long-termers for the ideas and plans Debbie was putting forward, it took some time to generate optimism that any of them would come to fruition.

> Fred: I was very reluctant at those first meetings. I was – am – Sister Saint Cynical, and I thought, who is going to listen to us? It'll never work. And Deb said, well, you've got to stand up for something, otherwise you're going to fall down for nothing, Drac. I thought, all right, but I'm going to play devil's advocate, anyway.
>
> So I did, and she'd howl me down. She was like this power-

house coming in, this powerhouse of 'do good, do right by the women', and 'I remember where I came from'. And that was the most important thing. After all those do-gooders coming in, here was this woman saying, yeah, well, I had a really rough time in prison, but I remember where I came from and I remember who you are. We weren't so close then, but a couple of meetings later, something clicked. She walked in and we gave each other a big hug. And it was just – click.

At first there was some argument about whether the new, as yet unnamed organisation would run as a collective. But Debbie was adamant: that wouldn't work. The backgrounds of those involved were too different. A hierarchy, even if it was one with a consensus style, was necessary. And the voluntary management committee, made up of women both inside and outside prison, needed to operate separately from the paid workers who would run the proposed programs. The first and most urgent of these, the women decided, would be the provision of sexual assault counselling.

To help identify the gaps in the system, the group conducted a survey of prisoners' backgrounds and needs. Apart from a low rate of literacy, and the varying problems of Indigenous women and those from non-English-speaking backgrounds, the survey revealed an astonishing 89 percent of women inside had been sexually assaulted. This galvanised the group's thinking and approach: applying for program funding was now an urgent priority. And to do that they needed a name.

'Sisters Inside' was the short, snappy version of suggestions like 'Sisters Behind the Walls' and 'Chicks Behind Bricks' that the original group toyed with while they worked out how this new organisation might work. No one remembers who put it up; the name simply grew out of the endless, ongoing discussions. But they all liked its powerful simplicity, and its quiet reference to the group's origins and real ownership.

The act of naming gave them new confidence and energy. For the next eighteen months, they set about investigating every possible avenue of funding, and taught themselves how to write professional and persuasive applications. And tentatively, they began to take a public stand on the issues that had brought them all together. Politicians, journalists and people outside the small world of prisons heard the name 'Sisters Inside' for the first time.

Throughout this period, Debbie continued her full-time work at Centre Ed as well as her part-time social work studies. She was also playing touch football every week, after organising a Centre Ed team to join the Logan Touch Football competition, looking after Joshua and trying to keep tabs on Jody. All this while still trying to come to grips with her new identity, her brand new open heart.

The Gestalt counselling was helping to unlock some of the emotions and vulnerability she had so carefully locked away as a child. She was beginning to see how women in prison might benefit from its here-and-now approach, and from its emphasis on personal responsibility:

Debbie: Gestalt is working with people where they're at, now, and that's why I liked it. They don't say, tell me what happened when you were three. It's about dealing with the here and now, which is connected back, for sure. Women inside like it because of that, because they've all been boxed in by psychiatrists and psychologists, and this isn't about a box. You can go anywhere and everywhere, start where you want, finish where you want.

In fact, Debbie developed enough faith in the therapy that, along with Greer, she decided to embark on the required two and a half years of training to become a qualified Gestalt therapist. As well as the theoretical elements, Debbie had to work hard on all the issues she and Mac had identified in her own past behaviour. Mac believes she did this so thoroughly that she became a 'highly effective counsellor':

One of the key issues she needed to overcome was her lack of confidence as distinct from 'front'. At first meeting, Deb presents as a force or a presence, someone to be reckoned with. Like everyone else, she needs to feel reassured that what she is doing is okay and that she is doing it to the best of her ability.

I see Centre Ed as the place where she started to come to terms with her own innate ability to deal with people and to be a mentor to disadvantaged youths. Instead of being held up as an example of someone no one should follow, she began to be praised for the constructive things she was doing.

Debbie has a good ear. But above all she has the personal life experience that allows her to empathise with many in dire trouble.

Somewhere in the middle of her busyness, her thoughts kept turning to Joe. By this time – 1994 – she felt she had proved to herself that she could make it on her own, and had finally put to bed Nana's dictum about the necessity of men. She even risked feeling proud of herself. But there were residual concerns about her marriage that wouldn't leave her alone. The most dominant was the ongoing hatred she harboured for Joe, and the unease she felt with it.

> **Debbie**: I did feel like I hated him then. I felt like he'd done me in. He was living up north, and he'd talk about us getting back together, and I'd just say, I hate your guts. But one day it just hit me, I don't know how: it was the behaviour I hated, not the man. There is this fine line between love and hate, and I figured out that I loved Joe, but hated the behaviour. When I could define that, that's when things started to move between us.

Debbie's epiphany was just one of the catalysts that led to the Kilroys' slow and tentative process of reconciliation. Around this time, Debbie abruptly took Joshua out of the local Catholic primary school he was attending after an argument that followed the sudden death of the school's principal. Joshua liked the principal, and knew him well: whenever he was taunted about his parents in the school-yard, the resultant scrum would see Joshua dispatched to the office. One way or another, the two spent a lot of time together, which they both seemed to enjoy, according to Deb. But when, in Joshua's fourth year, the principal suffered a massive heart attack and died, a teacher decided to lock Joshua in the library 'for his own good'. Later, a staff member told Debbie that she 'had better keep Joshua out of school for a week so that he did not get the blame for the principal's death'. Debbie was outraged. How could anyone suggest the mere presence of a seven-year-old child could prompt the death of a mature man? There were too many ghostly echoes of her own experiences at Wilson. She decided to remove him from the school.

Coincidentally, she had to attend a week-long camp with the

Centre Ed students, so Josh went to stay with Joe at Caloundra. On her return, Joe drove Joshua back to Brisbane, and he and Debbie began to talk. The long process of renegotiation began with discussions around violence. If their relationship was to resume, they decided, there would be no more violence between them, not one raised hand:

Debbie: I talked to him about Dad dying, and told him I knew now that I hadn't killed him. So I wouldn't be pushing any buttons to get a reaction and to get punished, because I no longer believed I deserved it. I didn't kill my father. So if you raise one hand to me, you're out. Joe wasn't really a violent person – but he had to take responsibility for the violence he'd inflicted.

He would say I was violent, but when it's put in context, he's the man, and in this world he has more power. I might have smacked him in the mouth a few times but that was nothing compared to what he did, and my fear of that. That's the power a man has over a woman. But obviously I had changed a lot, and he had changed, he was a lot more settled. And you could see that Josh needed his father and mother on a lot of levels.

Joe: I'd written to her just about every week in jail, but only got about two [letters] back from her. This one never gives anything away. I didn't know what she was thinking, she didn't tell me jackshit, so I just went away. Got on with my life. Then we had this conversation when I brought Josh back from Caloundra. When she told me she'd figured out the shit about her father I felt relief, because I felt I'd been wearing all the anger. So as soon as she owned all that shit, fuck I was happy. Because at least half of that button-pushing, imaginary stuff was wiped out. I could see it, a lot of the anger was gone. And so was mine. I was able to acknowledge and take responsibility for how violent I'd been, and for what I'd done. I had no excuse. I'd worked through my own issues and addressed them. There would be no more violence. I'm dirty it took ten years to work out though. Ten years of grief.

And then there was the matter of the missing finger. Through her work and training in Gestalt, Debbie was learning about her own habits and patterns, and the way these had adversely affected her emotional reactions in the past. One of the emotions she had buried was her grief over the loss of her finger, and the unresolved anger over the way it was lost.

> **Debbie**: I was learning about how I had protected myself. I could see I had steel doors in my head that just slammed shut, so no one could go there. One of the things I worked through was body awareness, body images, and I had this vivid visual in my head – it felt so real – that Joe had my finger in his back pocket. I wanted it back, so I had to go through this process of taking it back, getting it. And when I did I could let it go, let it resolve. I had to take it out of his pocket, and put it in my pocket. It wasn't about fitting it back on, because it can't be. It was about the fact that, in my head, he had ripped it off, he was responsible, and he's kept it all these years. I wanted it back.

Ironically, the reconciliation with Joe, and Debbie's willingness to expose her own vulnerability, coincided with yet another immense temptation to return to desensitisation mode: her daughter's apprehension and imprisonment for fraud. Despite all her better efforts, the terrible cycle of generational incarceration was about to be visited on her own family.

Apart from her credit card scam, Jody – now fifteen years old – had also run into trouble for impersonating police officers, as well as theft: all crimes of deception. 'I loved money, and I didn't really care how I got it,' Jody recalls now. 'And money also meant getting away from them.' Finally picked up in Sydney, Jody was incarcerated once more at Yasmar, a detention centre. On a trip south for football, Joe and Debbie visited her – at Joe's suggestion. Debbie's anger at her daughter was still too fresh. 'Joe's always been the "yes" man for me,' Jody says. 'Mum's the "no" woman. I always go to Joe first, for help or for money or if I've done something. I always ask for Joe if I'm ringing from the cop-shop. I say, *can you just tell Mum . . .*'

The deep hurt Debbie felt from Jody's behaviour would not go away. It was exacerbated, too, by Jody's refusal to allow her mother into her heart and mind, to confide in her or trust her.

'She was in detention down south for a long time then, but she would come and stay on home detention. She didn't want anything to do with me though, and I was traumatised by her behaviour,' she says. 'I kept it close to my heart, as mothers do when their kids are in trouble. You just feel powerless and hurt.'

Debbie's learning curve – in both the personal and professional spheres – paralleled the growth of Sisters Inside as it gradually found its feet as a professional organisation. It quickly became obvious that Debbie was and would be the nerve centre of the organisation, because of the implicit trust invested in her by women inside and prison management, and because her leadership skills, confidence and charisma were already attracting admiration and support for the work Sisters had set out to do.

But she had been careful, from the beginning, to pace herself, knowing she had to acquire a certain degree of confidence in her outside life to make revisiting the prison possible. She knew she had to have her feet planted solidly in her new life, and to feel unre-servedly that 'home' was on the outside, not in prison. The early meetings of SIS, as it became known, at Boggo Road were difficult for her for that reason; she felt the insidious familiarity, almost comfort, of the place, and interacted with the women as if she was still living inside, along with them. It would take her a while to let go of the institutionalisation she had absorbed since childhood.

Her personal growth also affected the way SIS operated in those first couple of years, in some very significant ways:

Debbie: It had been mainly focused around the long-termers and lifers because that's the group I was part of, that was the dynamic. But after we got funding, and then staff, we knew staff weren't going to be working much with long-termers and lifers because they would only connect with me. So the dynamic had to change in regard to acknowledging short-termers, which is against prison culture. Short-termers are whingers. So we had to say, no, these are women we need to be involved with too, no matter how long they're serving, all trauma is trauma.

I had to change my thinking on that and so did the long-termers. Before it was set up so it was one group against the other, you know, short-termers stay away, but we changed it to focus on the system. The system is the enemy, not each other. It was difficult at first because that's the environment they're living in day to day.

They'd be going off about short-termers getting this or that or whingeing and I'd say, yeah, well, what are you in here for, slitting someone's throat? Well, they didn't. I'd have to throw the reality in, because they end up forgetting what they're in there for. They're on one level, and they compare themselves to someone who hasn't paid a traffic fine. And they say, oh yeah, I suppose.

The first funding granted to Sisters Inside came through in early 1994. Debbie, Gabe, Kate Harrison and two local Murri women, Melissa Lucashenko and Odette Murphy, who formed the first outside management committee, had written countless funding submissions, a process aided by Lucashenko's experience working in the Queensland health department. Lucashenko remembers meeting Debbie for the first time just prior to this, with a group of others on Kate Harrison's front verandah at West End. After some discussion Lucashenko, who was then doing her PhD at the University of Queensland, said she had to leave to go to a class. 'Deb made some crack about "the shit they teach at uni", and I thought, just who is this bloody loudmouth?' she recalls. 'But I liked her.'

The first grant did in fact come from the Women's Health Policy Unit of Queensland Health under the Prevention of Violence Against Women program, to provide a sexual assault counselling service in Queensland prisons. There was also money to rent office space and employ an administrator. Sisters was on its way. The management committee inside – which became the 'steering committee' to fit the requirements of legislation, and included Fred, Karine Heath, Spider, Kim Jervis, Cheryl Murray and Margie Blair – celebrated by smoking lolly cigars.

Two counsellors were employed for the new service. Greer White was approached to apply while she was still away studying in Boston, and returned for an interview before the steering committee. She remembers being 'sussed out' by the women, who all, nonetheless, readily accepted her because she came with Debbie's seal of approval. A Murri woman, Shirley Blackman, was employed to work with the Aboriginal women. Subsequently, Sisters consistently employed Aboriginal workers to work with Aboriginal prisoners.

Shortly afterwards, Sisters was also funded to conduct a research project into women prisoners and their experience of domestic violence. The project was triggered by the shocking death, the year before, of a woman who was released from Boggo Road and returned to live with her violent partner. On her release, she had apparently told prison staff that she could not go home to him, and needed alternative accommodation. Not our problem, she was told. Within twenty-four hours, he had murdered her.

The project, which involved prisoners in the design and direction of its research, revealed that the vast majority of women in prison had experienced domestic or family violence and that for many, it had contributed to their incarceration. These women reported that for them, prison was 'safer than home, the safest place to be'.

Midway through 1994, Sisters moved into its first office in Walton Street, Dutton Park (opposite Boggo Road) amidst great joy and celebration. In what would be an unthinkable act of trust and charity these days, prisoners on the steering committee were allowed out to attend the opening party, escorted by prison officers. There were balloons, streamers and a cake – inscribed 'Congratulations Sisters Inside. To the women, by the women, for the women' – was ceremonially cut by Debbie and Fred. The general manager of the prison, Paul Severin (who had succeeded George Brand), made a speech, and all the inside committee members were given T-shirts that read 'What part of the word "no" don't you understand?'

The fact that, on the same day, Sisters had received funding for an innovative 'Kids of Mums in Jail' program added to the poignancy, especially for Debbie. Separation from her children is usually the first and biggest loss a woman experiences when she goes to prison. Both the woman and her children are catapulted into a cycle of grieving that starts with the shock of arrest and the trauma of a trial, and continues on through the stages of imprisonment and gradual release. Women are often overwhelmed by guilt and anxiety about the children; they have lost their parenting role and identity along with their freedom and dignity. Children of all ages suffer dislocation (if they are placed with a carer) and teasing at school; they feel anger at their mother for the separation and shame; and pain at the separation from her and often from their siblings.

Debbie had experienced first-hand the shock and grief of being locked up away from her children, and knew the pitfalls of trying to keep her relationship with them alive and healthy. Some kind of intervention was essential, she knew, to allow women and their children to keep communicating, to express their emotions about the situation, and to ease the way for reunion when the women were eventually released.

Sisters Inside used their new funding to run a series of camps for women and children at The Outlook – the outdoor recreation centre near Boonah. In this distinctly non-institutional setting, the women and children could enjoy programs and activities unavailable to them in the strict confines of prison visits areas, and reflect individually and in a group on the effects of imprisonment on them. Activities included canoeing, rope-work, bushwalking, T-shirt printing and drawing, and barbecues. Organisers also made sure there was unstructured time for families to spend together, as well as discussions on topics like having or being a parent in prison; responsibility issues; the needs of young people and of mothers; parenting strategies and the fears and hopes of parents and children for when women were released.

After the first two camps it became clear, through feedback and evaluation, that the initiative was a big success. Women and their children said they felt closer to one another, were more aware of one another's feelings and thoughts about the imprisonment and had new perspectives. Sisters Inside were able to work with their specific feedback to design future camps and to enrich staff members' knowledge about the ongoing impact of the imprisonment of women.

For Debbie, the success of the camps was bittersweet: if there had been a similar program when she was in prison, she and Jody might have had a better chance of re-establishing a warm mother–daughter relationship. It had been the very absence of such programs that had led to the birth of Sisters Inside.

Debbie continued to work at Centre Ed. James Finn, who had admired her approach from the beginning, recalls her turning up to the health service, bringing a crowd of young people with her. 'She was like no other youth worker I knew,' he says. 'She'd just turn up and say, okay, I've got a kid who wants to do a home detox; I'll support him through it. Will you just give me the medical advice I need? She'd do things, rather than talk about it. She was instinctive.'

At this time Debbie had asked James to be her supervisor

through her social work placement, and he readily agreed. She agreed to offer him in return the same kind of support and debriefing. 'Since that day, that's what we've done – we debrief each other in everything we do, work, our practice, personal issues. It's become the basis of our friendship. We had a hoot.'

But while she loved the experience of interacting with and challenging the young people, the downside was watching as some of them struggled with the hand life had dealt them, and lost. Some would run foul of the criminal justice system, and some, tragically, would find the struggle too hard and take their own lives. While the atmosphere at the centre was always positive and up-beat, the shadow of pain and loss was a constant one. Although each loss was hard to bear, there was one that lingered in the hearts and memories of everyone in that circle, one that would produce enduring images not just of terrible loss but of Debbie's extraordinary compassion and courage.

At the end of 1994, tragedy struck during a camp on Moreton Island, off Brisbane. Debbie and several other staff members had joined eighteen young people swimming, surfing, snorkelling, sand tobogganing and playing beach volleyball. Spirits were high. But late on the second day of the camp, around midnight, fifteen-year-old Joel Byrne collapsed and died after an asthma attack.

Debbie and two other staff members administered CPR to Joel, desperately trying to revive him. The young people held Joel's hand, trying to comfort him and each other, and begged loudly to the sky for the emergency helicopter to arrive. But when another staff member made contact with emergency personnel, she was told they would not come if the patient had died. 'Is there a pulse?' Debbie was asked. She already knew there was no pulse, and also knew the answer she had to give. 'Yep, a faint one,' she lied.

Debbie knew CPR was no longer needed. But she also knew how traumatic it would be for the other young people to have to sit with Joel's body until the morning, waiting and grieving. Rejecting that option, she continued to pump air into Joel's lifeless body, to press her lips to the boy's mouth, keeping the terrible spectre of death at bay for the others.

When the helicopter finally arrived, a doctor immediately pronounced the boy dead. The group was told the chopper could not transport a body. Debbie was outraged. What would you do, she wanted to ask, if someone died on your chopper halfway back? Eject the body? But they finally convinced the helicopter crew to take one of the Centre Ed staff members back with them so that his family could be notified and arrangements put in place.

Joel's body was then wrapped in sheets and placed in the back of a truck belonging to the local park ranger, who had also arrived in the middle of the drama. After the ranger departed for the other side of the island to wait with Joel's body for the first barge back to the mainland, the rest of the group was left to wait through the cruel leftover hours of the night and into the next morning for a later barge that could transport them all back to the mainland. The young people expressed their grief through talking and playing music, and covering the place where Joel had died with flowers.

Gabe Scattini, who had stayed at Debbie's house for the week to look after Joshua, and who had known Joel for years, vividly remembers Debbie's homecoming. 'I'll never forget how she looked,' she says. 'Her mouth was blue and her lips were really swollen from giving Joel mouth-to-mouth for hours. She said she had to, it would have been too traumatic for the young people to sit with a body all night. But she felt sick, too, because there was the taste of his death in her mouth and in her lungs.'

James Finn had also known Joel. 'Everyone was a mess,' he remembers:

It was horrendous. But even through that I could see this incredible sense of duty Deb had for the young people she was working with. I don't know how she did what she did on the island, knowing Joel had already died. But a couple of days later at work, she rang me and said, okay, the kids here want to talk about it right now, they've got questions about the health issues, about Joel's asthma, can you come right now?

There was a nurse I worked with and we jumped into the car and went over there. We seemed to just sit and answer questions for hours. Was he using his asthma puffer too much? Did that kill him? Should they have stopped him? They were feeling guilty that they hadn't taken it off him, or intervened in some way. It was incredibly sad and difficult, but also the most amazing piece of work I can ever remember doing as a youth worker.

It was much more difficult, he says, getting Debbie to think about herself in the process. Finally, they organised an HIV test for her, and some support and debriefing. 'It took a lot to get her to think about looking after herself,' he says.

There was a moving funeral at the Centre the following week for a boy who was genuinely loved for his vibrant spirit, energy and heart. But for Debbie, the funeral did not provide the kind of closure and comfort that it did for others. Joel's death joined the other unresolved deaths in her life, and it would take a traumatic session at the Gestalt centre for her to approach some kind of healing.

> **Debbie:** At this stage Jody was in and out of detention, running around, getting into trouble. I did a weekend session with another counsellor who'd come from overseas. I don't know what triggered it, but the murder came up. He suggested I needed to throw up the murder, literally go through the process of feeling I had to throw it up – he even gave me a bucket. And I was going through the emotions of throwing it up, in absolute grief, and it wasn't just the murder, it was Joel. I'd given him CPR and I'd swallowed all that death. I had to get it out of my body, go through the process of throwing it all up, and Dad too – Dad, Debbie, and Joel, all the death, throw it all up and get it out. And I did. And it actually felt good to get it out.

The social work degree seemed the perfect foil to the way her life was shaping itself. Although she didn't feel intellectually stretched by the demands of the course, she enjoyed the classes and revelled in the company of other students and some of the teachers.

> **Debbie:** I started out doing the course because all those dog social workers were the ones who made the decision to lock me up as a kid, so I decided I'd get the degree and tell them to get fucked, and dispute everything. I'd go to the library for assignments and look at these books – once there was one about the diagnosis of serial killers and it had one page of dot points, things psychiatrists identify. I could have been one!
>
> I was pissing myself laughing, thinking, all the psychs at Wilson thought I was mad, and they could have ticked off all these dot

points, but I didn't become a serial killer. I was antisocial, anti-authority, all the usual things, all the symptoms of ADHD [Attention Deficit Hyperactivity Disorder] – if I was a kid now, that's what they'd diagnose me.

Around this time, she met Jackie Huggins for the first time. Although Huggins had kept a weather-eye on Joe since their child-hood weekends together, and even visited him once in prison with Tich, she had never come face to face with Debbie, and had only the media's portrayal of her as the wicked, manipulative wife to go on. But with Huggins attached to the University of Queensland, and Debbie's frequent visits to the campus, they began to run in to each other regularly, and a firm friendship was formed.

'I'd always ask how my brother was – because by then I was seeing more of Deb than of Joe – and gradually, of course, she got me involved with some Sisters stuff,' Huggins recalls with a smile. 'It was a bit uneasy between us at first, but I just thought, gosh, what an incredible woman, what amazing energy. She was a ball of energy and spirit, and it was a spirit you could absolutely warm to.'

Although Huggins' work with Sisters remained limited, she grad-ually slipped into the role of chief supporter and intermediary for Debbie with the local Indigenous community. As the numbers of Aboriginal and Torres Strait Islander people in prison continued to escalate throughout the nineties, this would become a crucial rela-tionship for Debbie as she strived to ensure Sisters' services were relevant and seen as legitimate among Murri people. Meanwhile, she worked to make her own studies relevant to her own life, and to extract the maximum benefit from them:

Debbie: I did this one subject with a lecturer who was fantastic. He'd get speakers to come in every week and talk about the most horrific experiences – one woman spoke about how her daughter was murdered and they couldn't find the murderer, Aboriginal women spoke about being stolen, and sexual abuse. The lecturer got us to identify three things these speakers triggered in us and write about it. It was great – although some students freaked out and complained about him.

But I loved it, I think I wrote about ten thousand words over the semester. I owned it all, the perpetrator in me, the mass murderer

– it's in all of us – it was this process of identifying, being aware. And in the end he said to me, how do I mark this? He gave me a 7 out of 7. And that's what I did the degree for, that sort of thing. But the biggest thing about being a social worker was that I got to work in their court, on equal footing with other social workers. These are the people who took me away from my family, and who still take kids from their families. I needed the degree so they would recognise me, give me some credibility.

Very early in the piece, she'd worked out where the degree fitted into this new life shape and what its value was to her. But she was also given a wry insight into its converse: what her life was worth in social work. One semester, the main assignment involved students attending a court hearing to listen to a domestic violence order or a criminal matter, watch the procedure for detaining a young person in the Children's Court, visit and speak with an elderly, bedridden woman and a young single mother on the dole.

Debbie puzzled over the ironies of the assignment for her and finally approached the lecturer. 'I've got a bit of a problem with all this,' she said. 'I've actually been there myself, I've been that person in every one of those situations, except for the bedridden old lady, and I expect I'll eventually experience that too.' The lecturer thought about it briefly, and then told her not to worry about doing the assignment. She would give her the five credit points automatically. 'So that's what my life was worth in the university system,' she says. 'Five credit points.'

12

Friends

Debbie had always called Tracy Wigginton 'Drac'. Her penchant for nicknames – and for puncturing anyone's inflated sense of self-importance – made it inevitable that the woman dubbed the 'Lesbian Vampire Killer' would be rechristened Kilroy style. And although Wigginton says she was 'floored' the first time Debbie casually flicked the new name at her, she was also impressed by the chutzpah of the woman. Everyone else at Boggo Road gave the 'Vampire' a wide berth.

But as Debbie's confidence grew in her life and role outside jail, she began to feel uneasy with the title she'd flippantly given Wigginton when they were both prisoners. An early trigger for this unease was a story about the 'Lesbian Vampire' on the current affairs show 'Sixty Minutes'. The journalist had visited the jail and over-heard a mention of the nickname, and duly reported that 'even one of the women calls her Drac'.

It prompted Debbie to think about how powerful the media's influence had been on the public's perception of Wigginton, and how equally powerful the simple act of naming could be. Now that she was established firmly in her new life, the nickname, she realised, was not even in context anymore. She decided to approach Wigginton. What followed changed the nature of the friendship between the two women forever. They were already close allies, sharing a toughness, a warmth and a screwball sense of humour, as well as the unshakeable connection that comes when two people serve time together. 'When you've been through so much shit with someone,' Debbie says, 'three months in prison can be equal to three years of your life on the outside. You've known each other through thick and thin.' But after this conversation, according to Wigginton, Debbie Kilroy became her 'friend for life'.

One night, before a meeting of Sisters Inside at Boggo Road, Debbie called Wigginton aside near the chapel where the group usually gathered. The exact words she then used are lost to her, but they were simple, she says, something like: 'I'm not going to call you Drac anymore, because I don't believe you are Dracula. I'm going to call you Fred.' Wigginton herself recalls the event in more detail:

> She said, 'I've got a favour to ask you.' And I thought, what, you? Asking me a favour? And she said, 'I'm not going to call you Drac anymore. I'd like to call you Fred. I'd like to give you back your name.' She had a couple of tears, and I was dumbfounded.
>
> And slowly, very slowly – it probably took me ten to twenty seconds – the meaning of what she'd just said and done hit me. She'd given me back my identity. She'd given me back my human-ness. This one person said, okay, here is your key, you're now allowed to be human. I see you, I don't see your crime. It was as if she'd gone over to reception and stolen it out of the safe and said, here it is back again, I've kept it safe until now.
>
> And I think that for her, too, it was a letting go of a part of her that still lived in jail; it was almost as if she was giving herself permission to leave that part in prison, and to go on. But for me, she was giving me the foundations of who I am, and of who I would become. I wasn't willing to do it for myself, because we didn't even know we had the right to give ourselves back our humanity, and she showed me. It was as if she was saying: well, if I can go out there and get my shit together, and give myself back my humanity, then you guys can too. You don't have to remain animals, or criminals, or female prisoners, you can be human. Let's try it.

Wigginton says now that her sudden understanding of how the media had created and perpetrated the 'Vampire' persona was like 'being hit over the head with a sledgehammer'. For Debbie the epiphany was similar. Her own use of 'Drac' had, at the time, been a kind of test, she says, to gauge how Wigginton would react and deal with it, but Debbie now realised, living on the outside, how damaging the image of the vampire had been.

The murder and attendant media hysteria surrounding Wigginton's crime had caused a sensation around the world, providing endless newspaper and radio copy and television footage, so naturally, the continued evocation of the vampire myth was in the interests of all sections of the media. Any move to alter or deny it would be extremely difficult, especially to a sceptical public – but at least between Wigginton, Debbie and the members of Sisters Inside, the term would no longer exist.

The programs run by Sisters Inside at Boggo Road proved immensely popular with the women. Because they trusted Debbie and therefore the organisation and those involved in it, women inside were willing to go against their own instincts as prisoners and trust those who worked under the Sisters name. Some were even beginning to feel that here, at last, was an organisation they could own, one that spoke with and for them, one that might actually 'walk its talk'.

But outside the high walls of Boggo Road, the organisation's first major threat was looming. In 1996, a newly elected conservative government in Queensland had begun to slowly wind back the prison reforms of previous Labor governments and to review the funding decisions of its predecessors. Late in the year, without warning, the Coalition government announced by letter that, because Sisters Inside did not appear to 'fit into any category of service' offered by the health department, their funding would be removed.

Everyone in the group, inside and outside, was devastated, but unwilling to go down without a fight. In the political climate of the time, services for prisoners were obviously not a priority, not in the corridors of power, nor in the community where fear of violent crime and 'home invasion' was growing alongside the new gated communities and personal burglar alarms. There was little that Sisters Inside could do about the latter in the short term, but they knew the minds of ministers and bureaucrats could be changed with persuasive argument. What they needed, they decided, was some external muscle, someone who knew how to lobby, someone who knew about the way government worked.

A tentative list of possible consultants was drawn up. Debbie looked at it and immediately zeroed in on one name: Anne Warner, ex-government minister. 'We want her,' she announced. But Warner, who had served as family services minister in the Goss Labor government between 1989 and 1994, wasn't so sure. Political lobbying was the last thing she intended after retiring – especially among conservative politicians she still saw as the enemy. Summonsed to a meeting at Sisters' Walton Street office, she sat on the windowsill, smoking, and told them she doubted she was the person for the job. 'I was a Labor minister,' she said. 'I'm still in the Labor Party. This is a Coalition government.'

Debbie wasn't fazed. 'Do you know how it works?' she asked. 'Yes,' Warner replied. 'Well, you're in,' Debbie said. 'Let's go.'

Warner: I went to do a consultancy for what I thought was a crackpot little organisation called Sisters Inside. I thought it was going to be another fuzzy welfare organisation because that's what the name suggested, and at that stage I'd had welfare groups up to my chin. So I went along almost reluctantly, and what I found was a hard-nosed organisation doing it tough. With the most dispossessed section of the population.

And they weren't soft, they were real, they were real prisoners, a real situation, and they were interesting. That was my first reaction. They were interesting, fascinating. It was just so hard-core compared with a lot of other welfare organisations. And Deb and I connected straight away, although I didn't know anything about her, couldn't even remember her trial, only something vague about Joe Kilroy.

Warner and the committee decided on a limited media strategy to draw attention to their cause followed, if possible, by a meeting with the minister who had effectively signed Sisters out of existence. Warner believed that, with prison conditions deteriorating again, and the hardy annual issues of overcrowding and pre-Christmas tensions, they were likely to get some media interest. She nominated Debbie as the media spokesperson because of her first-hand experience behind bars.

A media sensation, they knew, would not endear them to ministers and bureaucrats, and Debbie finally settled on one interview with ABC radio and one with the local newspaper, the *Courier-Mail*. Together, she and Warner walked down George Street to Parliament House to meet up with the journalists, comparing notes, Warner remembers, 'about the respective institutions we'd both just been released from'. As they walked through the imposing iron gates, she said, 'I get the horrors every time I come in here,' and Debbie replied, 'An institution is an institution – you get institutionalised whether it's a parliament or a prison.'

Two days after the interviews were broadcast and published, Sisters received a phone call from the office of the health minister, requesting a meeting that week.

Warner: On the way to the meeting we happened to get into the lift with the head bureaucrat and Deb gave her a gob-full. So that was good. Then she gave her another one across the table in the meeting. As it turned out the minister didn't come, and we sat there with this insipid-looking minder and this bureaucrat who was doing the strategy on cuts to funding. Debbie explained to her why we needed services in prison, that she'd been through it herself and been lucky enough to get some support and advice that allowed her to be rehabilitated.

She went through her whole life and the bureaucrat was saying, oh yeah, I know, and Deb said, I've just laid out my whole life for you and you've trampled all over it, and besides that you've cut our funding, so don't give me all this 'I know' stuff. And then the bureaucrat said, well, we're not going to cut your funding, you can have it back. I was thinking, well, you're piss-weak, what about a fight? And then we went down to the pub.

I was having a Bailey's and ice, I think, and Debbie said, do you want to come onto the management committee? And I said, yes, I do. I'd been having fun. They were a good bunch of people and it was a bit of risk, a bit of argy-bargy. For me it was about cutting away the trappings, I'd had enough of trappings, I wanted to get back to something that was mean-ingful at a very basic level.

But their elation was short-lived. Within weeks, the trouble Debbie had publicly warned was brewing in the jail materialised in tragic and dramatic circumstances. A severely disturbed young woman, who had been in care for most of her life, arrived at the Wilson Juvenile Detention Centre (where Debbie had spent much of her troubled youth) to visit some staff members who, unfortunately, had been transferred elsewhere. Those she did see called the police, and the young woman was arrested and placed on remand in a cell with another prisoner at Boggo Road.

The two women had soon started a fire from which they could not escape because prison officers could not find the key. The door was eventually kicked in but the young woman was badly burned – the older prisoner had taken refuge in the shower. Incensed and distressed at the system's failure to protect this young woman, and at the thoughtless housing of prisoners with different backgrounds, the management committee immediately swung back into action, making official complaints to the department.

With more articulate, assertive and high-profile women on the committee, it was becoming clear that advocacy and the push for reform would be the outside committee's main role, separated from the service delivery role of those whom Sisters employed. Along with Pam Searle, whose knowledge of organisational structures and policies was invaluable, and Bino Toby, whose experience in domestic violence and sexual assault services made her a strong voice for Aboriginal prisoners, Anne Warner suggested inviting Bernadette Callaghan to join. Callaghan had enjoyed a long and influential career as secretary of the powerful Clerks Union, and had been active with Warner in the ALP. After being sworn in as a barrister, however, her political connections had been severed.

Callaghan: Anne rang me up and said, they need a lawyer at Sisters Inside – but to get onto the management committee you have to be checked out by Deb. And I was coming in as a lawyer, and most of the women didn't trust lawyers. So I went to dinner to meet Deb, and although I don't remember the specifics of the conversation, I remember her sitting and looking at me, and probably thinking, who is this yuppie lawyer? She was very guarded, hardly said anything.

But I was impressed with her, she was strong, and she knew what she was doing. I liked her straight away. I realised she was the key to this organisation, that it revolved around her.

I was also impressed because Deb didn't seem to have had the advantages that someone like me had had – education, a family and friends who surrounded me completely. I was a rebel at school, but was guided through it by my family and friends; I ended up a lawyer and she ended up in prison.

Callaghan remembers the trepidation of her first meeting with the committee inside the prison. Tracy Wigginton, she says, walked in and immediately made a comment designed to scare her. 'She walked up really close to me – and she's a big woman – and made some comment like, "I don't have a knife",' she says. 'That was Fred's way of testing, of shocking, of checking to see if I could cope. Deb told her to sit down and shut up.'

Callaghan wasn't put off by the swagger, but the structure and philosophy of the organisation worried her immediately: 'I wanted the organisation to be clear and direct, not wishy-washy, or involved in wishful thinking. I've never been interested in navel-gazing and at that first meeting I thought, if this doesn't improve, I'm not going to be around long. Some of the others had reached that point too, where the organisation had to move forward or it would collapse. We had to make change – and we wanted that change to empower women. I'd come out of a hard-nosed union background.

The combined power and assertiveness of Kilroy, Warner and Callaghan came into its own not long afterwards, when a newly appointed manager at Boggo Road refused outside management committee members access to the jail for the regular SIS meeting. He accused the group of being disruptive to prison routine, and specifically targeted Debbie, accusing her of verbally abusing prisoners on a particular occasion, and banning her from the jail. All witnesses to the supposed event rallied behind Debbie, outraged at the claim, but the ban stood.

At a scheduled meeting with the manager a week after the lock-out, Debbie, Warner and Callaghan readied themselves for an old-fashioned battle. Callaghan arrived straight from work, dressed formally in a suit, and immediately began taking notes. According to Debbie, the manager asked Callaghan if she was there to take minutes of the meeting, to which Callaghan replied, 'No, I'm taking notes.' The manager then became visibly nervous.

Warner: We went into that meeting knowing we had to absolutely back each other up, and we did. We were incensed by the injustices of the decision. We were at a very crucial stage and I was glad Berna was there. Politics is a good grounding; you know how to put a forceful case.

The ban on Debbie was lifted soon afterwards. But for Sisters Inside, a line had been drawn in the sand. Along with other minor scuffles between prison staff and SIS staff over petty problems, and lock-outs for often spurious reasons, the row with the manager had removed any confidence the organisation had in bureaucratic fair play. They had won that one, but nevertheless they decided to fight fire with fire: no longer would they play the game according to prison management rules. There was no integrity there, they decided. They would use their growing strength and voice to effect change where it was needed.

Despite initial concerns to the contrary, Sisters' funding did not come under scrutiny again and, within a year, it had actually expanded to include a research project on the needs of prisoners of non-English-speaking backgrounds and the production of a kit to be distributed to women on their release.

The kits, which are still produced with regularly updated information, provided a crucial lifeline for women on all aspects of life outside, including information on housing, parole and home detention; parenting and relationships; domestic violence; education and financial support; using banks and Centrelink; safe sex, drug and alcohol issues – even a map and transport information. Apart from a plastic rubbish bag containing spare clothes, toothbrush and a tiny cash allowance, this kit is often the only thing a woman possesses when she walks away from jail.

With the expansion of funded programs, and the continuation of existing ones, Sisters entered a busy and volatile period in their development. More programs meant more staff, and a move to bigger premises in Gloucester Street, West End. In 1997 the opening of a low-security facility for women at Numinbah Valley, over an hour's drive from Brisbane, meant programs were more spread out and, of course, that the composition of the inside steering committee would change, as prisoners became eligible for transfer.

Technically, steering committee members retained their positions at Numinbah, perusing minutes of meetings and trying to stay involved. But the geographic dislocation – both from Sisters and from their families – made many activities impractical for them.

Within the organisation, too, there were growing tensions between staff and management committee members over decision-making and staff performance, tensions that, for one protracted and ugly period, erupted into a personal dispute that split the committee and threatened the structural viability of Sisters. There was a lengthy mediation process and a settlement was eventually negotiated after the staff union was called in. Although problems with dispute procedures for staff were identified, it became obvious that some staff misunderstood the realities of prison culture in their service delivery, and miscalculated the paramount importance of loyalty within that culture and, indeed, the culture of Sisters Inside.

'At the time there were some people who wanted to keep it as a quiet little organisation doing services for women, who didn't want to do advocacy. It was like a bunch of social workers doing good once a week,' Callaghan says. 'It had to change, to do the good it had to do, to really change things for women in prison. And it did that. Now it has leadership and direction.'

It also became obvious at this time that Debbie Kilroy was uniquely able to straddle the two worlds that Sisters represented inside and outside prison. She alone provided the bridge of trust necessary for Sisters staff to operate within the prison, and for management members to enjoy any level of credibility about prison issues on the outside. As such, she had been elevated to the highest category of mateship by the women inside: a person they trusted implicitly with their lives. Many would have killed for her – literally. When she was personally attacked verbally by a staff member during the dispute, prisoners threatened to 'belt' the woman if she ever stepped foot inside the prison again. 'She actually thought they would align themselves with her,' Debbie remembers. 'People don't understand the link we have. It will never be severed, until our last dying breath.'

Early in 1999, Debbie was appointed acting coordinator of Sisters Inside, and later in the year became its director. She had left Centre Ed at the end of 1996 and was studying full time to complete her social work degree. Naturally, life as a student did not consume all her boundless energies; she worked part time for the Christian Brothers, training some of their people in youth work. She had also become involved in the Youth Affairs Network of Queensland – YANQ – becoming its chair between 1997 and 2003 and proceeding to flip the organisation 'on its head'.

In the years before her appointment as coordinator at Sisters, Debbie worked tirelessly (and, of course, voluntarily) at YANQ, reorganising all its processes and honing her own management philosophy as she went. When she'd arrived, the peak youth group was in disarray, with bitter infighting among staff and a split executive team.

Debbie: Members of the executive were making decisions without other members knowing. And they were based in the city, where it was easy to waste time sitting around at coffee shops, and where it was also easy to fall into the trap of working in too closely with the government.

I didn't like the processes which left people in the dark about what was going on. All of the management team needed to be consulted. And they needed to get out of the city. So we moved it out to West End, rewrote the constitution, and started to move and shake outside the government. It was the peak youth organization, after all – you consult youth first, not the government first. We had to be there for the young people. Fundamentally it had to have the same sorts of values that Centre Ed had run on – respect, safety, participation and loyalty, always. My values, I suppose.

Debbie would remain chair of the organisation until 2003, when she was forced to stand down because of legislation prohibiting anyone sentenced to a prison term of thirty months or more from serving on a corporation's management committee. She made sure her resignation had some effect, though. The legislation in question, she told local media, made a mockery of the 'rehabilitation' supposedly achieved by prisons, and which the government was so fond of trumpeting. What did she have to do to prove she had moved on from her conviction?

But she remained chair of YANQ when, in 1999, she became

director of Sisters Inside. This was also the year Sisters became incorporated, with a constitution that saw members on the inside become the steering committee, a legal entity of the management committee. The steering committee has real authority in the organisation, directing and advising management on all prison issues. They make decisions on matters of policy, politics and lobbying, as well as undertaking practical tasks like writing submissions, position papers and a newsletter, writing accommodation applications and serving on interview panels for new Sisters staff.

Tracey Leivers joined the steering committee shortly after beginning a life sentence in 1997. At her first meeting, she and Debbie clashed – neither remember the reason – but despite that the two women forged an immediate and firm connection, and Leivers became a vocal and fearless advocate for other women and the work of Sisters Inside.

> Leivers: We found each other very quickly. I think it was a personality thing. Not many people will go back in my face, and I tend to respect them more if they do. Deb did. And I liked what she stood for. She wasn't afraid to speak up at a time when others were. At the time things were getting tighter in the prison, there was heaps of tension and everyone knew it was going to blow. No one was game to step up and speak except Deb. I was in for a long stretch so I wanted to put my hand up too – what can they do to me? I'm already in prison for life. We had the same attitude – why just push one button, why not push all ten at once?

Through a long and agonising process of workshops and meetings facilitated by Suzi Quixley, Sisters also formulated its own 'values and vision' statement that would clarify for all current and future staff and management members the philosophy and goals of the organisation and the separate roles of each. The ability to 'walk the talk' underpinned the group's expectations of anyone who believed they wanted to join:

> At Sisters Inside, we believe that no one is better than anyone else. People are neither 'good' nor 'bad'; human behaviour is circumstantial, environmental, transformable and fallible . . .

We aspire to a society that meets the social and individual needs of the full diversity of its members. While each person has some opportunity to make choices, our individual and social context plays an important role in determining the extent of these choices. 'Choice' must be seen in the context of the situation, the social views being advocated, access to information and the personal experiences/values/beliefs of each individual . . . This belief is fundamental to Sisters Inside's commitment to challenging and changing the context in which women live.

We believe . . . that one small group exercises dispropor-tionate power in all areas of society. In fact, the whole society is constructed in the interests of this dominant group . . . this results in imbalances in social and economic power, including different levels of access to justice for different members of society.

Prisons are an irrational social response. Prisons do not achieve their intended outcomes – they neither 'correct' nor 'deter' law breaking. In our society, prisons only function to punish and socially ostracise law breakers. This generates alien-ation and further criminal behaviour. It also explains the disproportionate numbers of people from socially margin-alised groups, particularly Aboriginal people, in the prison population . . . Every member of society is entitled to have their human rights protected . . . However, in our society, prisons have been demonstrably unsuccessful in achieving this. Alternative means must be found for protecting society against destructive behaviour.

Sisters Inside strategically advocates for the collective inter-ests of women in the criminal justice system, and provides services to address their more immediate needs. Our service provision informs our social change work. While our lobbying role is designed to address the oppression of women in the criminal justice system, we recognise this is a long-term preventative strategy. Women in this system have a wide variety of unmet needs. That's why Sisters Inside will continue to offer a combination of services designed to address current gaps in services.

Loyalty, honesty and trustworthiness underpin all our

actions ... We will only continue to deserve the trust of
women in the criminal justice system for as long as we walk
the talk ...

The workshops also marked nearly a decade of Debbie's friendship
with Quixley, who continued to be impressed with the way Debbie
had maintained her own personal integrity since her release from
prison, and the brokerage role she now played between those two
very different worlds. 'She wasn't – and isn't – a sucker for either
side,' Quixley recalls. 'She doesn't take shit from anyone. She's got
the best bullshit barometer of anyone I know.'

Quixley was also impressed with the way Debbie had not
discarded her past, but built on the strengths she had always had.
Anne Warner agreed. 'Deb has an innate intelligence. She picks
things up very quickly, and deals with the environment she's in,' she
says. 'As a younger person she used that intelligence in the criminal
environment, in prison she used it politically. She just transferred the
skills she already had to the outside world.'

One of the most remarkable changes during this time of growth
and upheaval occurred through a particular addition to the management committee. It was an appointment that would shake and alter
the attitudes of everyone involved with Sisters, and illustrate the
extent of Debbie's personal and professional growth since her release
from prison.

Debbie: If Sisters Inside was going to be about *all* women, then
we had a challenge. First, to include the short-termers, and
acknowledge their trauma as we did any other trauma, no matter
what the length of the sentence is. We had to really support the
long-termers inside to acknowledge the others, because it was
against prison culture to consider short-termers, and it was difficult for them because they were living in that environment day to
day.

And then there was Storm: If we were about all women, we
couldn't say, well, all women *except* ... The values had to be
solid. I had to do the hard yards too, to show the example.

So I just decided that Storm had to come onto management.
Fred said, *fuckin' hell!* It was a big no-no to them. They thought
Storm was too cocky, and wouldn't pull her head in, wouldn't

come into line with the other long-termers. But Storm and her mates were still locked down behind the gate, and she had a lot of personal power. Things were happening down there, beltings, and I knew the only way to pull them all in, to have all the women onside, was to pull Storm in, because she had a following. I told them I had to sort it out with Storm, and then other women could see you can fix things up, and life can go on. There doesn't have to be this shit. The others couldn't argue with that.

One day I sent one of the staff down there, and she said to Storm, do you want to come up to this meeting of Sisters Inside? Apparently Storm said, who told you to come and ask? When she was told it was Debbie, she immediately agreed to come. She walked in and we asked each other, how are you going? And I asked her if she'd like to join the management committee. Then for the next few months we sorted through our issues.

The implications of Debbie's astonishing gesture would play out for a long time. Every time the management committee met, Debbie and Storm would spend time negotiating their way through the horrors of Debbie's murder, moving slowly towards a place in which they could both feel comfortable. It wasn't easy for either woman: the conversations they had were, according to Debbie, 'strong', and both had to redefine their ideas about trust, about friendship, and about forgiveness.

But by then Storm, for her part, had the hard evidence of Debbie's work with Sisters to gauge her by. Debbie had, after all, kept her word: she had said she would not forget the women, and she hadn't. Storm knew that when Debbie said she wanted her on the management committee, she meant it.

It was an extraordinary declaration of truce from the woman whose best friend Storm had murdered, and who had plotted single-mindedly to kill her in revenge. For everyone who observed it, Debbie's gesture became an emblem of Sisters' raison d'être: walkin' the talk.

Storm: The day I was invited up there, I was pretty suss about it. I was nearly going to go armed up – you get really paranoid in there, especially if there's old blood. Even though we'd had a kind of truce, we'd never really sat down and talked.

We'd look at each other when she walked past and there wasn't hatred anymore, just a look, then the glances would separate. So that day I ummed and ahhed, then thought, I'll go, but arming up isn't the way to solve anything. Let's see what happens.

When I got up there Deb came out and greeted me. She said, I want to ask you if you want to be part of Sisters. I just said, yeah, I'll give it a go. But I walked into the room very cautiously, watching my back. I didn't take my eyes off Deb, and I sat closest to the door. Back then you thought along the lines of 'kill or be killed' – I'm not saying you plan to kill everyone, but you fight to win. If you show a weakness, you're picked on severely.

We talked about the murder in that first meeting. Debbie said, we have to sort Debbie's death out, Storm. Everyone else melted into the walls, Anne smoking out of the window, Fred with her worry beads. I just listened more than anything that time, gave a response when I felt a question mark was there. And then every meeting after that we'd discuss it more, in the group and on our own – that's where the nitty-gritty came out.

But it took a bit of time: neither of us wanted to be alone in a room together at first – what happens if one us says the wrong thing? It was pretty strained. After that first meeting, though, I knew she was genuine. When it was over and she said goodbye to everyone, she treated me like everyone else – she came up and put her arm around me.

The process of reconciliation between the two women continued slowly but steadily over the next few years. Watching them, the other women on the committee were astounded and admiring. They would talk about their issues openly, without rancour, and also in private. Astonishingly, for two women who would never before have shown each other their vulnerable sides, they would emerge from these private sessions with tear-stained faces.

Tracey Leivers: I remember watching them over that time, working it out. I don't know if 'respect' is the right word for how I felt; the whole thing dumbfounded me a bit, because

I thought it was such a huge step on Deb's behalf. To forgive. I don't know if I could do it. So just seeing that process actually made me question a lot of things about myself. About my own stuff. The whole thing still amazes me, it really does. And something happened in Storm too. I don't think there is a self-forgiveness in her, because I just don't think Storm will ever forgive herself for what happened. But I think Deb's forgiveness filled a gap in Storm's life.

Those who knew Storm's whole story, however, also understood there was more to her than a rough street-fighter who could kill in cold blood. Storm was born in Russia, in 1969, to a Maltese father and Russian mother. The family migrated to Australia when Storm was five, but she has clear memories of St Petersburg, where she spent her early years, of toboggan sleds and snow, of reindeer on the tundra where her grandmother lived. Her memories of this time are positive and happy; there were none of the signs of the horrific abuse which would scar her life in her new country.

Storm: Dad was really dark-skinned, and I've always been fair, like my mum, and he always treated me differently to the others. I think he believed I wasn't his child because I didn't have brown eyes. I was seven when I had my first shot [of heroin], but younger when he first abused me sexually. If I said anything about it I'd be belted black and blue.

But I thought this was what happened in every family. People say, you must have been traumatised, but I wasn't, not then, I thought it was normal everyday life. Mum knew about the abuse, but she didn't give two hoots – she was just worried she wouldn't get a shot herself. She didn't care at all, even when he held me down so his mates could rape me. But again, because I wasn't allowed to knock around with other little kids, I didn't know what was normal.

That went on until one day when I was about nine they had to take me to hospital, because I'd been flogged so badly that I couldn't wake up. They said I'd fallen down the stairs or something. But when I still didn't regain consciousness they did all these blood tests and found opiates in my blood. They checked my arms then and saw the track marks. And that was it. They took me away and put me into kids' homes and foster families. The first family, I lasted two days; they took me back, said I was uncontrollable. The second family, I didn't even make lunch. They were trying to show me discipline, tell me what to do, and I'd arc up, get really aggressive.

In homes I was more controllable, they could just lock me in rooms when I misbehaved. They'd give me injections if I was going right off, and didn't even worry about rolling my sleeves or pants up, they'd give it to me right through the material. Pin me down, bang. I'd go all ga-ga and wake up hours later in a room, all dry-mouthed and dribbling.

Later, I used to get a certain type of angry, and it would turn into a rage because, I think, I'd go back to my childhood, and it would be like I was attacking my father or something, for all the pain he put me through. That hasn't happened for years, though, I've learned to control my temper.

The cognitive skills programs I've done have really helped me to figure out a way to try to talk out a problem instead of using your fists, like when I was growing up. If I ever dobbed on my sister, my dad would punch me out, blacken my eyes and give me a blood nose. You were supposed to fight it out, not tell tales.

Before the murder in the jail they had me drugged up. I was only twenty, and I was being used by one of the groups as their enforcer, I was fighting all their battles. And I was getting more and more worked up. The amount of people I flogged for them. They'd say, do this, and I would.

And McDougall was running back and forward between the two groups with her lies. I don't know why we took the carving forks. I think because the opportunity was there. We hid them under a long bench, where there was a board missing. When they talked about the forks, I was thinking, that won't do much damage, just make a little stab mark.

But there should never have been a murder. It was supposed to be a punch-on. I mean, I liked Debbie Dick. I remember once, when I was doped up, she tried to help me up the stairs and we both ended up falling back down, laid there laughing at the bottom. And Debbie Kilroy – I'd always looked up to her, admired her, even when we were supposed to be in two different cliques.

I still don't remember the actual stabbing. I remember having the forks and stabbing twice, and the next thing I realise I've been hit over the head with a chair by Deb. Then I ran out through the dining room door. I'd just blacked out – it had happened before – I don't know where I go, but it always happened when I was really angry.

When I snapped back in, I went back through the kitchen, palmed off the forks and went out and sat down. At one stage I stood up and saw Debbie Dick lying there, and I didn't see any blood so I thought, oh it's right then – no blood so I thought it was sweet. Then I sat back down. Then we were all sent to our rooms.

When I heard she was dead I freaked out. And Amali was yelling out, I'll lose my kids for sure. That's when I thought, I'll put my hand up for it, so she doesn't lose her kids. A bit later, they came to our cells, stripped all our clothes off and put them in bags for forensics. They gave me a really thin nightie, and that's all I had for months. Took us over to men's, stayed there for four months. They made me more bitter over there. They'd come in and flog me, cuff my hands behind my back, made me drink toilet water or my own piss. Wouldn't let me see my solicitor.

Then I was brought back down here and did another nine months in isolation. They'd throw the food in. I had nothing, no power, only allowed two magazines a week and basic toiletries, tobacco, a pen and paper. I wasn't allowed anything on buy-up, no lollies or anything.

But George Brand used to buy me little model cars out of his own pocket. He'd sit and talk to me, see how I was going, talk about his wife and son. I wasn't even going out into the exercise yard I helped them build, my own exercise cage. I was turning into an animal, going mad. I remember looking in a mirror once and thinking, that's not me. My eyes are blue. Those eyes are grey. They'd literally lost their colour.

After fourteen months they said I could come out, but I didn't want to then, I'd huddle in a cupboard, in tears. I can't forget what they did to me, the torment. But now I've learned about violence and that how I was brought up wasn't right at all. I've stopped thinking about myself.

Now the people I care about are my main priority, and I want them to be proud of me. My mum (my foster mum who I regard as my only mum) said to me once, I'm not proud of what you've done, but I'm proud of who you are. So I want to go out there and make her proud of what I do. That's what's in my heart. I want to show them that they've put a lot of time and effort into me, and I can be a success.

And for Katie, Debbie Dick's daughter, I want to do that victim-offender mediation because she deserves answers. I don't care if they yell or throw things at me – I can't imagine how it's affected them, and I deserve what they'll throw at me. But if I can help them in any way, I want to. I'm not violent anymore; I know it doesn't work. I want to resolve things in a positive manner – that's how Deb and I resolved our issues. Punching is the easy way. But no one could lay more blame on me than I do myself. I know what I've done, and the emotion of it is really raw in me. I know, because the blue is starting to come back into my eyes. I can see it.

At home, Debbie's life still seesawed between contentment and anger. On the positive side, her renewed relationship with Joe had finally hit calm water. They'd found a house to rent together on half an acre of land at Tingalpa, between Brisbane and Moreton Bay. Here, the couple were able to just be themselves, and to rediscover the joy they had once found in each other. Joe was happier than he had ever been, enjoying the new domestic bliss so much that he hadn't even bothered to leave the house long enough to attend meetings at the Uhlans' clubhouse.

Debbie: Joe was over the moon. Then one day a few of the Uhlans turned up to get all his stuff – if you haven't turned up regularly for meetings, that's what they do, they take away your colours until you get your act together. And it was very funny, because there was obviously this myth about me being this big monster, and these guys had never met me and are freaking out.

I'm just lying there on the lounge in my pyjamas and Joe says calmly, oh yeah, I'll get the stuff, he wasn't worried about it. While he was out of the room something came up about trafficking smack, and I told them no, I had never trafficked smack. They looked at me and said, that's what we were told. And we laughed, they thought I was going to be really scary. It was hilarious.

Pat and Nana had remained Debbie's staunch supporters throughout the ordeals of the previous ten years. Pat had held her breath a little in the first few years after Debbie's release from prison, hoping for the best, but by now always fearing the worst. It was difficult for her to know exactly what her daughter was thinking, because Debbie had never been the 'drop in for a cuppa and a chat' type. But the relationship strengthened and mutual trust began to grow as Debbie proved, again and again, that her life was on track.

'That was one of the best things about that time,' Joe Kilroy remembers. 'Deb's relationship with her mother. I really enjoyed it, because it meant I could have that relationship with Pat, too.' They were good days, he says, and 'they got better, because we got older and smarter'.

But the lives of the Kilroy children were in disarray. Jody was back in Brisbane. She was twenty now and still in and out of trouble, and in and out of prison. In between she lived with her family at Tingalpa, but rarely harmoniously. 'She was an adult by then,' Debbie recalls, 'and I couldn't control her as my child. She didn't want it. When she was in prison I visited her every Saturday and when she was at Albion [the half-way house] I'd pick her up and bring her home every weekend. But she kept breaching her orders. Our whole lives were being smashed to pieces because she just kept going back to prison.'

Josh was miserable too, reeling from repeated outbursts of racism at school. In one of the worst instances, according to Debbie, a teacher had encouraged 'free speech' around the issues raised by Pauline Hanson in her early campaigning against supposed 'benefits' enjoyed by Aboriginal people. As the only Aboriginal child in the class, Joshua was bombarded by racist allegations and jokes from insensitive classmates. Desperately unhappy, he cut his wrists, only to be interrogated by the teacher about 'his part in all this'.

Debbie was furious. She immediately withdrew Joshua from the school – just as she had removed him from several schools previously – but not before demanding the teacher display leadership over the Hanson material, and get her 'facts right', rather than 'pushing a scumbag, racist line'. Josh would run the racist gauntlet of cruel classmates and insensitive teachers again and again, however, despite Debbie's loud objections and willingness to withdraw him from class. By the time he reached year ten, he'd attended eight different schools.

'Kids would call me Smokin' Josh, and say my dad only got that name from smoking weed. They'd call me lots of names, say I licked toilet seats, things like that,' Josh remembers. But he was more distressed, he believes, by his sister's ongoing problems, and the spectre of prison looming over the family yet again. The resentment between the siblings festered as Jody ricocheted in and out of custody. Josh dealt with it by flirting with trouble himself – 'all the stupid things you do when you're fifteen'. It came to a head at around this time – 2001 – when Jody was on home detention, and Josh was caught shoplifting in the city.

'Jody came into my bedroom, big-noting. I started swinging,' he says. 'We were slamming each other's heads against walls, screaming. It started again the next day when Mum went out, and the cops came that time. They said they'd had noise complaints. But it was all bullshit stuff. I was so sick of her and she was so jealous of me. It's hard. I can see her point of view now, but it's not my fault.'

It was around this period that Debbie can, with hindsight, see the second big mistake she made with Jody.

Debbie: I was seeing a female counsellor at the time when Josh was having a few problems. She told me to cut Josh off. I was really distressed – he was only doing normal teenage rebellious stuff. But this counsellor had also advised me to cut Jody off. I though, oh God, I've made a big mistake. So I went to see Anne, and we had coffee and I told her what the counsellor had said. She was horrified. She said, no way, at these times you hold your kids close, you don't let them go. It was so distressing, because I had trusted this counsellor and what she said about Jody. In hindsight, I see she had no kids herself and no idea.

I could see it was history repeating itself again, too. Mum and Dad had trusted other people's advice about me; had believed them, had wanted to believe that locking me up would help me. But it was too late for Jody and me – I'd let her go. There was a lot of heartache in realising what I'd done. She'd run away, and I'd become so desensitised that I just wasn't in touch with my own grief over it, so the relationship virtually ceased. And it all happened just after I'd come out of prison, whereas with Josh I was strong, on my own feet by then. I realised you can never assume what it's like with someone else's kids.

Well before then, however, Debbie was thinking hard of ways to channel any residual problems Joshua might have not just with his treatment at school, but from the still-raw trauma of his parents' imprisonment. In 1999, as Sisters were refining their programs for helping children of women in prison, she asked Joshua if he would like to write down his memories of the difficult years when he was separated from her and from Joe, with a view to producing several books for children who shared similar experiences.

The result was *Joshua's Books*, self-published by Sisters Inside one year later. Written in a child's hand, they are a simple but harrowing reminder that more than 80 percent of women in prison are the primary carers of children, and that those children are the innocent victims of the jailing of their mothers.

13

Katie

It was one hell of a year to be appointed director of Sisters Inside. Nineteen ninety-nine was a bumper year for crises and change across the prison sector and, within the organisation, a year of extraordinary growth in programs and staff. And while the growth was exciting, it was overshadowed by two deaths that occurred within months of each other, tragedies that galvanised Sisters and catapulted its members into the arena of hard political advocacy. Simultaneously, the group was forced to re-examine one of the founding principles – the refusal to 'dog' – when they decided to go to the media and use inside information about the deaths to highlight poor jail management.

The first death was that of a baby inside Boggo Road, stillborn after the appalling neglect of its mother in the twelve long hours she spent in labour, hours in which prison management insisted she was not experiencing contractions, but merely had a urinary tract infection. Despite complaining about cramps and pain all day, she was ignored by prison officers until the afternoon, when she was dismissed by nursing staff with two Panadol, and told to puff on her asthma spray.

Back in the block where she lived, the woman was in obvious distress. Other prisoners timed her contractions at one minute apart. Still they could not interest staff in the woman's condition. Finally, at six in the evening, the labouring woman went to the toilet, and there, alone and frightened, she delivered her very premature baby. The presence of a dead baby in a toilet bowl, and the screams of other prisoners as they tried to assist the distressed woman, finally gained the attention of staff.

Debbie: They pulled the baby from the toilet, put it in a garbage bag, and shackled the woman round the wrists to an ambulance trolley. They put the bag containing the baby's body between her legs. Meantime, they cleaned up the blood, the towels, everything, before the coppers came in to investigate. The next day I went up to the hospital to see her, and she's still shackled to a bed, absolutely devastated. And I said, that's it, fuck all this secrecy, this is bullshit, something needs to be done about this. And all the women agreed. This was a baby's life.

The secrecy Debbie spoke about was the unwritten law in prison culture that forbids a prisoner from telling tales about anyone or anything that happens inside prison – or, for that matter, anywhere else. In their world, information is the most valuable commodity, and one slip of the tongue – unintentional or otherwise – can have disastrous consequences. Inside prison, anyone who tells tales, especially about other prisoners' activities, is labelled a 'dog', and can often end up in a protection unit. A 'dog' is never safe.

So up until the shocking loss of the baby, stories about mistreatment or brutality were kept within the circle of knowledge held by the women. Even tales about prison officers' misdemeanours were not countenanced, nor were those about prisoners who were most reviled, the child molesters. It was all part of being 'staunch' in the system, but the baby's death forced a rethink about what constituted 'dogging' and what didn't, and the possibility that such blind loyalty to a code might be misplaced.

Debbie: Before the baby, we'd shackled ourselves internally to the prison culture, to say nothing. We were actually protecting the perpetrators, and protecting a system that itself perpetrates violence. After the baby died that was broken down, and I had the women's endorsement to open it up, to challenge the injustices.

We had all these discussions about dogging, what it was and wasn't. We realised we'd been brainwashed to protect the system, to keep everything inside and not talk about anything. So they gave me permission to talk. It allowed me to launch into these broader policy issues too, whether it was strip-searching or mental illness or whatever.

The incident was widely and sympathetically reported, with Debbie's quotes, and re-visited months later in the investigative magazine *The Eye*, under the heading, 'A Baby Should Never Be Born Like This'. But in the closer circle of Sisters Inside, it contributed to a sense of unease among staff, some management members and prison workers, who were worried about the new emphasis on advocacy in the organisation. People employed in the rehabilitation process, Debbie remembers, began to 'get shirty' with her, because she was diverging from their line. 'Sparks started to fly,' she says, 'and do-gooders were dropping off left, right and centre. They thought I was losing the plot.'

But the newer, vocal members of the management committee had never seen Sisters' role stopping at service delivery. That was important, but there was a bigger picture, and after the death of the baby it began to assemble itself clearly in Debbie's mind. It wasn't just about prison reform. It was about prison abolition. The events that followed in the next twelve months would entrench that view.

The old Boggo Road prison had been crumbling for years. Bound by a railway line, arterial roads and, on one side, a primary school, it had no potential for expansion, but given its proximity to the centre of Brisbane, the hillside site did have potential for significant commercial development and gain.

In the 1990s, all the right ingredients were in place for the prison to move: governments everywhere were expanding their prisons, building new complexes and leasing them to private concerns, and demand for prime inner city land was climbing. In Queensland, several new prisons – including Woodford, Borallon (the first private prison in Australia) and Sir David Longland, as well as Numinbah Prison Farm, the new facility for women – opened over a period of fifteen years. Male prisoners from Boggo Road were moved in 1992, and the men's section of the historic prison was officially closed. And then, by July 1999, the new women's prison was ready for occupation at Wacol, with a capacity for 272 beds.

Like other new prisons around the world, the new Brisbane Women's Correctional Centre was high-tech, with keypads instead of keys, modern equipment, and cameras at every turn. The blocks crouched low behind razor wire fences, spread out and separated by stretches of grass (not to be walked on) and covered walkways. It was

clean and modern, with vocational and educational facilities, but its
setting, in the dry, flat lowlands chosen for psychiatric institutions,
detention centres and men's prisons, was forbidding, and for visitors
without cars, difficult to get to.

Debbie and many of the women inside were dismayed and
worried by the layout and atmosphere of the new jail. Its geographic
isolation seemed amplified by the distances within its fences – particularly those between accommodation blocks, which separated groups
of women who had previously spent years living in close quarters
together, able to yell out and communicate to each other from their
cells. When George Brand opened the infamous gate, women could
move around the old Boggo Road complex and visit each other. In
the new prison that was no longer possible. Here, ironically, the feeling
of restriction and confinement was deepened, and the omnipresent
cameras soon began to further erode the women's sense of self, any
sense that they had any control at all over their daily lives.

> Tracey Leivers: Leaving the old prison was sad for me because
> I'd always had this idea that when I finally walked away, it
> would be from Boggo Road. And then, when we got there,
> they wanted to split us all up – some to Residential, some to
> Secure. The ones going to Secure were supposed to be escape
> risks. Escape risks? There were all these boxes, and women
> weren't boxed at Boggo.
>
> All of a sudden all these women who had been free to mix
> came to this new fandangled prison with new rules and labels
> that make no sense at all, and get locked up, isolated. At the
> old prison you could just cruise on out of your block, and see
> who you wanted to see. Here, you're very restricted, there's no
> interaction, not even with the screws. Even they talk about
> feeling isolated.

But the most isolated and most chilling area of the prison was the
detention unit (DU), small, secure punishment cells where women
were placed for breaching prison rules. In the DU even the shower
is monitored, but while a prisoner is aware of being constantly
watched, she cannot glimpse her jailers. Staff are not visible in the
DU, and nor are any other human beings. Any outside sounds are
muffled. The conditions only intensify the atmosphere of isolation as

well as the feeling of desperation among women who might already be feeling depressed and utterly powerless. Prisoners described the detention cells as cages, and the unit as a zoo.

From the time the women were moved from Boggo Road to their new home on 'institution alley', Debbie had been warning prison authorities that this atmosphere of alienation, combined with several other factors, would result in tragedy. The women were reporting that more frequent strip-searches at the new jail were triggering flashbacks to earlier sexual abuse for some.

And the teams of new staff, some unschooled in prison culture and uneasy in the presence of prisoners, added tension to an already stressful situation. Sure enough, there was an increase in the number of incidents of self-harm among the women in the first two months, and Sisters staff were dealing constantly with uncertainty and high levels of distress.

But even then, everyone was shocked when, in September, Debbie's original prediction proved right. A woman who had been locked in the DU suicided the day after she was released back to her cell. Prison officers did not open the door of the cell for an hour and a half, despite the fact that she had not responded to raps on the wall and shouting, instructing her to come out. While they hesitated, fearing she was waiting behind the door to jump them, she was suffocating on the end of a rope made of plaited wool.

Outrage built on outrage. From the women inside, Sisters knew that the first response from a senior prison officer to the death was a lament for the reputation of the new institution. 'How could she do this to my new prison?' Since the death of the baby, the women were willing to tell Debbie what they knew, but were not willing to provide written statements. Debbie understood. She tucked the information away for later use.

There was one more, final cut. Debbie's daughter Jody, refusing to react to the suicide the way authorities wanted her to, was locked in isolation for five months. 'She refused to cry on demand,' Debbie says. 'That's what they demanded. I engaged solicitors to fight to get her out, but to no avail. But I knew what it was about. Whenever I opened my mouth about something, Jody copped it.'

Debbie had always known that, one day, her path would cross that of a young girl who would have questions to ask her about the murder in 1990. Debbie Dick's daughter was just five at the time her mother was killed. Debbie Kilroy had never met her. But she sensed that, because of the circumstances of the murder, Katie would one day want to find her. And she would want answers, some of which Debbie could not provide.

The phone call came early in 2000, at the Sisters offices in Gloucester Street. Katie Cooper asked if Debbie would see her. Debbie had been partly prepared for the call, after hearing about Katie from some girls inside the youth detention centre, who had asked Debbie unceremoniously if she knew Storm Brooke. She killed our friend's mum, they told her, and went on to say Katie would probably be joining them in detention soon. She'd been running around the streets in Ipswich, getting into trouble.

Debbie could see the likeness as soon as Katie stepped into the room. She was small and finely built, as her mother had been; it didn't take long to see that Debbie Dick's wry sense of humour had been passed on too, as well as a fierce loyalty to those she loved.

Debbie: She wanted to know all about her mum. The family hadn't talked about her much. And at first she wanted to know all about the murder. But I wanted to spare her the grim details. I also had to tell her that Storm and I had resolved our issues, that we had made peace around the murder, that we had worked it all through. There was a full-on energy in the air.

I'd guessed too that she was on a mission. To go to jail herself, to find Storm, to see where her mother was killed. I had to tell her she couldn't, there was a new jail, and that Storm too was different, a different person. I could see that was a relief for her, in a way. Her subconscious had been driving her to go to Boggo Road. At the time she was only fifteen or sixteen, living in a shelter, in and out of a violent relationship.

Katie had lived with the shadow of her mother's memory since her violent death, hearing snippets from family members before silence once more descended over the topic. At thirteen, angry and resentful and not understanding why, she'd begun to search out the very people – her mother's criminal contacts and friends – her family had hoped she would not.

Katie: Everyone tried to keep that part of her life a secret from
me, but I needed to know. I think they thought if they spoke
about it, I'd want to go out and explore it, and talk to people
in the wrong scene. But not telling me about it forced me to
go to the people they didn't want me to. I wanted to know
everything. I was going through the terrible teenage years and
I was angry, sad – all the emotions mixed around. I went off
the rails a bit.

When I was fifteen or sixteen I contacted Debbie. She
seemed to be the person closest to her, someone who could
tell me. I was nervous about going; I didn't know what to
expect. But after all that time thinking about it, there I was,
and suddenly I didn't want to know. I couldn't face it, or hear
about it. And just seeing Debbie was a big relief to me. I didn't
need to ask so many questions then; just seeing someone who
knew my mum seemed to be enough.

Katie left soon after, pledging to stay in touch. Debbie hoped she
would, feeling she had a responsibility for her dead friend's child, a
need to watch out for her. But it would be several years before
Debbie saw her again, and when she did, Katie would need more
than Debbie's help. She would also need the professional services of
Sisters Inside.

The programs provided by Sisters inside the jail continued to
expand. Between 1999 and 2000, the crucial and well-received
'transition' program was introduced, along with programs focusing
on women with hepatitis C, on youth crime, child protection, and
on drugs and alcohol. By now, the organisation had developed more
sophisticated processes for obtaining funding and received grants
from a variety of sources, including state and federal governments,
Jupiter's Casino and the Gaming Machine Community Benefit
Fund. More people in Queensland and in other states were
becoming aware of the outspoken organisation that took its arguments to the highest levels, and the woman at its head who seemed
genuinely unafraid of anyone.

Debbie was passionate about the transition program. Since the
first domestic violence programs in 1994, Sisters had been gathering
alarming statistics about what happened to women in the early

months after their release from jail. The figures varied, but in the two years up to March 2000 – just after the new transition program started – eighteen women died just after release, from overdoses, suicide, and extreme domestic violence. The transition program was designed to cover not just the transition from prison to the outside, but the reverse, including changes and movements that affect women after their sentencing. It also covered transitions in a woman's personal life, changes in relationships with friends and relatives and her engagement with the past and the future.

Although leaving jail is cause for celebration, it is also a time beset with huge challenges for most women as they try to reintegrate into the broader community and their own lives. They have roles to reclaim: that of mother, primarily, wife or girlfriend, of daughter, sister and friend. Jail impacts hard and usually negatively on families, and long-termers especially need to renegotiate the relationships that were abruptly curtailed when they were imprisoned. Even if family members have been regular visitors, imprisonment effectively removes a woman from her place among them. Resuming that place and role can require delicate negotiation, and for women who have spent years desensitising themselves to pain and fear – and sometimes love – the process can be long and complicated.

Even the practical steps to resuming outside life can be fraught with difficulty: everything is mined with problems when you have a prison record. Finding accommodation, finding work, accessing social security and banking, regaining custody of children from care become mountainous obstacles to your best intentions: to lead a blameless life. For many women, the seemingly insurmountable difficulties can make the path to re-offending or drug use look very attractive indeed. The transition program, at its best, would aim to stop women going back to jail because they resorted to the easy path. Tragically, that still means well over half of the women released from jail.

The hepatitis C program, which began in early 2000, was aimed at the astonishing fifty percent of women who SIS discovered had injected drugs while they were in prison. With syringes shared between five to seven women, and washing only in hot water, the program aimed to reduce transmission of hepatitis C and to provide harm minimisation strategies. Kim McNeil, who took on the job, also provided group and individual counselling, helping women deal with their diagnosis and educating others. She also began counselling on drug and alcohol issues, seeing up to thirty women every week.

As the new millennium approached, with all its attendant symbolism, Debbie's thinking around the wider issues of imprisonment was deepening and acquiring a sophistication not always appreciated by those close to her, both inside and outside jails. While she was still keen to ensure women inside could access services, her experiences and her research were pushing her beyond the need for reform, beyond merely applying bandaids to what she increasingly saw as a broken system. By the time she became director of Sisters Inside, she was convinced the very foundations of the system were rotten. Prisons, she believed, did not work. She had the stark evidence, in the numbers of women who returned to jail time after time, neither rehabilitated nor able to cope with life outside. It was the beginning of her transition from reformist to abolitionist.

> **Debbie**: Up until then I didn't have my head around how much I'd been brainwashed, like other women, to say, well, if it wasn't for prison, I wouldn't be here where I am now. But I also knew, all along, that it was a highly traumatic system – couldn't we do it a different way? Do you have to be so traumatised to get something decent out of life? I knew it was bullshit, it couldn't be the answer. Jail doesn't work – not for me or any of the other women in there who had walked the same path: from foster families to juvenile lock-up to prison, drugs and violence.
>
> Prison just covers up the atrocities women experience, and that sometimes they're party to, because they're about protecting their home environment. It's hard for some of them – when you're inside you'll fight for the stuff to make life better inside, because that's the life you've got. And when I started talking about abolition, for them it means their homes aren't going to feel like homes anymore. I knew we'd have to straddle that.

In 2000, with these thoughts coalescing in her head, Debbie travelled to Adelaide for 'Women in Corrections', a major conference organised by the Australian Institute of Criminology. Women and community groups from all over Australia, and some from overseas, joined the academics and senior corrections staff for the formal speeches and workshops. But the Australian prison activists, including Amanda George, a long-time activist and community lawyer from Melbourne, were determined that the real issues for incarcerated women – like the trauma of strip-searching – would be aired.

The Adelaide conference would prove to be a watershed for Debbie and Sisters Inside. An active coalition against strip-searching would be formed and Debbie would be introduced to Kim Pate, a Canadian activist whose work and thinking almost mirrored her own, and who would become one of her closest friends and allies. But before any of that, the activists' group – including Amanda, Kim and Debbie – would stage an audacious and controversial protest before shocked participants at the conference, an action that still reverberates in the memories of those who saw it and those who performed it.

On the day, the auditorium was full, with more than three hundred participants anticipating a keynote address and the media, alerted to the nature of the coalition's plans, expecting something with a bit more punch. A group of female corrections managers were assembled on the stage. But no one could have guessed what would unfold when, instead of a speaker, Kim, Debbie, Amanda, Karen Fletcher (coordinator of Queensland's Prisoners' Legal Service) and prison support worker Jade Blakkary took to the stage and assumed the roles of prison officer, prisoners and observers. They didn't delay.

From behind a microphone Karen, the 'prison officer', ordered the two 'prisoners' to strip. 'Shirt!' As Amanda and Jade removed their shirts, the first statistics were read out: 89 percent of women prisoners have been sexually abused. 'Trousers!' More stats: 98 percent of women prisoners have been physically abused. 'Bra!' And so on, until the two women stood naked on the stage, their ordinary, female bodies exposed and vulnerable.

Journalists and television cameras from the ABC moved in closer. The group on stage stood firm, unrepentant: they had done nothing that was not done in most prisons around the country every day, and they'd been careful to keep within the protocols of strip-searching in prisons in most states.

Amanda George remembers that the room was so quiet 'you could have heard a pin drop'. 'The 300-odd suits – they were mainly suits – were gobsmacked. We'd removed our bras and pants, and held our arms out. We didn't bend over and part our cheeks – that humiliation I couldn't stand,' she says. 'The girls handed out our leaflets, there was a smattering of applause, and then we left. I think it's fair to say the whole session was completely distracted by the action.'

Cathy Pereira, from the Prisoners' Legal Service in Brisbane, described the action in the second edition of Sisters' new *Women in Prison* journal. She spoke of the 'enormous courage and commitment' shown by Amanda and Jade when they volunteered to strip in a meeting of prison advocates the day before. George remembers that planning meeting for other reasons.

> George: It was an amazing discussion because, when we were deciding who would strip and who would be the prison officer, some women were saying they couldn't strip because they were too fat/too skinny/had been sexually abused/were too shy. That really put into focus what women in prison must feel when they get strip-searched, without choice.
>
> But when someone suggested Debbie as the prison officer, I saw tears welling in her eyes instantly. She said, I could never do that to a woman . . . not even for this. I was really shocked. I suppose for a long time I had been fooled by the veneers of strength and bravado that Debbie had obviously layered over the memory and pain of the strip-searches she had undergone. And I was also shocked because I thought perhaps she would use it as a revenge against the system that did it to her. But all she could see was that it was women being strip-searched, and it hurt her.

Pereira agreed: 'Everyone involved in the discussion preceding these women's decision to publicly act out a strip search were acutely aware that it involved a process which, however much a protest, still constituted a form of abuse,' she wrote.

From her place in the audience, Pereira could see the reaction to the strip-search was mixed. The chilling reality of two real women – Amanda and Jade – being coerced to strip naked publicly, the odd conjunction of pathos and terror, was extraordinarily confronting and moving for many. Some sat silently, obviously in shock. Many were in tears. Predictably, the prison managers showed little emotion on stage, apart from a couple who, according to Pereira, 'smiled and laughed'.

For the protest group, both the strip-search and the presentation of statistics had one aim: to give a voice to women in prison. And to underline the notion that the majority of women prisoners have endured sexual assault or abuse either as children and/or as adults, and are therefore the most vulnerable of all women. The strip-searching they endure on a weekly basis – if they want to touch their children – is hidden from the public eye.

The group was at pains to point out that, if making a woman strip publicly was unacceptable by wider community standards, then it should be unacceptable inside jails. And if sexual assault was not acceptable and, in fact, required punishment, then it should be unacceptable inside jails. Invisibility did not make a woman in prison any less a woman. 'We felt it was particularly important that the suits and bureaucrats saw a strip-search,' says George. 'They are the people who write prison policy, and who want more and more strip-searching. Prison officers do them all the time and many of them say it is one of the worst bits of the job. But the suits . . . they're distanced from the abuses they authorise and enforce.'

When the procedure was complete, the group gathered around Amanda and Jade to form a protective wall while they dressed. Several then handed out more material they had prepared on the trauma of strip-searching headed 'Sexual Assault by the State', and Debbie and Kim went outside to deal with the media.

Pate: I'd just arrived the night before, and Amanda took me to the room she and Deb were sharing and told me about the action. She asked me if I'd do media and I said sure, even though I wasn't really clued in, I was still half asleep and thinking about the paper I was going to deliver. Deb wanted to know who the hell I was; she was checking me out. But for myself, I was absolutely in awe of this amazing group of activist women who had decided to do such a clear and concise direct action at the conference.

When Amanda and Jade removed all of their clothing, I remember having a visceral response of wanting to leap in and stop the entire thing. It started out as a desire to intervene to protect both women from the humiliation and degradation of having their naked bodies observed by not only a roomful of correctional authorities, but also the national media and the general public. My initial reaction was quickly replaced by anger and revulsion as I heard some of the reactions from the officers. One male officer sarcastically intoned: 'If they were going to do it, then they should do it right and they should do it all – bend over, spread their cheeks and squat and cough, too.'

I found it disturbing that the officers could distance themselves from the very acts they were involved in almost every day, and I was repulsed by the way they dealt with the situation so cavalierly. For those of us who were there, whose life work is trying to alleviate the oppression experienced by the most vulnerable members of our communities, the memory is seared into our consciousness. It's a chilling reminder of the extent to which otherwise calm, caring and humane individuals are capable of some of the most degrading, inhumane and humiliating interactions with others.

But the other thing that is seared into my emotional memory is how Deb and I were able to support each other when we spoke to the journalists. This was a woman I had met barely twelve hours previously and I quickly realised we were both saying basically the same thing, even though we hadn't rehearsed anything.

For Debbie, too, even the re-enactment of a strip-search was horrifying. She supported the action absolutely, and knew the significant media coverage would raise the issue more effectively in the public arena. But the reality of the event shook her. When one prison general manager approached her afterwards, telling her emotionally, 'My prison officers don't do that,' Debbie replied: 'Well, what the hell did you think a strip-search was like?'

The international coalition against strip-searching became active immediately, with all groups, including Sisters, arguing that the process represented a breach of prisoners' human rights as well as cruel and unusual punishment, and that it was intended as social control and demoralisation rather than an attempt to control drugs in jails.

Despite the strident views of government that the act was a legitimate part of the war against drugs, Sisters Inside continued to raise the issue with ministers and bureaucrats and to expose its short-comings. Freedom of Information statistics obtained by the group showed that prison authorities conducted 12 136 searches within Brisbane Women's Correctional Centre between August 1999 and August 2000. Of those, 5346 were full body searches, one of a baby. Contraband unearthed included a pair of earrings, some tobacco, cigarettes, and an unused sanitary pad – but no drugs. How then, Sisters argued, did women continue to access drugs in jail?

But for the women, the humiliation and serious after-effects of strip-searching has led to many forgoing regular contact visits with their children and loved ones. In Queensland, strip-searching is mandatory after every contact visit. For the 89 percent of women prisoners who have been sexually assaulted or abused, the process can trigger terrifying flashbacks, and can, according to counsellors, delay the long path to recovery. Given the choice between cuddling their children and enduring the trauma of removing their clothes publicly, or missing out on both, many women choose the latter.

By the close of the Adelaide conference, Debbie had a new, wider context for her work. After long discussions with Kim Pate and Amanda George, the bigger picture of prisons and the growing culture of incarceration around the world began to form in her head. She could see that her work, and the work of Sisters, had a global agenda, and was tied not just to international systems of justice but to the underlying political and economic structures on which they were built. Her wider reading, contacts and research were also revealing something no one, until then, had suspected: that Sisters Inside, with its power invested firmly in the hands of women in prison, and its growing political clout, was unique in the world. Debbie began to see its real potential to achieve change.

For Amanda George, the Adelaide conference and its aftermath combined with the stress of her long-running prison work to provoke a personal crisis from which she only emerged, she believes, because of Debbie's 'enormous support'. The night after the strip-search action in Adelaide, she was out with other delegates and inter-vened in an incident between police and an Aboriginal man. 'They were trying to get him into the paddy wagon and were slamming the van door against his ankle. His offence had been urinating at nine thirty at night in a dark alley. I told them I was a lawyer and wanted to chat to him, but ended up being arrested myself,' she says.

In the Adelaide watch-house cells, she 'hoped against hope' she would not be strip-searched. 'What an irony that would have been. Fortunately I wasn't, but I could hear the screams of the fellow who was arrested as he was getting and resisting the search,' she says. Back in Melbourne, she 'fell into a complete heap'.

> George: I had just been involved in a very lengthy inquest into the death of a young Indigenous woman who hung herself in the private women's prison in Melbourne. What precipitated her decline had been a forced strip-search where four officers – two male, two female – held her face down on a bed and used a cutdown knife (used to cut down hanging bodies) to cut off her clothes, bra and undies to retrieve a drink can she had concealed. Only six weeks before when she had been out, she had been held face down and anally raped.
>
> The conference strip-search, the arrest, the night in the cell was the trigger for the burnt-out me to implode into a teary, shaky, unconfident, inconsolable self. I felt extremely embarrassed that such a small incident tipped me over, when I had worked with women who had spent years and years enduring the awfulness of incarceration.

What sustained her over the next twelve months, she says, was the compassion and understanding and support from Debbie, who telephoned her constantly and visited. Without that, George believes, she would have 'lost the heart and energy to keep doing the prison thing'. 'She made my work feel valuable and valued,' she says.

In July that year, Debbie's horizons were further expanded when she was invited to visit East Timor. Anne Warner was already there working on a four-month contract, and set up meetings for Debbie with an organisation providing sexual assault and trauma counselling. Debbie loved the experience. She made close contacts and became part of the provision of those services for a week.

'It was a time in East Timor when people were hungry for information and experience around the provision of those services because assault was endemic,' Warner says. 'Deb's skills were invaluable. And for her it also meant realising things weren't centred in Brisbane, that human beings were human beings everywhere. She did a lot of reading around the East Timorese experience, which really enriched her understanding of how the world works. It was an opportunity for her to understand the world as a bigger place, and a richer and more varied place, and at the same time the same.'

Sisters Inside had already decided to conduct its own conference the following year, one that would not be slave to the agendas of corrections agencies, universities or governments. It would bring together women working at the coalface of prison issues – activists, service providers, academics and writers, and would provide an arena for challenging the stereotypes and assumptions about who was in jail, why, and the repercussions for individuals and societies of the growing practice of incarceration.

The Canadian Association of Elizabeth Fry Societies (CAEFS), where Kim Pate was director, was also having a conference in 2001, entitled 'From Victimisation to Criminalisation', and Kim and Debbie immediately invited each other to their events. (Elizabeth Fry was a Quaker woman born in 1780, who was a strong proponent of humane treatment for prisoners and led major reforms in the treatment of women and children inside London's Newgate Prison. She was regarded as a shining light in prison reform.) For the rest of 2000, they kept in touch via email, exchanging ideas and plans, both realising the power of the connections they were making, and the great potential for cross-fertilisation between the two organisations.

Debbie fully understood the importance of legal knowledge and power to the fate of women in prison, both at an individual level and in the wider context of imprisonment – the reasons they were there, and how the system often worked against them. But in 1999, when she had returned to university to study law, it was a personal decision, a rare impulse to do something for herself.

Debbie: Years before, all these people had told me, only certain people can be doctors and lawyers, and they're not people like you. You're too stupid. So I thought, I'm going to prove you wrong. I wanted to prove something to myself, too. I'd swallowed a lot of things back there – that I was bad, and couldn't do this or that – so it was also about breaking down those walls for myself. I'd wanted to do social work because social workers had locked me up, and getting the degree meant I could play in their ballpark easily. Then the law locked me up. So that's next.

But I also wanted to challenge the system, to say, if you really believe in rehabilitation, then you will allow me to practise law. Or will you insist that I carry these criminal convictions for the rest of my life, and it's all just rhetoric? So it's a test; I want to set a precedent. And to show the women inside: you can do anything you want to do. Law, or medicine. Do it. Just be consistent yourself, and challenge their inconsistencies along the way.

She enrolled in law at the Queensland University of Technology, and began with two subjects, hoping to move steadily through the units and – with summer school thrown in – to graduate within six years. But the enormity of the issues faced by Sisters that year and in 2000 forced a slower progression. She completed two subjects in one semester, one in another. Always, her involvement with Sisters took precedence.

But the more frequent contact with the lawyers in the new international coalition – Kim Pate, Amanda George, Karen Fletcher – convinced her the effort would be worthwhile. Intellectually, she had no trouble dealing with the subject matter. The big hurdle was time. The Catch-22 for Debbie was becoming all too apparent: the growth of her profile and that of Sisters Inside matched the reduction in her available time. And she and Sisters were only just hitting their stride.

14

That Prison Cell Coldness

Debbie can't remember when the name Angela Davis was first mooted in connection with the approaching Sisters Inside conference. But she does know that, despite other gaps in her memory and education, she knew the name as soon as it was mentioned. In Debbie's mind, it was straightforward: Angela Davis was a woman who had been in prison, and who wasn't afraid to speak out about her experience. Davis had provoked worldwide controversy and debate in the late 1960s and early 1970s with her involvement in the radical Black Panthers group, and her imprisonment on charges of murder and kidnapping. She had spent sixteen months in prison until she was eventually acquitted on all charges in 1972. In the process she had become a heroine of the black revolution and the fight against injustice.

Davis was someone known to be honest about the issues. Debbie wasn't aware, at that stage, of the celebrity status that attended Davis's name, or the huge reputation the black activist had built in the days following her arrest in the United States. She knew only that Davis was well known for speaking out against prisons. That was enough.

Debbie: We were talking about a keynote speaker – I think it was Anne who suggested Angela – and I said, let's get *her*. They all said, you won't get Angela Davis. I said, I'll email her. She'll come. I was thinking, she's been in prison, I've been in prison, I'll write from one woman who has been inside to another. So I got on the Web and found her email address, wrote to her and she responded. *Yes.*

No one could believe it. Angela told us later that she gets thousands of emails; she doesn't usually read them herself, her assistant does. But for some reason she saw this one, opened it and read it. The letter just explained who I was, what Sisters was about, that women inside were the steering committee. And invited her to come over and speak at our conference. Apparently, she'd never even heard of Brisbane – she knew of Sydney and Melbourne and assumed they were the active spots.

But when she got here and saw what we were doing, she changed her mind. When she spoke at the conference she said this was where it was all happening in terms of prison issues, here, in Brisbane. There was nothing like it in the rest of the world. So it almost seemed as if she was meant to come here.

Amanda George still smiles when she recalls hearing about the guest speaker Sisters had managed to lure. 'The audacity and coup in getting Angela Davis! I thought it was extraordinary. Angela gets three hundred emails a day. Debbie's energy and passion must have flashed like a beacon in an in-box crowded with competition,' she says.

The inclusion of Angela Davis on the conference program added a certain gravity to the three-day event, scheduled for the end of November 2001. Registrations began to roll in from women and community groups all over Australia, as well as one from New Zealand. Although the other national and international speakers – including Amanda George, Kim Pate, and academic and poet Jean Trounstine from the United States – were also regarded as draw-cards, it was the reputation and charisma of Davis that attracted the attention of prisoner advocates and the media.

By the time of the Sisters Inside conference, Davis had become an iconic figure in academia and in the resistance movement across the United States, where she had continued to campaign and advocate on political and social issues. But it was what she eloquently described as the growing 'prison industrial complex' that still captured most of her attention, and that was also the major theme of her writing, including the books *Women, Race and Class* and *Are Prisons Obsolete?*.

Even high-ranking bureaucrats inside Corrective Services – who were officially invited to register – were excited at the prospect of hearing Angela Davis. But at the highest levels, they were also very worried about the conference, and the issues that might arise. In the days leading up to its opening, the serving director general summonsed Debbie and Anne Warner (by now president of Sisters Inside) to her office in the city, where Debbie was warned off a repeat of the Adelaide strip-search and told that she should in no circumstances take off her clothes.

> **Debbie**: We laughed. I said, it's *our* conference, we'll walk around naked if we want to. Don't try to tell us what to do. Then we were warned not to abuse Corrective Services staff. I said, we won't, but if they're going to take things personally, tell them not to come. But don't read us the riot act, it's *our* conference. God, they thought they had control. It was hilarious.

There was another new addition to the management committee in the lead-up to the conference. Janine Walker was well known in Brisbane for her involvement with the right wing of the Labor Party, her statewide morning ABC radio program and her membership of the board of the ABC. As Walker remembers it, Anne Warner telephoned her early in 2001 and said, do you want to come on to our committee? We need someone with your connections and expertise.

She wasn't surprised to hear from Warner, who is firmly on the left. 'I'd always been associated with the right, but in the Labor Party the women have always been friends across those factional boundaries, we've always been connected with each other,' she says. And it was fortuitous timing for Walker, who had just divested herself of various committee memberships and was convinced something 'interesting' would come along. She knew about the work of Sisters Inside, and also knew the Kilroy name: 'I grew up in a rugby league mad family; my uncle writes books about league,' she says. 'I remembered Joe Kilroy as the most wonderful footballer. Despite having known prime ministers and others, I am only now seen as a person of consequence to my uncle because I know Joe Kilroy.'

Walker submitted herself to the usual 'suss-out' by Debbie and, looking back, is still surprised that the two of them have become such close friends. 'I'm a good girl,' she smiles, 'I keep the rules. If they say, walk on the left hand side, I walk on the left hand side.

And Deb is the sort who, if you tell her to walk on the left side, she'll go straight to the bloody right. So I was puzzled at first about what Deb saw in me. We're very different, at least superficially. I love my lipstick and high heels. But we began to explore how we weren't different, the things we have in common – the ways we mother, for instance, and our love of buying bargain Versace.'

Throughout 2001, planning for the conference occupied much of the attention of Sisters' administrative staff, particularly Rebecca Draper and Natalie Bell, both of whom had worked in the office for several years. By mid-2001, however, two other issues were diverting Debbie and her growing number of staff. The first was the need to once more find bigger premises.

With increased funding, more programs and eight or nine people employed to run them, Sisters Inside could no longer be contained inside the Gloucester Street office. Debbie knew she had to plan for expansion. Throughout 1998, 1999 and 2000, she had lobbied hard with funding bodies and government agencies, with generally positive responses. From experience, she knew the incubation time for funding was usually two years. Some of it had arrived already, and they had to be prepared to employ more staff over the next twelve months.

> **Debbie**: I'd planted the seeds and I wanted to make sure we'd be ready when the fruit hit the ground. The lobbying had been heavy-duty, especially with the bureaucrats. In the meetings I tried hard to help them understand the issues, and convince them these programs were needed. It's important to get them onside because then they become your agents internally, to advocate around the issues.

Debbie began the hunt for bigger premises in West End, but quickly came to the conclusion that for $40 000 a year – the going rate to lease office space in the area – Sisters could conceivably buy their own place. She and Natalie Bell began to look closely at the idea, researching loans and mortgages and repayment rates versus the costs of long-term leasing. The results convinced them: purchasing would put the organisation well ahead, and give them an asset too. Their lack of a deposit, however, proved a major stumbling block: as an incorporated body, they would need 20 percent of the purchase price.

The breakthrough came when Debbie approached ANA, the Australian Natives Association, which was known for providing 'ethical' loans and superannuation in the community sector. By now Debbie and Natalie had found the property they wanted, a roomy cottage in Victoria Street in West End in Brisbane already fitted out with offices, one hundred metres from the Brisbane River in a residential/commercial zone. The price: $307 000. They took the proposal to ANA. A mortgage was organised immediately, and Sisters Inside moved to its new, permanent home in August. According to Debbie: 'Buying Victoria Street was big for everyone, particularly the women inside. It was just great: now we knew no one could pull the rug out from under us anymore. It was ours. Even if we lost all our funding tomorrow, we own that property.'

For long-termers and steering committee members like Tracey Leivers, Storm Brooke and Tracy Wigginton, the purchase of the house was not just financially advantageous, but enormously symbolic. Stripped of just about everything they own in prison, the house gave them possession of something solid on the outside, a real and tangible object that they, as the drivers of the organisation, had and were a part of.

'Buying the house was one of the biggest things for me,' says Tracey Leivers. 'In jail, shit happens and Sisters can be booted out. But no one can boot you out of what you own. It's solid, it's ours.'

The second major concern that year was the health of one of the Sisters staff members, Kim McNeil, who had been working since 1999 on the hepatitis C and alcohol programs. Debbie had met Kim when Kim was studying at the University of Queensland with Joe Kilroy, who had relinquished all interest in football in favour of working in Aboriginal health. They'd made an immediate connection: Debbie describes Kim as 'honest, feisty, upfront, no bullshit', a woman who had done time in prison herself and lost her five children to the care of the government. When she began work at SIS, Kim had already survived one bout of cancer, and was 'virtually living at the health food shop' in an apparently successful campaign to keep the disease at bay. But midway through 2001, while Debbie was in the throes of investigating mortgages and loans, a shocking and debilitating personal crisis sent Kim spiralling back into ill-health.

She told Debbie in a distressing midnight phone call that one of her children – she had managed to retrieve two of them from care – had been sexually abused by someone she knew. The news took a terrible toll on Kim physically. She told Debbie she could no longer face life; she wanted to give up. 'You're not checking out on me, are you?' Debbie asked her when she dropped in to see her. 'Yes, I am,' Kim told her. Within days she was looking less and less like herself, like the robust and voluble Kim that Debbie knew.

Kim was admitted to hospital and Debbie warned staff to expect the worst. Within five days of telling Debbie she was ready to 'check out', Kim was dead. Debbie received the news early on a Friday morning; numb, she went back to bed and 'cried for an hour'. Joe, who had also been close to Kim, sat crying beside her. It then fell to Debbie to pass the news to Sisters' staff and the women inside, all of whom had loved Kim, she says, and admired her hugely successful work inside the prison.

James Finn, who had been helping Kim complete her work in the weeks leading up to her deterioration, remembers Kim's funeral as the first occasion on which he had seen Debbie cry openly. He was shocked, but realised Debbie must have crossed some personal threshold: 'You only did that behind closed doors and with certain people,' he says.

Debbie recalls only the large number of people at the service. 'Even Corrective Services staff came. Everyone liked her,' she remembers. 'People at Sisters still cry about Kim; her death had a huge impact on everyone.'

There had never been an intention to repeat the public strip-search staged at the Adelaide conference. That initiative had been enormously successful in raising awareness of the brutality of strip-searching, but the two conferences were too closely spaced to ensure success again, and besides, Sisters Inside believed their program was strong enough to attract attention on its own merits.

Along with Angela Davis, the program featured Jean Trounstine, whose book *Shakespeare Behind Bars* described her ten years teaching Shakespeare and facilitating drama workshops and performances at Framingham Women's Prison in Massachusetts; feminist criminologists Dr Suzanne Davis and Sandy Cook, who had also been at the Adelaide conference; Prisoners' Legal Service director Karen Fletcher; Amanda George; high-profile Aboriginal women including writer and academic Jackie Huggins, high-ranking bureaucrat Kerrie Tim, and novelist Melissa Lucashenko; and, of course, Kim Pate, whose Canadian Association of Elizabeth Fry Societies had just hosted a controversial conference in the deep shadow of the September 11 attacks on New York and Washington.

Also on the list was the then chief magistrate in Queensland, Di Fingleton, who would make sensational headlines twice in the two years that followed: initially, with the release of a movie, which depicted the violent upbringing Fingleton and her brothers had endured; and soon afterwards when she was herself imprisoned for twelve months in controversial circumstances on charges of 'threatening a witness'.

Despite the calibre and profile of some of the keynote speakers, there was one group Debbie was most keen to see take the podium: several of the women from Brisbane Women's Correctional Centre. Right up until the week of the conference, she held out hopes that, despite the tough policies of the most recent regimes, long-term, low-security prisoners like Tracey Leivers and Storm Brooke might be given leave to attend and to speak to delegates. No one was surprised, however, when that permission was withheld; only two women each day from the open security halfway house at Albion were allowed to attend. Those inside Brisbane Women's Correctional Centre were invited to write down their speeches for others to deliver for them. Even the proposed video link-up to allow them to speak for themselves was cancelled.

In the end, although the women from Albion duly arrived, they declined to speak. 'They wanted to,' Debbie says, 'but by then they were terrified. They'd been threatened, in a nice way: be careful what you say because you've got to come back here, you know. And we had to tread really carefully too because we wanted approval to take delegates into the prison. They could have knocked that on the head. But they didn't.'

Indeed, the prison visit would prove to be the emotional pinnacle of the conference, of three days of anger, joy, laughter and tears, as stories were told that gave the dire facts around women's incarceration an unforgettably human face. The visit was what the women inside had been waiting for. Here was firm evidence that they had not been forgotten, despite their invisibility, that they had been heard, despite being deprived of a voice. The visitors did a tour of inspection and then were ushered into the work area to meet some of the women. There were warm and tearful greetings all round. Angela Davis took the hands of each woman in turn, embracing them. Tracy Wigginton, Tracey Leivers and Debbie hugged each other, crying.

> Tracey Leivers: That day, I realised what SIS had become. Not when they were actually there: it was too overwhelming. Meeting them, then all the questions, I didn't have time to take it in. I wanted to cry but there were too many people. But afterwards – wow! I saw that we had grown up. Being in here, I don't get to see the bigger picture all the time. I hear about it, but because I don't walk it out there it isn't my reality. But then all these people came in, and I saw that we weren't this little organisation anymore. We were more than the sum of our parts, bigger than the individuals. Bigger than a dozen people sitting around in a room once a month.

But for Tracey, the success of the conference was a double-edged sword. The paper she had written about the inadequacies of the medical services in prison caused a minor uproar after it was read to delegates – she had faxed off both the officially authorised version and an unauthorised one – and she spent two months in the prison's secure section as punishment. 'It was all worth it,' she says now. 'I'd do it all again, because it's the truth. And they didn't want the truth.'

Tracy called her story the 'Two Panadol' story. This was its un-official version:

> Before my incarceration, I was totally frustrated with the public health system, and now I take back every nasty word I ever said. The health system within the correctional centre makes the Dark Ages look advanced.
>
> My first big encounter with the medical system was while I was trying to cope with coming to prison – confused, stressed and scared. I was sent off to the psychiatrist who diag-nosed depression – although I thought it was quite normal to experience a period of shock. But it fast became clear to me that I was no longer in control of my body, which had become

the property of the government. I was put on high doses of three drugs, which seemed to be a regular practice then – putting inmates on such high doses of psychiatric medication that it's hard enough to function let alone create trouble. After months of functioning just above a catatonic state, other women strongly advised me to stop taking the medication. I did.

Some time later, I was called for a pap smear and, having returned positive tests in the past, I knew the procedure. This time, the positive result required treatment which took so long to organise that the operation I finally had took four hours and left me with virtually no cervix. Most recently, it took the intervention of the Minister for Corrective Services to get treatment after I developed a lump in my breast, then began to lose blood and produce milk from both breasts.

After ascertaining I could not be pregnant (my medical file would have shown I was unable to conceive) the doctor expressed some concern and said I'd need an appointment at the hospital. Ten stressful months later, still no appointment. I raised the issue with Sisters Inside. They contacted the Minister who requested my file, and within days I was at the hospital and the tests began.

Between fortnightly appointments, I was given various amounts of medication, and I am grateful to nursing staff who pointed out that one of them should not be taken by people with hepatitis C or stomach ulcers. I have both! But finally my operation was done, and my life now is somewhat normal. I find it sad, though, that nobody employed by the correctional centre has been near me to ask how I'm coping with the effects of the operation.

Leivers finished off her paper with an account of a woman who had experienced a rough day in court and, feeling 'a little teary', asked centre medical staff for something to help her sleep. For her trouble, the woman was placed on suicide watch overnight – her clothes were taken and she was forced to wear a suicide gown – despite her protestations that she merely wanted to get a good night's sleep. 'At no time did she mention any self-harm,' Leivers writes. 'No wonder nobody requests their help and would rather try and deal with life on their own. What if it was your mother, or your daughter?'

To an already tearful audience, two other papers were also read out – one criticising the lack of programs for women released to the low-security Numinbah Prison Farm, and the other about the effects of institutionalisation on long-term prisoners. The latter was written by Tracy Wigginton, who gave a moving account of how, with the removal of all her decision-making opportunities in prison, she had assumed an 'almost robotic' approach and behaviour, and had actually begun to *want* to stay inside. To that end, she realised she had unconsciously sabotaged her own progress through the system, even breaking the rules to ensure she was not given the 'privilege' of transfer to a low-security facility:

> I rely on the system for all my needs, both physical and mental. They tell me where to work, what to wear, what I can eat and within the scope of the programs run within the system, what I can think.
>
> Other aspects of my life have also become institutionalised. In general conversation another woman and I realised we no longer knew what size clothing we wore, or our shoe size. I do not know what our currency looks like or how to use new telephones. I have forgotten what it is like to go shopping.

But for Wigginton, the most devastating realisation was that she no longer knew her place within her own family unit:

> For twelve years, my life has been in here, and theirs has been outside, so my real family and I are literally worlds apart. I find it more and more difficult to have visits and phone calls with my parents because I don't know what life is like out there, and they have limited knowledge of life in here. I have lost my sister, not because of the crime or length of time I have still to spend in jail, but because of the things I have done to remain here. Trying to explain why I want to stay is almost impossible, they cannot understand, although my parents do try.
>
> If women – like me – are to become 'productive members of society' again, then changes must be made so that they don't return because they can't cope with the outside world. The

system has recently made me low-risk, and while this pleases me, because it means I have conformed and am no longer a risk to the community, I can't help but wonder if this is because I am so heavily reliant upon the system, and that I could not function out there by myself. I identify myself, not as an individual any more, but by my place in the system. It is very hard to see myself differently.

Other speakers raised issues about private prisons, the over-representation of Aboriginal women in prison, the treatment of women with mental illnesses and post-release options. But Angela Davis managed to galvanise delegates with her observations that the globalised 'war on drugs' begun in the United States had 'demonised people of colour' everywhere, by setting up victims of illegal drugs to look like criminals, and had ensured the numbers of women in prisons had skyrocketed. The numbers of women in Queensland prisons, she pointed out, had increased fivefold over the previous six years.

In the prison industrial complex, she said, the 'penal equivalent of ambulance chasing' had seen architectural and construction companies vying to build more prisons all over the world, and an increasing number of corporations dependent on supply of goods and services to those prisons – food manufacturers, software and even soap suppliers. Because prisons had become an important source of profit to these companies, it was in their interests to push racism and sexism, because it involved the very groups – blacks and women – most likely to go to prison.

For Janine Walker, the first SIS conference was a stark reminder of how many people's lives are touched by prisons:

I was lining up to get lunch one day with this very nicely dressed older woman. She was an average woman – you would have seen her in Myers, shopping, someone's mum, or grandma. I asked her if she was interested in prisons, and she said, 'Yes, luvvie, I do a bit of work with girls up around Bundaberg. And I was in there myself a couple of years ago.'

She'd done twelve months for social security fraud. I suspect she couldn't have talked to anyone up there about it. Prison is this powerful, unspoken thread in our community.

Anyone could be there. And no one talks about it; it's one of the big silences in our community. If a friend or family member goes to jail, you think you're the only one, you feel very isolated. So you keep silent. And Deb, and that conference, gave people the freedom to talk about it. I realised that one of the most powerful things Deb has done is to gain the support of ordinary people, particularly women, for issues around women in prison. They now have a face, and its name is Debbie Kilroy.

The 2001 conference proved to be a significant milestone for Sisters Inside. Delegates who came expecting a rabble or one long protest rally found instead a three-day event dense with measured debate and run with faultless professionalism. While emotions ran high throughout many of the sessions, there was no hysteria; rather, a sad and dignified recognition of the cruelties society insists on inflicting on those born into disadvantage, abuse and poverty. By the end of the three days, it was obvious the conference had been a brilliant vehicle for highlighting that. Sisters Inside had come of age. 'That conference rocked people off their socks,' says Amanda George. 'It was palpably powerful, and run like a military mission. Everyone who left it had the power and passion of it written on their hearts.'

Debbie: It was the first time we'd all come together and really gelled, all of us across the sector. We'd done something we'd all dreamed about when we first started – and we realised we'd created something huge. We'd cemented all the relationships too: from the beginning, when Anne and I had gone to meet Angela at the airport, we'd just clicked. Bingo. It was like we'd known each other for a million years. Then everyone else clicked too. That was so obvious at the prison visit. Thinking about that still brings tears to my eyes. But it was all so big, and it had been such a huge year, a big emotional roller-coaster. I felt wiped out.

But with that kind of impetus, the roller-coaster wasn't about to slow down. Debbie could not know it then, but when a large group of asylum-seekers on a ship called the *Tampa* was turned away from Australian shores in late 2001, followed by the controversy of the 'children overboard' allegations – both of which propelled John

Howard back into government at the December 2001 elections –
she would soon become caught up in the heated debate.

After the initial outrage from refugee support groups settled, that
debate centred on the incarceration of asylum-seekers of all ages in
remote detention centres, where conditions were rumoured to be
worse than in mainstream jails. Because the media was refused entry
to the centres, information was limited, but reports soon emerged
about the desperation of some inmates who had attempted suicide
or self-harm by swallowing soap or sewing their lips together.
Advocacy groups became particularly alarmed about the health and
welfare of children locked up with their parents for months and
sometimes years.

For Debbie, the very words 'locked up' were enough to fire a
deep anger at the trauma and desperation that was surely being
visited upon the detainees, many of whom, like mainstream prisoners, had already suffered through years of abuse, poverty and terrible
disadvantage. When Anne Warner and her daughter Kate suggested
joining a protest at the Woomera detention centre over Easter 2002,
Debbie readily agreed to go. Siyavash Doostkhah, then (and still)
director of YANQ, and who had escaped from Iran several years
earlier, also joined them.

The group flew to Adelaide where they planned to hire a small
bus for the drive into the desert, but for Debbie the emotional pain
of the journey began on the aircraft. The award-winning Australian
film *Rabbit-Proof Fence* was about to premiere around the country,
and trailers were being screened on longer flights. Debbie watched
the wrenching scene in which the Aboriginal children are torn from
their mother's arms, and felt her heart begin to beat fast. The
circumstances were different, of course, but all she could see was
Joshua being dragged away from her after a prison visit, his little
boy's face crumpling as he sobbed and pleaded to stay, her own sense
of bereavement on the face of the black woman. She felt reluctant
tears well in her eyes.

These were the feelings – loss, anger, grief – that accompanied
her on the long drive across the desert, feelings amplified by the vast
emptiness they journeyed through. But they would not prepare her
for the scenes they would encounter when they finally arrived at
Woomera late on Good Friday. Just as they parked the bus and began
to walk towards the razor wire of the detention centre, the crowd

that had gathered around the perimeter fence suddenly broke apart, and people began to run away, and towards them. 'People were yelling at us: *run!* They were everywhere,' says Debbie. 'Then we noticed there were asylum-seekers amongst them. It was a break-out.'

For the next two days, the protesters' camp buzzed with plans and rumours. Some of the escapees were being sheltered in tents, and argument raged about how the situation should be handled. Debbie was impatient and becoming increasingly angry at the prolonged talking and lack of action. Through Siyavash, who spoke Farsi, she knew that some of the escapees wanted to return to the detention centre, frightened by the dramatic events and the likely consequences. Others wanted only to leave, even if that meant walking for days through the desert.

Debbie made a passionate speech to the gathered protesters, urging an end to the prevarication. Finally, on Easter Sunday, some of the escapees walked back through the fences; others were successfully spirited away. That day, Debbie joined a group walking around the perimeter of the centre, communicating with those inside via loudhailers. They knew that, behind the rear wall, water trucks lay in wait, their powerful hoses at the ready. But it was another sight, another sound, that reached Debbie first: all along one wall, behind the wire, banks of women and children were wailing and sobbing.

Debbie: That did it for me. Those sounds hit the core of my being. That night I sat down and started to cry, and couldn't stop. Their trauma just connected to mine. It affected everyone – Siyavash just stood at a lean, not quite touching a post nearby, staring and smoking. He hadn't smoked for years. But some of the men inside had come from the same part of Iran he'd escaped from, so that was very hard for him. And Kate was wandering the desert in her socks. Anne was running around trying to console everyone – delaying her own reaction until she got home.

Next morning, my rib cage hurt from crying. That was Monday, and we drove out, all of us in a state of shock. On the way out we found a river, and we stopped and just threw ourselves into it, to get it all off us. But leaving those people behind, out there in the desert, wrenched our hearts.

But it was anger, too. About what they were doing to these

people who had come over here in leaky boats, seeking asylum. How dare we? We see these things happening day in, day out in the prison system – and here are these people captured for political gain, put out in the desert, isolated from everyone. I knew what that experience was like.

In June that year, Debbie flew out of Australia for Canada and the United States. She would spend three weeks visiting prisons across Canada with Kim Pate, and speak at a 'prison round table' in New York at which Angela Davis was guest speaker. The time in Canada was an important building block for both Debbie and Kim: it would bring to fruition their dream of creating a truly international anti-prison movement, and forge one of the closest friendships in their lives.

Kim: When Deb was in Canada I was doing my regular visits to all the prisons – it wasn't just a tour around – and it was incredible for me to have someone in the prison with me who worked the same way I did. Even in my own organisation, I can't say there's anyone I've gone into a prison with who works so clearly in tandem with me.

Early in the piece, I was seeing one woman and another one was waiting for me, calling out to me. Debbie said, I'll go. By the time I got there Deb had laid out exactly the same kinds of things I'd been talking about to the other woman. It soon became clear that the ways we worked were eerily similar. We'd be driving along, two to three hours in the car at a stretch, and suddenly we'd start talking about the same thing.

The way I introduced her in Canada was as a woman who has both the lived experience of prison, and now has been accumulating the academic experience and the 'straight' credentials people look for. But she's never let go of the lived experience as the thing that informs everything she does. I'd been talking for a number of years about women organising within the prisons, and it was after Deb visited that people started picking up on that in a way I couldn't give life to, and she could. It's about what it's like to have been in prison and come out, and to work against the system.

On that trip Debbie paid me the second-best compliment

I've had in twenty years. The best was from a woman serving
a life sentence in the infamous Prison for Women in Kingston;
she asked me when I had gotten out. Deb told me that 'you'd
think you'd done time, the way you move through the
system'. It was no doubt a typical, maybe even offhand
comment from Deb, but she has no idea the impact it had on
me. I never presume to understand what being locked up is
like, but if I have even a semblance of appreciation that
permits me to better support, advocate and generally walk
with the women, then I'm grateful and honoured.

Debbie and Kim were also joined on the long drive by Karen
Fletcher, from the Prisoners' Legal Service (PLS) in Brisbane.
Fletcher had been a close friend of Debbie's for over five years,
despite a shaky start. As a new lawyer at PLS in 1996, she had organised a public forum on prison issues, only to receive an 'irate' phone
call from Debbie (who she'd never met) complaining that there was
nothing specific to women prisoners on the agenda. 'I considered –
and still consider – myself to be a feminist and I was a bit miffed to
be dressed down by Deb about neglecting women's issues,' she
recalls. 'Deb had argued that women prisoners were different and I
didn't agree with her. But it didn't take long for me to warm to Deb
and after working with and for women in prison, I came to agree –
prison is different for women.'

The three women, along with Pate's baby daughter Madison,
forged an enduring friendship during their drive across Canada.
Fletcher was delighted when Debbie told her how a Canadian lifer
they had visited had mistaken Debbie for the Australian lawyer and
Fletcher for the ex-prisoner. 'It was a proud moment for me,' she
says. 'Most lawyers take great pains to differentiate themselves from
their prisoner-clients. With Deb I was able to walk into prisons as a
woman amongst women.'

Debbie had felt a close emotional and intellectual connection
with Kim from the first days of their acquaintance in Adelaide. The
trip through Canada consolidated that, but for Debbie, it also
stitched a frame around the big picture that had been forming in her
mind for years. 'You're so concerned with your own backyard that
you often don't even get to look closely at other places in the
country,' she says. 'But after Canada I began to seek it out, every-

where, and I've realised that it's all the same, in terms of prisons, everywhere. There's little difference. And the world ain't that big.'

In New York, however, the first hints of the acknowledgement and praise that awaited her work came when Angela Davis singled her out during her speech to the hundreds at the five-day round table. She asked Debbie to stand up – which she did, shyly given the T-shirt she was wearing proclaimed 'George Bush – International Terrorist' over a photograph of the President of the United States. Davis then introduced her, declaring Sisters Inside the 'best practice model throughout the world' for those working in the field. Debbie blushed and hurriedly sat down. But it soon began to dawn on her that the work she was doing in Brisbane had a real global agenda. And that, just ten years after her release from prison, she was at its helm.

Back in Australia, the work of Sisters Inside was still expanding. Eight programs were now running with fourteen staff and six volunteers, and the house in Victoria Street was beginning to fill up. Debbie began to make plans for the next meeting of the international coalition, which they'd decided would take place in December on Stradbroke Island, where Debbie and Anne went to fish whenever a weekend was spare. On Straddie, the whole group assembled once more: Debbie, Amanda George, Kim Pate, Angela Davis, Sandy Cook, Karen Fletcher, Anne Warner, and members of Sisters' management team. The talk ranged over the usual topics: strip-searching, the abolition agenda, as well as a complaint Kim was planning to lodge against the Canadian government for systemic discrimination against women in prisons. As always, the discussions were robust.

The group challenged Kim about the realities of attempting change through such a complaint: many hours were spent negotiating the expected benefits or otherwise. Kim Pate loved the debate. 'In Canada I didn't really have peers to bounce things off, no one to push me and hold me accountable. That's one of the strengths of us all working together,' she says.

For Debbie, though, there is one clear and lasting memory in her head about that first summit on Straddie:

Angela and me were swimming in the ocean. She and I often have little conversations about our time in prison. I said to her, do you get that really core, ice-cold, freezing sense in the pit of your guts, that real prison cell coldness? And you know you could sit on top of a heater and you'd still be cold? Sometimes I feel so cold my teeth chatter. Even years later, I can get cold to the bone; I can stand so close to the heater my legs are burning but I'm still cold. And she said, no, I don't get that, but I know what you mean. I'm still afraid of mice coming under the door, nibbling on my fingers. I can still be terrified of that.

15

Celebrity Prisoners

It took Debbie some time to realise the significance of the letter that dropped through her mailbox in late December 2002, the crisp envelope stamped with the seal of the governor of Australia. She looked around the room, as if the answer might be on the walls. She picked up the phone. 'What's an Order of Australia?' she asked Anne Warner.

Later, Warner and Bernadette Callaghan looked at Debbie across a coffee table and said, with wide grins on their faces, 'You *really* don't know what this means, do you?' 'Nope,' Debbie replied. 'Well, it's big; big, big, *big*. It's fucking *huge*.' Then, silenced by the confidentiality imposed by the governor's letter, they stopped talking about it until, on Australia Day 2003, Debbie was presented with her medal at a ceremony at Brisbane's Government House. The citation read: 'for services to the community, particularly through providing assistance to women in correctional facilities'. 'At the time my reaction was: 'well, that's fantastic,' says Debbie. 'But I wasn't jumping out of my skin. I don't allow myself to get that excited; I guess I haven't for a long time. But Mum was excited – I think she could see that finally, everything was going right. Here was the proof.'

With the announcement of the award came a wave of media attention. Who was this ex-crim, people wanted to know, whose achievements were being recognised with one of the highest distinctions in the land? What was her story? Profiles in the *Courier-Mail* and smaller local papers, and a spread in the colour magazine of the *Weekend Australian*, fleshed out Debbie's life for people for whom she was either totally unknown, or a half-familiar name in their memories.

In their wake she received dozens of letters from across the community, from acquaintances and strangers. Some came from those who still remembered the comet of Joe Kilroy's talent blazing across the football field, and some from young people who had known neither Joe nor the reign of Joh Bjelke-Petersen and his personal 'war on drugs' that the Kilroys had fallen victim to. The electronic media followed with stories, too. Channel 9's 'Sixty Minutes' wanted Debbie to appear on their program, and the ABC's 'Australian Story' began the long process of interviews and research that precedes one of their popular features. (Debbie's story went to air in March 2004.)

Debbie took the attention in her stride. Her confidence in dealing with interviews and cameras had skyrocketed over the previous three years. Now she knew many local journalists by name, knew their particular deadlines and needs, and was relaxed in their company. She was also developing a nose for the '30-second bite', and could deliver succinct summaries of an issue that endeared her to both broadcast and print journalists. And that was just as well – before the year was out her face would be a familiar one to anyone watching the news or reading a newspaper.

Before the next big prison stories of the year blew, however, there was another accolade for Debbie. In March 2003, she was surprised to be told she had been short-listed for the Telstra Businesswoman of the Year award. She had no idea she'd been nominated. At a gala ceremony at the Sheraton Hotel in September, with Pat and a table full of tearful and cheering friends around her, she was announced the winner of one of the four main sections, the government and community award. Her moving acceptance speech, in which she told her story and urged listeners to remember that anyone – anyone – could find themselves in jail, reminded the large gathering of women of the momentous events that had recently taken place outside the ballroom, in their own judicial system. Just down the road, in the Supreme Court of Queensland, a woman regarded as perhaps the most unlikely of anyone to find herself in jail had three months earlier been given a twelve-month sentence, and was now behind bars.

The then chief magistrate of Queensland, Diane Fingleton, had been charged in sensational circumstances earlier in the year with making a retaliatory threat against a witness after a dispute involving several other magistrates. The 'witness' in the case was a male magistrate who had supported another female magistrate when she appealed against being transferred by Fingleton to north Queensland. The Crown alleged that when Fingleton sent an email to Basil Gribbin, giving him seven days to show cause why he should not be demoted, the action represented a retaliatory threat. Ironically, Fingleton had recently helped draft the law she was now accused of breaking, which was passed by Parliament in 2002.

The case resulted in weeks of state and national headlines when, despite defence arguments that Fingleton's actions were part of a 'workplace dispute' rather than a criminal offence, the jury in the trial could not reach a verdict. Unusually, a retrial was scheduled immediately. When the new jury brought down a guilty verdict, shock waves reverberated around the country. Shock was replaced by disbelief when Justice John Helman sentenced Fingleton to a year behind bars, describing the offence as 'an extremely serious one'. Even her fiercest critics – and the majority of commentators – felt the sentence was extremely tough punishment. Fingleton and her family were clearly distraught. After a night in the Brisbane watch-house, two strip-searches and the allocation of a 'double P' – highly protected – classification, Fingleton was taken to Brisbane Women's Correctional Centre at Wacol.

It was an extraordinary fall from grace for a woman who had survived an abusive and difficult childhood to become a respected community lawyer who fought for the needy, and who leapfrogged several more senior and more experienced magistrates to become the state's first female chief magistrate in 1999. Just months prior to her trial, she had walked the red carpet with actors Judy Davis and Geoffrey Rush at the world premiere of *Swimming Upstream*, the movie Fingleton co-wrote with her brother Tony about their childhood, which was dominated by their violent, tyrannical and drunken father. Now her life was being laid bare in a dramatically different way.

Debbie Kilroy understood Fingleton's distress better than most. She knew the horror of the holding cells, the crash of the prison doors behind her. But this was personal for Debbie as well – Fingleton was a close friend of Anne Warner and others in her circle. She wanted to minimise the trauma of the coming months both for Fingleton's sake and for her friends'.

Debbie: We had these mutual friends and we all used to go deep-water running at a pool nearby on Saturdays, then have breakfast at West End. And Di had also spoken at our first conference. None of us wanted to see her in prison – Di, or anyone else. After she was sentenced I went straight in, because I told her I'd make sure I was there.

But what Fingleton didn't know was how Debbie rallied the women inside not to touch her:

Debbie: I went in there and advocated on her behalf – I said she's another woman in prison who shouldn't be there, just like you, and we have to stick together, not pull apart. I particularly targeted lifers and long-termers and told them she's a no-go zone, and to make sure she's a no-go zone. And they did. If I hadn't spoken to them I think she would have got hung out to dry; people would have had a go, left, right and centre. As it was the women were all calling out to her, hey, Di, come over here and live with us – they were going to look after her, because I'd asked them to.

But she spent all of her time in protection. After three months, she wasn't looking good, I can tell you. I was seeing her nearly every week, and she was very fragile. Not long afterwards, she was transferred to Albion. We'd made some calls about that too.

Fingleton probably has little real idea of what was done on the outside to get her moved to low security. Debbie never told her.

One of the major roles that Debbie played was as a kind of cultural interpreter, translating Fingleton's experience inside prison to an outside world still disbelieving and hungry to know about it. Both as the director of Sisters Inside and as a woman who had also been to prison, Debbie was identified by the media as the one person, apart from Fingleton herself, who at that time could give an open account of Fingleton's life in prison.

But while Debbie liaised with Fingleton about what might and might not be said, it was the directness of Debbie's own experience and her ability to contextualise it that lent the whole episode clarity. An example is an interview she gave on ABC radio the morning after Fingleton's imprisonment when, before the interviewer could ask the first question, Debbie got her own in. 'Well, are you feeling a whole lot safer this morning, now that the chief magistrate is behind bars?' she asked.

But Fingleton was barely out of maximum security and settled at Albion when Queensland's second celebrity prisoner was sent to jail, with all the controversy and outrage that had attended Fingleton's incarceration. Like Fingleton, Pauline Hanson had not expected to be dealt such a difficult sentence – three years – and had never contemplated the notion that she might one day fall so far. The community was once more treated to the dubious spectacle of one of its high-profile women disgraced, deprived of her liberty and relabelled 'criminal'.

Founder of the right-wing One Nation Party, Hanson had been charged, along with her One Nation co-founder David Ettridge, with defrauding the Electoral Commission by lying about the size of their party's membership and receiving $500 000 in electoral payments. After a trial lasting more than three weeks, the jury delivered a shock guilty verdict.

Hanson and Ettridge were each sentenced to three years imprisonment. Media reports detailed Hanson's disbelief and anger as she was led away, first to the watch-house and then, next morning, to the Brisbane Women's Correctional Centre where she spent her first night heavily sedated and under 24-hour observation. She was then transferred to the protection wing while she waited for the outcome of her appeal.

It was difficult for Debbie to ignore the irony of Hanson's plight: here she was, locked up, just as she had urged for others in the tough law and order campaign she had run as an aspiring politician. Still, she knew the distress Hanson would be in, the shame she would feel, the humiliation she would share with all women subjected to mandatory strip-searches after contact visits with people she loved.

Unlike Fingleton, Hanson had not asked to see Debbie or to be supported by Sisters Inside, so the two women had no contact. But the pattern had by now been set: journalists bombarded Debbie with phone calls about Hanson, assuming she would know her condition and her likely release dates. She couldn't help them with specifics, limiting her remarks to general experience, but it delighted her to see that Sisters Inside had become acknowledged as the conduit between the community and women in prison.

Pauline Hanson would serve just three months in prison, her entire time at Wacol, like Fingleton's, spent in the protection unit. But when her appeal was upheld and she was acquitted of all charges late on 6 November 2003, it was a very different Pauline Hanson who emerged from the gates of the Brisbane Women's Correctional Centre to tearfully hug her sons. Thinner and with the trademark red hair faded, she looked haunted and vulnerable. Her voice cracked as she spoke with a large group of journalists who had been closely monitoring her appeal process to ensure they could record her first moments of freedom: 'I got caught up in a system that I saw fail me, and I am so concerned for the other women behind the bars . . . and men,' the 49-year-old said. 'The system let me down like it let a lot of people down.'

In media interviews in the following days, Hanson said she had been shocked at what she had found inside prison. 'I'm the first to admit when I'm wrong,' she said. 'I'd assumed the system found them [inmates] guilty, so they must be, but there are so many girls in there who shouldn't be there.' She also spoke of the serious trauma she experienced the day she was imprisoned, and revealed she had at times felt suicidal. 'They destroyed my life, my career, my future, my family has been absolutely devastated, and my children – what it's done to them,' she said.

> **Debbie**: When Pauline got out you could see she was absolutely traumatised by the experience, and I know that feeling and know it well. Many women do. And for all she is and all she isn't, that hit a chord with me, just as Storm screaming in her cell hit a chord. Just seeing her like that.

Earlier in the year, Debbie had attended a conference in New Orleans, organised by the group Critical Resistance, to speak on a panel with Angela Davis, Gina Dent, Kim Pate and a number of women from New Orleans who had been in prison. It was the school holidays, so Debbie took the opportunity to take Joshua with her. The theme of the conference was the prison industrial complex, and the arguments for abolition. Many of the American delegates had been astounded to hear Debbie speak about the services provided by Sisters Inside, and the model on which the organisation operated. Service and advocacy groups in the United States are almost uniformly locked out of prisons so, to them, the notion that an independent group – and one that frequently criticised the governments and policies of the day – had workers inside women's prisons almost every day seemed extraordinary. The fact that women inside had a real and meaningful role in running the organisation left them gobsmacked.

In between sessions Debbie and Josh went shopping and sight-seeing around New Orleans, sampling the music and food. The teenager had by then become firm friends with Angela, Gina and Kim, and, like Kim's daughter Madison, was a fixture at social occasions wherever the women happened to meet up.

Naturally, Debbie took the opportunity in New Orleans to invite anyone who was interested to the next international conference run by Sisters Inside, timed for November that year. Once again, Angela Davis, Gina Dent and Kim Pate would headline the program, which would throw down the gauntlet by using the title of Davis's recent book: 'Is Prison Obsolete?'. By September, at least two more women from the United States had accepted Debbie's invitation – Andrea Smith, a member of the Cherokee nation and co-founder of Critical Resistance, and Shalom Odokara, head of 'Women in Need' in Maine.

The remaining months of the year were mainly spent in organising the conference, and negotiating once more with Corrective Services for a video conference with women inside – if not their physical presence. In September, Debbie took a rare three days off to go sailing and fishing in Moreton Bay. Her friends were amazed: no one could recall Debbie taking *real* days off. Even in summer, when the offices of Sisters Inside are closed for two weeks, Debbie is rarely in holiday mode.

'Sitting down to contemplate the navel, or losing yourself in a long novel is not her thing at all,' says Amanda George. 'She is always scheming, talking, plotting, thinking about funding submissions or strategies. I think fishing is the most relaxing thing she does. One weekend when she and Kim were in Victoria, and down visiting me at Aireys Inlet, a place by the beach, I think she was bored. "What do you do here?" she said.'

George was right about the fishing. When both of them have coinciding weekends off, Debbie and Anne Warner will stow the fishing lines and head for Stradbroke Island. They fish, Debbie drinks beer and Anne drinks tea. They have long conversations, which rarely veer away from the politics of prisons, future directions for Sisters, the behaviour and attitudes of various people in corrections.

In 2003, however, Debbie had two other claims on her attention. One was soccer. With another management committee member, Paulette Dupuy, she had joined the Pineapple Rovers, a south-side soccer team in the Brisbane women's league. Made up of lawyers, teachers, IT experts and students, the team trained twice a week, a physical commitment Debbie enjoyed despite the disparity in ages – most of the team were twenty years her junior. The team took the game seriously, and no one was surprised when they made it to the grand final, only to be beaten in extra time.

That year also saw Debbie and Joe's son, Joshua, complete year twelve at Coorparoo Secondary College. Bright and artistic, Joshua had done what his parents could only hope and wish for: finished school without encountering any kind of trouble with teachers or (with the exception of one bout of drunken shoplifting) the police. And he'd done so well academically that, when his results came out, he was offered places at Griffith University, the University of Queensland, and at the prestigious Aboriginal Centre for Performing Arts in Brisbane.

Josh had enjoyed the kind of 'normal' teenage life Joe and Debbie had always hoped for him. He was close to both his parents, but had an easy, confiding relationship with his mother that Debbie took real joy in. She spent a lot of time with him being 'the usual mother-taxi', driving him to and from school, to friends' houses and to casual jobs. The Tingalpa house quickly became a refuge for any of Joshua's friends who might find themselves homeless, even temporarily.

Debbie: Sometimes there would be five or six of them at a time – some would stay a day, some a week. Our home was always home to his mates, it's always been a place where they could come. We have big weekend barbecue breakfasts they would come to. Our relationship was and is close, a confiding one, and it's developed into a friendship. We're easy in each other's company. I encouraged him to apply for uni, along with his other Aboriginal friends who thought they didn't do well enough to apply, that they weren't good enough. I told them it was about equal opportunity, especially if they'd suffered disadvantage. But Josh said, I haven't had a terrible childhood or anything Mum, I've had a fantastic childhood. And I said, what? Your parents both went to prison when you were a baby, you were separated from your sister, you went to eight schools in ten years because of racism – you call that easy? I don't think so. But it was really good for me to hear that from him, because I knew then he had come through to the other side of the trauma.

It all hit home for Debbie in November, when she and Joe watched Josh, suited up and grinning widely, step into the electric blue 1957 Chevrolet Joe had organised for Josh's senior formal. At the pre-formal drinks, they watched their son mingling effortlessly with his friends, saw how well he was liked and accepted, and breathed out the breath they'd collectively held since he was small. They'd done it. Joshua had come through, unscathed, happy, successful. The cycle of institutionalisation had been broken.

Jody, however, was still behind bars at Brisbane Women's Correctional Centre, waiting out her release date: February 2005. Although Jody had matured significantly since her last incarceration for fraud, Debbie had stood firm. She'd told her daughter previously that, if she went back to prison, Debbie would not be making the weekly trips for visits. She had done that before and Jody had taken her loyalty for granted.

It would have been a difficult decision for any parent to make, but for Debbie it was double-edged: she was also painfully aware of the added difficulties Jody had faced in prison because of her mother's activism around women prisoners, the name-calling and slurs on her mother's reputation, the five months in isolation she'd once endured after leaking to Debbie the true circumstances surrounding a prison suicide. But this time Debbie's closest friends watched as she hardened her heart and let Jody do her time, determined not to make it easy for her to keep going back to prison. 'I used to hear her on the phone to Jody,' says Natalie Bell. 'She was impersonal – "yes, no, yes". But I could see it was killing her.'

'There is only so much you can do when they don't want your help,' Debbie says now. 'The pain ran so deep, and the cuts from the relationship were so raw, that I knew Jody had to do it for herself.

I could only help her when she decided to accept help from me. What could I have done – tied her up?'

Debbie was also aware of the two very different roles she played when Jody was in prison: she was Jody's mother, and she was director of Sisters Inside. 'I knew how different the roles were and I had to make sure the prison knew it too. I had to draw boundaries,' she says. 'She copped the retribution for everything I did on the outside. On the other hand, there was the enmeshment of the mother–daughter relationship. If Jody didn't want my help and other young women did, well, so be it. I'm not their mother. I'm the director of Sisters.'

Karen Fletcher acted as Jody's solicitor during some torrid legal times, and remembers Debbie's mix of 'worry and anger' over her daughter. 'She wanted to be clear about being both Jody's mum and her public, Sisters self. Like everything she does, she thought it all through very carefully and even though she was ripped up emotionally, she didn't stop walking her talk, behaving ethically and in Jody's best interests as she saw them,' Fletcher says. 'We talked about the legal issues and about Jody's welfare, but her daughter is the most difficult subject to talk to Deb about. She can talk about the most horrific things that have happened in her own life, but talking about Jody can make her cry. I was really proud that she trusted me to help Jody, but Debbie was clear that no one could actually save Jody but Jody.'

Otherwise, Debbie's home life had become surprisingly calm, even predictable. She drove to the office every day in West End, and Joe climbed on to his Harley and rode to work. After 25 years in the youth sector and in Aboriginal health, Joe took a change of direction and was now happily ensconced at Barhoppers Custom-Built Choppers, a motorcycle shop on Brisbane's south, where he continues to spend his days with his beloved Harley Davidsons. During the week there was reading and studying for Debbie's law degree, a bit of television. Sometimes she and Joe would head off to the local Thai restaurant or the pub for a meal.

Weekends often meant picking up Nana from her Northside home, where she lived independently, and ferrying her to Pat's at Tarragindi for dinner or lunch. Josh, who had remained fiercely close to his grandmother and his great-grandmother, would often head off to Nana's or Pat's on the bus to visit them on his own. Few weekends would go by, however, without Debbie meeting up with some of the Sisters management committee for coffee or lunch and long, involved talks about the current issues for women in prison.

One other small diversion gave Debbie a lot of pleasure towards the end of 2003: a visit from 'The Hurricane', Rubin Carter, whose unjust imprisonment in the United States for more than twenty years and eventual acquittal and release had been immortalised in song by Bob Dylan. Debbie knew his story; knew that his promising boxing career had been cut short by a trumped-up murder charge; that he had spent ten years of his life sentence in solitary but had always maintained his innocence. When Brisbane's Griffith University invited Carter to accept an honorary doctorate in recognition of his struggle and his achievements, she thought about attending the gala dinner held in his honour. But at $200 a ticket, it was out of her league. On the day of the dinner, however, she was asked if she would attend as a guest of the university, and take her place beside Rubin Carter. Debbie happily accepted, and she and Carter entertained themselves for much of the evening trading prison stories in whispers, while high-profile admirers milled around hoping to be introduced to 'The Hurricane'.

The second conference had taken its name from the title of Angela Davis's new book, *Are Prisons Obsolete?*, which had been published that year and was described as 'an unflinching critique of how and why more than two million Americans are presently behind bars, and the corporations who profit from their suffering'. With her arrival once again in Australia, many audiences here heard for the first time the arguments around the abolition of jails. Angela, Kim Pate and Debbie all took to the airwaves to convince Australian audiences that their arguments had merit.

Debbie focused her line on the indisputable fact that 60 percent of all women released from prison return to prison. Sixty percent, she reiterated to radio, newspaper and television journalists. If any other major government body recorded that failure rate – if, indeed, Sisters Inside did – they would be de-funded, closed down. There would be ongoing questions about how and why this failure rate occurred.

If prisons are about rehabilitation, not just punishment, if the community is sincerely interested in ensuring the crime rate drops and the effects of crime diminish, then the efficacy of prisons as a deterrent must surely be examined, she argued. For the most part, women emerge from prison in much worse shape than when they enter: traumatised, stigmatised, their physical and mental health problems exacerbated, their children alienated and angry. Many will be homeless, jobless and penniless. How can we expect such women to return to the community as optimistic participants? How can we expect them to return effortlessly to their family lives? The place that was meant to 'correct' and rehabilitate them, to ready them for better times, instead betrays them, setting them up to fail once more. Prisons, Debbie told whoever would listen, do not work.

As they did during the first conference, the national and international guests visited Brisbane Women's Correctional Centre. Along with everyone else, Amanda George watched with admiration as Debbie did battle with the prison staff over missing paperwork authorising the visit. 'Deb never genuflects to authority or status,' says George. 'She would not see why you wouldn't approach the prime minister, a pop star or head of a government department to get the women's prison message across. I think she is probably incredulous about those people who don't do it. I was incredulous myself on that visit to Brisbane Women's. There had been a stuff-up with the booking at the prison end, and Deb just threw a total wobbly about how incompetent the prison was, etcetera. Which I was sure would get us no further than the Dr Who tube [laser security] and out again – but no, they let us in.'

When Kim Pate arrived back in Australia for the 2003 conference, she was in the midst of the tumultuous response to a human rights complaint against the Canadian government for systemic discrimination against women in prisons. The Canadian Association of Elizabeth Fry Societies, of which she is director, had launched the complaint in 2001, urging the Canadian Human Rights Commission to conduct a broad-based systemic review of the treatment of women serving federal sentences, and to issue a special report.

Throughout the three days of the SIS conference, and for a week afterwards on Stradbroke Island, Pate workshopped the proceedings with Debbie, Anne Warner and Amanda George. The complaint had been based on discrimination against women prisoners on the grounds of race, disability and gender: it claimed discrimination affected the way women were classified in the penal system, and the kinds of programs and treatment they received; that aboriginal women in Canada were over-represented in the system, and more likely to be classified maximum security; and that women with cognitive and mental disabilities experienced a lack of appropriate placement and treatment options. By the end of 2003, Pate had been travelling constantly across Canada garnering support for the complaint, and was expecting the public release of the report and a major response in the new year.

Debbie knew the issues in Queensland were almost identical to those in Canada, and consulted all the relevant legislation to confirm it. Sure enough, all the grounds were there. Perhaps a similar complaint could work here. To clear the way, she wrote to Corrective Services in Queensland on 10 December – Human Rights Day – calling for an inquiry into the discrimination against women prisoners and the publication of a report. She had to wait until January for the reply: the department found there was no discrimination, so calls for an inquiry were unfounded. With that under her belt, she began to gather the research necessary to lodge a complaint with the state's anti-discrimination commissioner, and to lobby groups in other states to do the same.

Debbie: The complaint detailed the systemic discrimination against women prisoners on the grounds of race, sex and disability. The main means are the tools by which women are classified; the low numbers of low-security beds, the high numbers of Aboriginal women in prison and particularly in maximum security; the discrimination faced by women who don't speak English; the lack of programs, industry and education; the use of strip-searching, solitary confinement and the crisis support unit.

An example is how the classification system works, supposedly to identify need. But if you get a tick in a box, it's about risk, not need, so the more ticks you get the higher risk you are. So if you live in Inala, or Ipswich, or Woodridge, low socio-economic areas, you would get a tick, because they assume that's a high crime area. But the question is supposed to be about where crime happens, not where they assume people with criminal convictions

live. If you have a psychological or psychiatric illness, you get
a tick. If you practise your cultural beliefs, you get a tick. What
hope have you got if you're black, have a mental illness and
live at Woodridge? If you've had a drug or alcohol problem you
get a tick, if you've been in a situation of domestic violence,
you get a tick. You get ticks for all the things disadvantaged
women experience.

Debbie was also angered by the way the classification system
concentrated on facets of women's lives that could not change –
their colour or race, episodes of domestic violence – but did not
take into account any achievements or changes women had experienced. To prove her point, she went through the classification test
herself: 'If I went back to prison today, I would still be at the highest
rung, still in maximum security. Everything I've done wouldn't
count: the fact I've got a social work degree, that I'm a psychothera-
pist, nearly finished a law degree, have a job and have lived in the
same place for years. I would be seen as a risk to the community.'

The complaint was lodged with the Queensland anti-discrimination
commissioner, Susan Booth, in June 2004 (and subsequently lodged by
groups in every state and territory). Copies were sent to the corrective
services department and other agencies, as well as service groups around
the country. Controversy wasn't far behind it. In a press release that
accompanied the launch of the complaint, Debbie had described the
treatment of women prisoners as having 'echoes' of that infamously
meted out to Iraqi prisoners at the Abu Ghraib prison and recorded on
camera. She'd been making similar comments for months: the forced
strip-searches, the women locked, sometimes naked, in the crisis
support unit, restrained with body belts, handcuffs and suicide gowns in
rubber rooms.

Debbie: I'm especially worried about the women with a mental
illness who are regularly locked inside the CSU – they use all
kinds of restraints on them to control their behaviour, and they're
kept for hours or days until their behaviour 'settles down'. But if
you've got a mental illness or disability, you can't just stop your
behaviour. So you keep being restrained. It's about the use and
overuse of those restraints. It's about punishment rather than
treatment.

I don't agree with prisons, but they're there; and I'd rather see a woman walk out the same, if not better, than she went in, not further traumatised and diagnosed with post-traumatic stress syndrome, which a number of women have been in the past twelve months. It makes no sense to go to prison to be further traumatised, but society allows it to happen by not asking what's happening in there. The more closed the system, the more grief we'll have, and the more we're locked out of the prison, the more it will happen.

It's like sexual abuse – women don't speak out about their perpetrator, and prisons are perpetrators in a systemic way. So women inside aren't going to talk – they're going to put their heads down, for fear. That's what they've learned from an early age – don't take on the perpetrator – they've done it before and been beaten. I know what it's like. But they're not going to beat me any more. I don't care. They won't shut me up. As soon as I become silent I become part of it. Complicit.

The Queensland government's immediate response to the complaint was to institute an inquiry of its own and to lock Sisters Inside out of Brisbane Women's Correctional Centre. Prison officers, enraged by the reference to Abu Ghraib and what they saw as a comparison of them with abusive US soldiers, threatened to strike if Debbie Kilroy's access to the prison was not stopped. The programs run by Sisters Inside ground to a halt. Management committee meetings were also prohibited. Despite loud and widespread protest from women inside – particularly those who relied heavily on Sisters for sexual assault counselling and getting their children to the prison for visits – the lock-out continued.

However, because several women had made direct allegations of abuse to the manager of the prison, Debbie accompanied an independent investigator appointed by Corrective Services into the prison to interview anyone who wished to come forward. The interviews were also conducted outside, with women who had been released. Outside management members conducted regular crisis meetings to decide how to proceed, and to devise strategies in the face of the biggest challenge Sisters Inside had ever faced.

Debbie: The government has always wanted Sisters Inside out, because we keep raising the issues for women inside. Secrecy breeds abuse. Prisons need to be open and accountable to public scrutiny, and I'm very worried for the women now that we've been kicked out and they have no one to trust and who will speak out on their behalf. I'm particularly scared for women who are in the dark corners of the prison – the CSU and the DU. And for the Aboriginal women, who always serve their time in maximum security.

Ironically, the strategy adopted by Debbie and the management team to deal with the lock-out in the first instance was to maintain their own thoughtful silence – a kind of passive resistance, while they awaited the outcome of the inquiry initiated by the department. Their own complaint to the anti-discrimination commissioner had a much longer timeline. Remaining silent in the face of potential disaster might be an excruciatingly difficult challenge for Debbie and for Sisters, but everyone was aware of the odds: the well-being, if not the survival, of many women inside.

16

Walkin' the Talk

It was typical of Debbie that, despite the distress of the lock-out and the obvious threat to the organisation, she continued to 'walk the talk' at a very personal level. Eight months previously, at the end of 2003, she had offered a home to a young woman who had been released from prison after four years, but had not secured accommodation approved by the government. Tash accepted the offer on a temporary basis, but was still living with the Kilroys in June 2004, on her twenty-first birthday, which was duly celebrated at a special dinner complete with flowers and presents.

Tash: I'd been offered home detention but had to get a positive home assessment. My mum's a user and I don't get along with my dad – I only met him last year – and they wouldn't approve a boarding house. My only option was to leave the job I'd got and go to my grandfather ninety kilometres north of Roma. And I knew if I went back there I might reoffend.

Then Deb rang me and said, no, you're coming to my place. And I just cried. I was shocked – that was her private life. I don't know anyone who would be able to do that – and I know she wouldn't do it for just anyone, I know how she feels about her privacy and personal space. I was so grateful – and nervous. I didn't know them very well. But we all got on really well. I talk to Josh for hours and Joe and I tease each other and go on with each other. I really enjoy it. It's the closest to an immediate family I've ever had. I'll always have that connection with them now. And if I'm ever half the woman Deb is, I'd be stoked.

273

Months before Tash was released, Debbie had begun supporting another young woman, Tia, who, at twenty-four, had just been released from prison after serving six years. Tia had secured work at an industrial laundry and, shortly after Tash moved in with Debbie, was hit by a personal crisis she found hard to cope with.

Tia: I was having a rough trot. I was hating my job, and then suddenly I started to feel I'd rather be back in jail. I told Tash, and she told Deb, and Deb came over straight away, picked us up and made us go out and have dinner with her. I broke down, sobbing my eyes out. But she knew what was wrong with me before I knew it. It was amazing. She said, you're institutionalised. I said, no I'm not. But she was right. I was subconsciously planning how to go back. And that's dangerous. If she hadn't said that I wouldn't have realised it. Something at work was triggering it, and I think I would have bashed my boss or something. If Deb hadn't been around I could quite possibly be back in jail.

She told me she still feels that way sometimes, even after fifteen years. She still goes through what I went through. When does it go away? She said it may never go away. So what do I do? Am I not normal any more? You feel like a freak sometimes, because people don't understand you. She told me it was important to identify it, and ride with it, go over the bump, cos it will happen again. But you'll be aware of it. And you look at her and she's so successful and you think, it can be done.

So I just got it all out with her, and she told me to ring her. She said she didn't care if we had to do this every month, every week, every night of the week. She's my number one person in my life at this point; the only one who understood what was happening. I know that wherever I am, or whatever state I'm in, that woman will dead-set drop everything and come, if I need her. And you just don't find that in people.

Slowly, Debbie's relationship with her daughter had also begun to strengthen again, as trust built up on both sides, and Jody was able to talk to Debbie more about her own experiences. Debbie was horrified when Jody disclosed to her that she had been sexually abused, but it finally assembled some of the shattered pieces of the relationship in her head.

'It all started to make sense when she told me what had happened to her twelve years earlier,' she says. 'It's taken all this time for her to talk about it, and for me to understand some of the reasons she was flipping out.' Debbie organised regular sessions for Jody with Sisters' sexual assault counsellor, sessions which still continue. Jody was then able to discuss the abuse more freely with her mother, alongside her plans for a more positive future. They decided that, once Jody was paroled, she would come back home once more, and apply for university. 'And we'll try again,' Debbie says.

There are endless examples of Debbie's intervention to help individual women who might otherwise fall through the cracks. Like Sharon Scully, who had known Debbie since childhood, and was released from prison after a long stint in mid-2004. Sisters Inside had organised accommodation for her, but it was Debbie who picked her up from outside the prison gates and found her a hotel room until the new flat was available; who talked to her constantly in those first few days when she knew her old friend was feeling vulnerable, who drove her around and organised some paid writing work that Scully could do while she looked for permanent employment.

And then there was Katie. Debbie had hoped her murdered friend's daughter would stay out of trouble after her initial meeting with her. But she wasn't very surprised when Katie turned up again at Sisters Inside. This time she was about to front court on a series of charges, but had been denied legal aid. With a small child and minimal income, Katie felt powerless and afraid. Once more Debbie turned to her friend Chris Callaghan, a solicitor (and Bernadette Callaghan's brother) who had previously come to the aid of women referred by Sisters Inside. He agreed to help Katie.

Debbie was unsure if Katie would face jail after her court appearance – 'These days any woman is likely to go to prison' – but the next time she saw Storm Brooke inside Brisbane Women's she had a quiet word to her. 'If Katie comes in, and anyone so much as touches a hair on her head, I'll be looking for you,' she told her. 'No one will,' Brooke replied.

Several months later, Katie visited again, bringing Tiana, her

twenty-month-old daughter. Debbie was happy to see them: Katie
seemed matured and calm, happy with her little girl, and determined
to put the past behind her. Although she was about to face a
committal hearing on the previous charges, she was optimistic they
would be dismissed, and that she would be given another chance to
live the 'straight' life her own mother never had.

> Katie: I was going through a rough patch right up until I
> found out I was pregnant with Tiana. She made me want to
> go straight, because I didn't want to be the mum in jail with
> my daughter being looked after by someone else. But then
> there was a custody battle over her in the Family Court, and
> I got a bit nasty and did something I shouldn't have, and I'm
> paying the consequences now. I came to see Debbie because
> she'd been on the other side of the law, and I thought she
> might have some advice. I'm really grateful for the help she's
> given me. But once all this is sorted out in court, that's it, for
> me. It's not going to be the way it was for Mum and me.
>
> I've got another mum now, who I call 'Mum'. For many
> years I was full of resentment towards her too, because she
> couldn't talk about my real mum either. I can see now she was
> trying to protect me. But looking back, now that I have my
> own child, I can see she didn't want me to be hurt. So I spent
> all those teenage years hating her. Now we have the best rela-
> tionship. And she's my mum, because she's the one who has
> looked after me.
>
> I can talk to people about my real mum without any
> emotion, it's like it happened to someone else. Obviously I've
> blocked it all out. Debbie says maybe I should deal with that,
> do some counselling, and I think I should too. But I'm a bit
> scared of that, because I'll have to bring it all up. I think it will
> be very intense.

Katie says she doesn't hold any feelings of hatred towards Storm
Brooke, and doesn't even really blame her for her mother's murder.
'It might sound weird but I don't blame her for some reason. I think
there's more to what happened than was said,' she says. I've thought
about her, and thought about going to see her, but I don't think I
ever will. If we were ever in the same room, I'd talk to her, for sure.

Maybe that will happen. I wouldn't go out of my way to meet her, but if she was there, I'd certainly talk to her.'

But for Debbie Kilroy she has unending admiration: 'She's turned her life around. Everyone says they want to do it, but the number of people who actually do . . . Once you're in there, it's so hard to do. It's easier for me, because I haven't actually been in there; I've been close many times, but haven't actually had anything to do with it, so I can stay clean.'

The stories behind these three young women help explain why, despite her heavy involvement in all facets of Sisters' operations, Debbie has continued to volunteer her time at the Youth Detention Centre at Wacol, where she spends one night every week talking to the young women, counselling them and often advocating for them on the outside. Despite twelve-hour days, she sees this as crucial intervention in the lives of young women who might be saved the trauma of incarceration in the adult prison with the right kind of guidance and opportunities. In 2004 she began a campaign to introduce soccer games inside the centre for the young women who, unlike their male counterparts, had no organised sport to participate in and learn from; to eliminate illegal strip-searching and even to ensure the young women had new and properly fitted bras. These are the kinds of actions that have galvanised staff and other management committee members of Sisters Inside to keep fighting beside her, and to support her without question, even when the odds look very grim indeed.

Natalie Bell thought her life was 'over' when she joined Sisters as an accountant and human resources consultant in 2000. Three years previously, the middle-class and well-educated young woman had been sent to prison for two and a half years for fraud and misappropriation of funds. It was as much of a shock to her as it was to her friends, family and boyfriend, a police officer. 'I was petrified,' she recalls. 'I thought I was going to be ravaged by lesbians and bashed, that all women in prison had two heads. I was quite stuck up. I had no comprehension that other people might not have had the same opportunities that I'd had.'

Released after four and a half months behind bars and three months on home detention, Bell found work with Second Chance, an organisation that assisted ex-prisoners. At one of her first meetings with other agencies, she listened to Debbie Kilroy tell those assembled that 'they didn't know anything about helping people in jail because we'd never been there'. 'I didn't say anything to her at that stage. I just thought she was a real pain in the arse, pushing this thing about women all the time,' Bell says. At a second meeting, however, when Bell confided to Debbie that she'd recently done time, Debbie's eyes widened. 'Her whole attitude towards me changed,' she grins.

Shortly afterwards, after Bell volunteered to do work on Sisters' accounts, Debbie convinced her she could set herself up as a consultant to community-based agencies. 'At the time I was thinking, I can't go out on my own. Coming out of jail, all your confidence is gone. I didn't even want to go out in public – I'd be petrified of seeing people I knew who might have read about me in the paper,' she says. 'But Deb said, you can do this. She reminded me I was capable, that I was good at it. So I did.' It was mainly due to Bell's efforts that the first Sisters Inside conference, in 2001, had been such a spectacular organisational success. Despite Bell's lack of experience, Debbie had convinced her she could pull it off. 'At a debriefing afterwards, in front of all the staff, she told me she couldn't have done it, or got through it, without me. I wasn't sure what I'd done,' Bell says, 'but it was obviously personal. She felt supported by me.'

Not long afterwards, Bell threw a party for her thirtieth birthday in country and western style, with bales of hay and a neighbour's very expensive saddle decorating the picket fence. Bell has two enduring images of the party and they both concern her boss: 'We'd been drinking cock-sucking cowboys in tall glasses all night. Deb was into it, having a great time. At one stage, though, a friend tried to get into our mobile coldroom to get a drink, only to be thrown out by Deb, who was sitting in there having a heart-to-heart with one of the girls from work,' she recalls. 'He was quite scared of her, I think.'

The other image is from later in the evening, when the party was in full swing with dancing, eating and drinking. Debbie was alone. 'There she was at midnight,' Bell laughs, 'up on the neighbour's saddle on the picket fence, yahooing away, with $1500 worth of leather grinding on the spikes of the pickets.'

Natalie Bell is not the only staffer at Sisters who feels she owes her livelihood and confidence to Debbie Kilroy. Jenny Speed, now second in seniority to Debbie in the organisation along with Bell, was in bad shape when Debbie invited her to do some casual work for her in 2001. She had returned to Brisbane several months earlier after a breakdown prompted by a savage and abusive experience in the workplace in Sydney. Unable to shake off a lingering and deep depression, she had barely been able to leave her bed or her house in West End. Anne Warner, who had known Speed for years, was shocked by the condition of her old friend, who she knew as a highly intelligent woman with an honours degree in philosophy and a string of high-powered jobs behind her. When she took Debbie along to visit Speed one day, Debbie decided to act.

Within days Speed was working – albeit in a desultory fashion, she concedes – in the Sisters office, but gradually, her mental strength began to return. Within twelve months she was working full-time again, with renewed energy and focus. Now an indispensable deputy to Debbie, assisting her to supervise staff and programs as well as working with individual women herself, Speed credits Debbie and the organisation 'almost 100 percent' for her recovery. 'This work has validated everything that had previously been negated in me,' she says. 'It's reminded me of the things I can do, the things I'm capable of.' She is convinced that the structure of Sisters Inside – 'women inside are our bosses as well as our clients' – is the secret behind the success of the organisation. That, plus the fact that Sisters is 'built on trust – and on Debbie's honesty'.

Management committee members, friends and acquaintances agree. 'Deb's got a heart bigger than herself. She just gives out, and you don't resist that,' says Bernadette Callaghan. 'I've gone from not knowing her at all to considering her one of my closest friends. I'm a much better person, having known Deb and having been involved with Sisters. I'm very proud of it.'

For Callaghan, this is perhaps a bigger call than for many others. In 2002, she was appointed as a magistrate and, as such, was forced to stand down from the management committee of Sisters Inside. (The writer of this book took her place on that committee.) Standing down, she says, was the saddest thing about an otherwise exciting appointment and, at first, she 'wasn't game' to tell Debbie about the move.

'Magistrates send people to jail. And there has been a time when I've had to deny somebody bail,' Callaghan says. 'I knew that was a potential conflict between Deb and me – but she thought it was great, as I should have known she would. She's a big-spirited person. So it didn't change our relationship a bit ... But I can say that Sisters Inside has an enormous amount of respect among judges and magistrates. They see the work they do. No one likes sending anyone to jail, so it helps if there's an organisation out there helping women prisoners.'

This commitment has been an important part of the friendship that still thrives between Debbie and Melissa Lucashenko, and with Jackie Huggins. Both have watched as Debbie fearlessly fought for services for Indigenous women, taking that fight to the highest levels when necessary. 'I've been in meetings where Deb has savaged bureaucrats and politicians about the services they don't provide to black prisoners, and you can see them sweating and thinking, who let this one in the building? At the end of the day, it's the services that get to the women that matter,' says Lucashenko. 'Deb's a rough diamond, and though she's completely legit, she still operates prison-style, so she will always rub some people up. But she's only white on the outside, and I'd trust her with my life.'

Huggins agrees:

I feel like she's coming into her own now, as a very strong woman. I feel my role is as a support person for her within the Murri community, telling people her work is so legitimate and so vital to our people. Because it's getting so that half the prison population is becoming Indigenous. It's quite a significant number and it's scary. Certainly in the juvenile detention centres it's over 90 percent. Those figures are so terrifying that, when you talk to people about them, they barely register on the psyche. People don't believe it.

Deb's not afraid of anything; she'll talk to anyone, from the premier down. She doesn't seem to see the levels – you and I might talk to a minister or the premier in a certain way but she doesn't. The lines are invisible. She's upfront and straight to 'em. And she has the most amazing sense of humour – it actually borders on blackfella humour. I've said to her, tell me you've got some blackfella in you. I can pick something. It's just like talking to another Murri woman. My suspicion is there's a bit of goanna there.

Both Huggins and James Finn say independently that, in meetings or on controversial issues, they will 'back Deb, and go with her' even if they're not entirely certain. They trust her absolutely. 'Trust' is another word that emerges repeatedly – and voluntarily – when people speak of their experiences with Debbie. 'I'd trust her with my life,' says Melissa Lucashenko; 'I trust her fully – I'd sleep in her house!' says Storm Brooke. 'If I was ever in trouble, or needed somebody, she'd be the first port of call. I trust her; I rely on her judgment,' says Finn.

And while everyone agrees that Debbie's confidence has grown markedly in the decade since Sisters Inside began, Finn believes that confidence often belies a real vulnerability that has always been at her core:

> She hasn't changed in that way. She's certainly grown; but the essential core of who she is is no different. She's more analytical, more book-smart, but I think she's always been politically savvy. The difference is that before she was savvy and powerless, and now she's in a more powerful position, it's more obvious.
>
> People have been a bit threatened by her as she's gathered more skills, and it's been very hurtful to her when she's lost people from her life. People assume she's a much stronger and braver person than she really is. But she's not as impervious as people think. She puts on that persona, wears it like a mantle. People assume there's been a transformation. But it's about learning. It's important to see that, when the time is right, you can be enabled to change your life – not to change yourself.

Debbie's brother Michael agrees. Michael, who has also found himself on the wrong side of the law in the past, knows how easy it is to talk about 'turning your life around'. Although he and his sister have 'different ideas' and 'agree to disagree' about many issues, he clearly admires her determination to build a new life and to support others as they try to do the same. 'Lots of men get out of prison with a dole cheque and nothing else – they're on the streets,' he says. 'No wonder they end up back inside. Debbie's work helping young girls to get employment and places to live is really important. I'm very proud of her.' Like many siblings with different personalities,

Michael and Debbie don't spend a lot of time together, but meet up regularly at Pat's for birthdays and special occasions. Pat remains a staunch – if quiet – supporter of her daughter, seeing her as often as she can. Len is now housebound, suffering Alzheimer's, and Pat is devoted to him. But her home, neat and welcoming, full of photographs of children and grandchildren, often rings to Debbie's and Joe's – and Nana's – very loud talk and laughter.

Amanda George is still awed by Debbie's courage – and her endurance – in a field which constantly throws up blockades and challenges to the 'extremely small and marginalised group' of women prison activists across the world. 'There are very few women who have been inside who go on to become activists. There are a million good reasons to leave prison behind, if you can,' she says. 'Women who have been in prison are considered low-lifes by many in our society – there is no positive status for women in being a former con. Whereas I think for men there can be: the good old double standard. So in that way she is unique. To stand up and shout, "Yeah, I've been in prison, so fuckin' what?" is extremely courageous. Another reason to leave prison behind is the pain. You get treated as a curiosity and untrustworthy, and many other shitful things. It is these shitful things – and the pain – that Debbie will not leave other women to bear alone.'

Denise Foley of the Catholic Prisons Ministry has watched with interest as the Debbie Kilroy she first met and sparred with has grown into her new life. 'I respect her hugely for the way she has turned things around,' she says. 'And she has done that through painful self-examination, and owning her own shit. We laugh now when we talk about restorative justice, about the new relationship between Debbie and Storm, and of a possible mediation between Storm and Debbie Dick's family. I had to listen to her for years railing against mediation. Now I say to her: who would have thought you would have turned out to be the biggest restorative justice advocate there is? You live and breathe it. She just laughs.'

But Foley isn't convinced Debbie's life has yet come full circle: 'Right now she's moving towards the person she will become. I don't think she is that person yet. She's evolving. She's in the midst of becoming a person who can articulate some of the really complex aspects of crime and family breakdown and prison and abuse, the real complexity of it. She's got the balls and the courage to do all of that, but she's only part of the way there, to becoming the person she was meant to be. And that might not be working around prisons. I don't live and breathe prisons, and I look forward to a time when Debbie doesn't either. And that's the rest of the evolution: what are the other parts of Debbie Kilroy?'

It's a view shared by others, not least Janine Walker: 'In a way, she did lead a protected life. And she's been so busy fighting that she's missed out on a lot. She grew up confined within those walls, and I worry sometimes that she's still confining herself. I don't want the women inside to lose her but I want her to have the opportunity to broaden what is there for her. She is such a clever, thinking, extraordinary individual.'

Today, the agenda for Debbie Kilroy is clearly the abolition of prisons. She has sworn to work towards it relentlessly, but in the meantime, existing prisons must be held to account for the treatment of women behind their walls, and made to fulfil the meaning of their names: corrections. If women – and men – are to be ostracised from their communities and families as punishment, then the time they spend away must be used to ensure their lives are improved, so that their chances of returning to prison are minimised and their children's lives left intact. To that end, she continues to lobby, negotiate, browbeat, harangue and question decision-makers at every level of government and in the community to consider the terrible failure that prisons have become.

With the 'normality' of prisons accepted across the community, along with the assumption that 'bad' people are made 'good' by incarcerating them there (hence relieving the rest of society of any responsibility or guilt) she keeps repeating the mantra of the institutionalised, those people we all expect to be grateful for the experience prison delivers:

They brainwash you from a young age, telling you the system will fix you. So you're going to fix me? Well, thank you! Thank you for locking me up as a kid, throwing me in isolation and drugging me all my teenage life, oh and thank you for telling me I killed my father, I'm so grateful. And thank you for double-cuffing me, putting me in a body belt and locking me in a rubber room; thank you for someone else's pair of jocks, someone else's shoes; thank you for the abuse and neglect. Oh, and thank you, Corrective

Services, for strip-searching me every time I have a contact visit, it felt so wonderful to hold my kids before the humiliation of exposing myself to you, of you inspecting my naked body – thanks for that. Don't know how I could have got on with life without you. Thank you for letting me see my mate murdered, for being brutalised. Thank you for locking me in a cell twelve hours a day. And thank you, really, on behalf of all the women who go to prison after lives of misery, only to endure more misery inside and then they're chucked out 'rehabilitated' with no job, no money, no house and no kids. Thank you for nothing.

Epilogue

As this book went to print, Debbie Kilroy, the staff and the management committee of Sisters Inside were still effectively locked out of Brisbane Women's Correctional Centre. On paper, the department of Corrective Services might say this was not the case. Staff of Sisters Inside have been permitted entry to the prison to see women who formally request assistance and receive approval from management to access Sisters' services. The weekly list of women provided by the prison manager contains, on average, two referrals. Prior to the lock-out, Sisters Inside was providing services to 190 women, about 90 percent of the prison population. That has now been reduced to less than 10 percent. Under these restrictions just four programs are permitted to run, and six more have been disallowed.

The internal inquiry conducted by the Corrective Services department about specific allegations of abuse inside the prison found the department and its officers had no case to answer. With the report of the Anti-Discrimination Commissioner still months away, prison staff demanded that Sisters' services remain curtailed, threatening to strike if their demands were not met. The services remained restricted.

In late November, Debbie wrote to the general manager of the prison, requesting permission to hold a meeting of the Sisters Inside management committee inside the prison. Monthly meetings of this committee, including the steering committee of prisoners, had been held inside prison since the inception of the organisation. These meetings, too, had been banned, and this request was also refused — the first time this has occurred in Sisters' history.

The on-going lock-out of Sisters' staff and its management team was, according to the general manager of the prison, in the interests of the 'good order and security' of the prison. Debbie could only assume the Minister for Police and Corrective Services and her director-general agreed – personal approaches to both had met with blank stares and with the issue being continually passed from one to the other and back to the prison manager. The outcome: no change.

A further irritant to the government was the release, in November, of 'Incorrections: Investigating Prison Release Practice and Policy in Queensland' by an associate professor of law from the Queensland University of Technology in association with a medley of groups supporting prisoners and their families. Sisters Inside was one of them. The report underlined many of the issues raised in the previous chapters of this book, emphasising how little had changed in the prison system since the Kennedy Report of 1988, when it was described as being 'completely ineffective at rehabilitating prisoners'.

This report also alleged regular rape and assault against prisoners and active drug smuggling by prison officers. The Queensland Public Service Union, representing prison officers, described the report as 'garbage' and 'a piece of pseudo academic nonsense' and singled out the involvement of Sisters Inside.

In response to a request from the general manager of the Brisbane Women's Correctional Centre, Debbie penned a letter outlining why Sisters should be permitted to resume its manage-ment committee meetings – and its regular services – inside the prison. She mentioned the importance of the involvement of the inside steering committee to the successful operation of Sisters Inside, emphasising they had more than a 'cosmetic say' in the organisation's procedures. She also reminded the manager that SIS 'now runs a large number of programmes that are an intrinsic part of the rehabilitative aspect of the prison', and that the organisation made a difference in the lives of women in prison and their children – enough to make their lives happier and more productive.

'Sisters Inside is a unique organisation that is internationally recognised as providing the best practice model for work with female prisoners. Sisters Inside's management structure has been cited in numerous international publications as the most effective model for supporting women in prison, improving their lives and preventing recidivism, family breakdown and the intergenerational cycle of crime,' she wrote.

At the time of writing, however, Debbie's pleas had fallen on deaf ears. For the first time in its existence, Sisters was indefinitely locked out of the prison and prevented from carrying out its roles. It seemed ironic to Debbie and to management committee members that this lock-out had been instigated by a Labor government, one which purported to have a social conscience, and a concern for social justice.

But Sisters is not known for rolling over. After months of peaceful and respectful negotiation with various arms of government, it was clear to all that public pressure was required – the community would be told in no uncertain terms that Sisters was being prevented from delivery of its services and advocating for women. Not to save Sisters Inside. 'We will be here long after this prison manager, this director-general, this minister,' says Debbie. 'We will survive in some form – we're not fighting for that. We're fighting for the women, for the better lives that they and their families deserve to have. That's what we're all about.'

One more, very powerful irony, was played out at the end of 2004. As the lock-out agony continued, with the inference that Debbie Kilroy and Sisters Inside were superfluous – even dangerous – in the prison system, Debbie was awarded the 2004 Australian Human Rights Medal by the Human Rights and Equal Opportunity Commission. In an emotional acceptance speech, Debbie described how many women in prison had no concept of the term 'human rights' – in their bleak lives they had rarely encountered them, and prison worked to remove both their humanity and their rights. She spoke of the work of Sisters Inside and thanked the Commission, but didn't pull any punches: ironically, she said, she had been given this prestigious award for work she could largely no longer do.

Acknowledgements

We would both like to acknowledge the courage and generosity of Debbie's family and her friends, both inside and outside prison, in speaking so candidly about issues and events many of them have long kept to themselves. Pat Harding and Joe Kilroy, along with Jody and Joshua in particular, have lent time, patience and good humour to the often painful process of remembering.

Members of the management and steering committees of Sisters Inside offered advice, support and warm encouragement to us throughout the long days of research and writing, as have staff members at Sisters Inside. Particular thanks are due to Jenny Speed, Natalie Bell and Rebecca Draper.

We are grateful also to Wally Dethlus, Marg O'Donnell and Denise Foley, who lent precious personal files to the writer; to Angela Davis for taking time out of her busy schedule to write the Foreword; and to the many people who have believed in this book and contributed in various ways to its completion, including Tony Chambers, Sandra Hogan, Fiona Inglis, Jo Jarrah and the enthusiastic team at Random House.

The following books have helped me tremendously in writing Debbie's story:

Justice in the Deep North, by Carole McCartney, Robyn Lincoln and Paul Wilson. Bond University Press, Gold Coast, Queensland, 2003

Walkin' the Talk, A History of Sisters Inside, by Kate Warner. Sisters Inside, Brisbane, 2001

One Step Beyond, The Story of the Centre Education Program. Church Archivists' Press, Virginia, Queensland, 1996.